MTTC

English as a Second Language (126) Secrets Study Guide

Dear Future Exam Success Story

First of all, **THANK YOU** for purchasing Mometrix study materials!

Second, congratulations! You are one of the few determined test-takers who are committed to doing whatever it takes to excel on your exam. **You have come to the right place.** We developed these study materials with one goal in mind: to deliver you the information you need in a format that's concise and easy to use.

In addition to optimizing your guide for the content of the test, we've outlined our recommended steps for breaking down the preparation process into small, attainable goals so you can make sure you stay on track.

We've also analyzed the entire test-taking process, identifying the most common pitfalls and showing how you can overcome them and be ready for any curveball the test throws you.

Standardized testing is one of the biggest obstacles on your road to success, which only increases the importance of doing well in the high-pressure, high-stakes environment of test day. Your results on this test could have a significant impact on your future, and this guide provides the information and practical advice to help you achieve your full potential on test day.

Your success is our success

We would love to hear from you! If you would like to share the story of your exam success or if you have any questions or comments in regard to our products, please contact us at **800-673-8175** or **support@mometrix.com**.

Thanks again for your business and we wish you continued success!

Sincerely,
The Mometrix Test Preparation Team

Written and edited by the Mometrix Exam Secrets Test Prep Team
Printed in the United States of America

Table of Contents

Introduction

Thank you for purchasing this resource! You have made the choice to prepare yourself for a test that could have a huge impact on your future, and this guide is designed to help you be fully ready for test day. Obviously, it's important to have a solid understanding of the test material, but you also need to be prepared for the unique environment and stressors of the test, so that you can perform to the best of your abilities.

For this purpose, the first section that appears in this guide is the **Secret Keys**. We've devoted countless hours to meticulously researching what works and what doesn't, and we've boiled down our findings to the five most impactful steps you can take to improve your performance on the test. We start at the beginning with study planning and move through the preparation process, all the way to the testing strategies that will help you get the most out of what you know when you're finally sitting in front of the test.

We recommend that you start preparing for your test as far in advance as possible. However, if you've bought this guide as a last-minute study resource and only have a few days before your test, we recommend that you skip over the first two Secret Keys since they address a long-term study plan.

If you struggle with **test anxiety**, we strongly encourage you to check out our recommendations for how you can overcome it. Test anxiety is a formidable foe, but it can be beaten, and we want to make sure you have the tools you need to defeat it.

Secret Key #1 – Plan Big, Study Small

There's a lot riding on your performance. If you want to ace this test, you're going to need to keep your skills sharp and the material fresh in your mind. You need a plan that lets you review everything you need to know while still fitting in your schedule. We'll break this strategy down into three categories.

Information Organization

Start with the information you already have: the official test outline. From this, you can make a complete list of all the concepts you need to cover before the test. Organize these concepts into groups that can be studied together, and create a list of any related vocabulary you need to learn so you can brush up on any difficult terms. You'll want to keep this vocabulary list handy once you actually start studying since you may need to add to it along the way.

Time Management

Once you have your set of study concepts, decide how to spread them out over the time you have left before the test. Break your study plan into small, clear goals so you have a manageable task for each day and know exactly what you're doing. Then just focus on one small step at a time. When you manage your time this way, you don't need to spend hours at a time studying. Studying a small block of content for a short period each day helps you retain information better and avoid stressing over how much you have left to do. You can relax knowing that you have a plan to cover everything in time. In order for this strategy to be effective though, you have to start studying early and stick to your schedule. Avoid the exhaustion and futility that comes from last-minute cramming!

Study Environment

The environment you study in has a big impact on your learning. Studying in a coffee shop, while probably more enjoyable, is not likely to be as fruitful as studying in a quiet room. It's important to keep distractions to a minimum. You're only planning to study for a short block of time, so make the most of it. Don't pause to check your phone or get up to find a snack. It's also important to **avoid multitasking**. Research has consistently shown that multitasking will make your studying dramatically less effective. Your study area should also be comfortable and well-lit so you don't have the distraction of straining your eyes or sitting on an uncomfortable chair.

The time of day you study is also important. You want to be rested and alert. Don't wait until just before bedtime. Study when you'll be most likely to comprehend and remember. Even better, if you know what time of day your test will be, set that time aside for study. That way your brain will be used to working on that subject at that specific time and you'll have a better chance of recalling information.

Finally, it can be helpful to team up with others who are studying for the same test. Your actual studying should be done in as isolated an environment as possible, but the work of organizing the information and setting up the study plan can be divided up. In between study sessions, you can discuss with your teammates the concepts that you're all studying and quiz each other on the details. Just be sure that your teammates are as serious about the test as you are. If you find that your study time is being replaced with social time, you might need to find a new team.

Secret Key #2 – Make Your Studying Count

You're devoting a lot of time and effort to preparing for this test, so you want to be absolutely certain it will pay off. This means doing more than just reading the content and hoping you can remember it on test day. It's important to make every minute of study count. There are two main areas you can focus on to make your studying count.

Retention

It doesn't matter how much time you study if you can't remember the material. You need to make sure you are retaining the concepts. To check your retention of the information you're learning, try recalling it at later times with minimal prompting. Try carrying around flashcards and glance at one or two from time to time or ask a friend who's also studying for the test to quiz you.

To enhance your retention, look for ways to put the information into practice so that you can apply it rather than simply recalling it. If you're using the information in practical ways, it will be much easier to remember. Similarly, it helps to solidify a concept in your mind if you're not only reading it to yourself but also explaining it to someone else. Ask a friend to let you teach them about a concept you're a little shaky on (or speak aloud to an imaginary audience if necessary). As you try to summarize, define, give examples, and answer your friend's questions, you'll understand the concepts better and they will stay with you longer. Finally, step back for a big picture view and ask yourself how each piece of information fits with the whole subject. When you link the different concepts together and see them working together as a whole, it's easier to remember the individual components.

Finally, practice showing your work on any multi-step problems, even if you're just studying. Writing out each step you take to solve a problem will help solidify the process in your mind, and you'll be more likely to remember it during the test.

Modality

Modality simply refers to the means or method by which you study. Choosing a study modality that fits your own individual learning style is crucial. No two people learn best in exactly the same way, so it's important to know your strengths and use them to your advantage.

For example, if you learn best by visualization, focus on visualizing a concept in your mind and draw an image or a diagram. Try color-coding your notes, illustrating them, or creating symbols that will trigger your mind to recall a learned concept. If you learn best by hearing or discussing information, find a study partner who learns the same way or read aloud to yourself. Think about how to put the information in your own words. Imagine that you are giving a lecture on the topic and record yourself so you can listen to it later.

For any learning style, flashcards can be helpful. Organize the information so you can take advantage of spare moments to review. Underline key words or phrases. Use different colors for different categories. Mnemonic devices (such as creating a short list in which every item starts with the same letter) can also help with retention. Find what works best for you and use it to store the information in your mind most effectively and easily.

Secret Key #3 – Practice the Right Way

Your success on test day depends not only on how many hours you put into preparing, but also on whether you prepared the right way. It's good to check along the way to see if your studying is paying off. One of the most effective ways to do this is by taking practice tests to evaluate your progress. Practice tests are useful because they show exactly where you need to improve. Every time you take a practice test, pay special attention to these three groups of questions:

- The questions you got wrong
- The questions you had to guess on, even if you guessed right
- The questions you found difficult or slow to work through

This will show you exactly what your weak areas are, and where you need to devote more study time. Ask yourself why each of these questions gave you trouble. Was it because you didn't understand the material? Was it because you didn't remember the vocabulary? Do you need more repetitions on this type of question to build speed and confidence? Dig into those questions and figure out how you can strengthen your weak areas as you go back to review the material.

Additionally, many practice tests have a section explaining the answer choices. It can be tempting to read the explanation and think that you now have a good understanding of the concept. However, an explanation likely only covers part of the question's broader context. Even if the explanation makes perfect sense, **go back and investigate** every concept related to the question until you're positive you have a thorough understanding.

As you go along, keep in mind that the practice test is just that: practice. Memorizing these questions and answers will not be very helpful on the actual test because it is unlikely to have any of the same exact questions. If you only know the right answers to the sample questions, you won't be prepared for the real thing. **Study the concepts** until you understand them fully, and then you'll be able to answer any question that shows up on the test.

It's important to wait on the practice tests until you're ready. If you take a test on your first day of study, you may be overwhelmed by the amount of material covered and how much you need to learn. Work up to it gradually.

On test day, you'll need to be prepared for answering questions, managing your time, and using the test-taking strategies you've learned. It's a lot to balance, like a mental marathon that will have a big impact on your future. Like training for a marathon, you'll need to start slowly and work your way up. When test day arrives, you'll be ready.

Start with the strategies you've read in the first two Secret Keys—plan your course and study in the way that works best for you. If you have time, consider using multiple study resources to get different approaches to the same concepts. It can be helpful to see difficult concepts from more than one angle. Then find a good source for practice tests. Many times, the test website will suggest potential study resources or provide sample tests.

Practice Test Strategy

If you're able to find at least three practice tests, we recommend this strategy:

Untimed and Open-Book Practice

Take the first test with no time constraints and with your notes and study guide handy. Take your time and focus on applying the strategies you've learned.

Timed and Open-Book Practice

Take the second practice test open-book as well, but set a timer and practice pacing yourself to finish in time.

Timed and Closed-Book Practice

Take any other practice tests as if it were test day. Set a timer and put away your study materials. Sit at a table or desk in a quiet room, imagine yourself at the testing center, and answer questions as quickly and accurately as possible.

Keep repeating timed and closed-book tests on a regular basis until you run out of practice tests or it's time for the actual test. Your mind will be ready for the schedule and stress of test day, and you'll be able to focus on recalling the material you've learned.

Secret Key #4 – Pace Yourself

Once you're fully prepared for the material on the test, your biggest challenge on test day will be managing your time. Just knowing that the clock is ticking can make you panic even if you have plenty of time left. Work on pacing yourself so you can build confidence against the time constraints of the exam. Pacing is a difficult skill to master, especially in a high-pressure environment, so **practice is vital.**

Set time expectations for your pace based on how much time is available. For example, if a section has 60 questions and the time limit is 30 minutes, you know you have to average 30 seconds or less per question in order to answer them all. Although 30 seconds is the hard limit, set 25 seconds per question as your goal, so you reserve extra time to spend on harder questions. When you budget extra time for the harder questions, you no longer have any reason to stress when those questions take longer to answer.

Don't let this time expectation distract you from working through the test at a calm, steady pace, but keep it in mind so you don't spend too much time on any one question. Recognize that taking extra time on one question you don't understand may keep you from answering two that you do understand later in the test. If your time limit for a question is up and you're still not sure of the answer, mark it and move on, and come back to it later if the time and the test format allow. If the testing format doesn't allow you to return to earlier questions, just make an educated guess; then put it out of your mind and move on.

On the easier questions, be careful not to rush. It may seem wise to hurry through them so you have more time for the challenging ones, but it's not worth missing one if you know the concept and just didn't take the time to read the question fully. Work efficiently but make sure you understand the question and have looked at all of the answer choices, since more than one may seem right at first.

Even if you're paying attention to the time, you may find yourself a little behind at some point. You should speed up to get back on track, but do so wisely. Don't panic; just take a few seconds less on each question until you're caught up. Don't guess without thinking, but do look through the answer choices and eliminate any you know are wrong. If you can get down to two choices, it is often worthwhile to guess from those. Once you've chosen an answer, move on and don't dwell on any that you skipped or had to hurry through. If a question was taking too long, chances are it was one of the harder ones, so you weren't as likely to get it right anyway.

On the other hand, if you find yourself getting ahead of schedule, it may be beneficial to slow down a little. The more quickly you work, the more likely you are to make a careless mistake that will affect your score. You've budgeted time for each question, so don't be afraid to spend that time. Practice an efficient but careful pace to get the most out of the time you have.

Secret Key #5 – Have a Plan for Guessing

When you're taking the test, you may find yourself stuck on a question. Some of the answer choices seem better than others, but you don't see the one answer choice that is obviously correct. What do you do?

The scenario described above is very common, yet most test takers have not effectively prepared for it. Developing and practicing a plan for guessing may be one of the single most effective uses of your time as you get ready for the exam.

In developing your plan for guessing, there are three questions to address:

- When should you start the guessing process?
- How should you narrow down the choices?
- Which answer should you choose?

When to Start the Guessing Process

Unless your plan for guessing is to select C every time (which, despite its merits, is not what we recommend), you need to leave yourself enough time to apply your answer elimination strategies. Since you have a limited amount of time for each question, that means that if you're going to give yourself the best shot at guessing correctly, you have to decide quickly whether or not you will guess.

Of course, the best-case scenario is that you don't have to guess at all, so first, see if you can answer the question based on your knowledge of the subject and basic reasoning skills. Focus on the key words in the question and try to jog your memory of related topics. Give yourself a chance to bring the knowledge to mind, but once you realize that you don't have (or you can't access) the knowledge you need to answer the question, it's time to start the guessing process.

It's almost always better to start the guessing process too early than too late. It only takes a few seconds to remember something and answer the question from knowledge. Carefully eliminating wrong answer choices takes longer. Plus, going through the process of eliminating answer choices can actually help jog your memory.

Summary: Start the guessing process as soon as you decide that you can't answer the question based on your knowledge.

How to Narrow Down the Choices

The next chapter in this book (**Test-Taking Strategies**) includes a wide range of strategies for how to approach questions and how to look for answer choices to eliminate. You will definitely want to read those carefully, practice them, and figure out which ones work best for you. Here though, we're going to address a mindset rather than a particular strategy.

Your odds of guessing an answer correctly depend on how many options you are choosing from.

Number of options left	5	4	3	2	1
Odds of guessing correctly	20%	25%	33%	50%	100%

You can see from this chart just how valuable it is to be able to eliminate incorrect answers and make an educated guess, but there are two things that many test takers do that cause them to miss out on the benefits of guessing:

- Accidentally eliminating the correct answer
- Selecting an answer based on an impression

We'll look at the first one here, and the second one in the next section.

To avoid accidentally eliminating the correct answer, we recommend a thought exercise called **the $5 challenge**. In this challenge, you only eliminate an answer choice from contention if you are willing to bet $5 on it being wrong. Why $5? Five dollars is a small but not insignificant amount of money. It's an amount you could afford to lose but wouldn't want to throw away. And while losing $5 once might not hurt too much, doing it twenty times will set you back $100. In the same way, each small decision you make—eliminating a choice here, guessing on a question there—won't by itself impact your score very much, but when you put them all together, they can make a big difference. By holding each answer choice elimination decision to a higher standard, you can reduce the risk of accidentally eliminating the correct answer.

The $5 challenge can also be applied in a positive sense: If you are willing to bet $5 that an answer choice *is* correct, go ahead and mark it as correct.

Summary: Only eliminate an answer choice if you are willing to bet $5 that it is wrong.

Which Answer to Choose

You're taking the test. You've run into a hard question and decided you'll have to guess. You've eliminated all the answer choices you're willing to bet $5 on. Now you have to pick an answer. Why do we even need to talk about this? Why can't you just pick whichever one you feel like when the time comes?

The answer to these questions is that if you don't come into the test with a plan, you'll rely on your impression to select an answer choice, and if you do that, you risk falling into a trap. The test writers know that everyone who takes their test will be guessing on some of the questions, so they intentionally write wrong answer choices to seem plausible. You still have to pick an answer though, and if the wrong answer choices are designed to look right, how can you ever be sure that you're not falling for their trap? The best solution we've found to this dilemma is to take the decision out of your hands entirely. Here is the process we recommend:

Once you've eliminated any choices that you are confident (willing to bet $5) are wrong, select the first remaining choice as your answer.

Whether you choose to select the first remaining choice, the second, or the last, the important thing is that you use some preselected standard. Using this approach guarantees that you will not be enticed into selecting an answer choice that looks right, because you are not basing your decision on how the answer choices look.

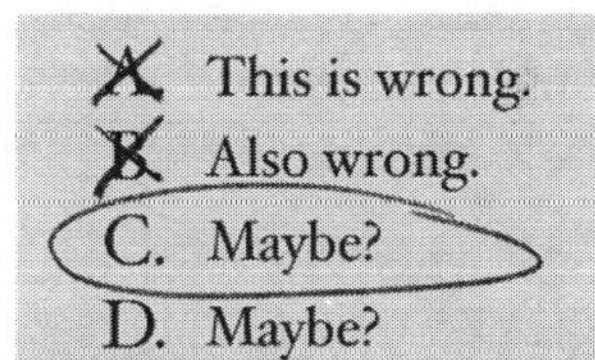

This is not meant to make you question your knowledge. Instead, it is to help you recognize the difference between your knowledge and your impressions. There's a huge difference between thinking an answer is right because of what you know, and thinking an answer is right because it looks or sounds like it should be right.

Summary: To ensure that your selection is appropriately random, make a predetermined selection from among all answer choices you have not eliminated.

Test-Taking Strategies

This section contains a list of test-taking strategies that you may find helpful as you work through the test. By taking what you know and applying logical thought, you can maximize your chances of answering any question correctly!

It is very important to realize that every question is different and every person is different: no single strategy will work on every question, and no single strategy will work for every person. That's why we've included all of them here, so you can try them out and determine which ones work best for different types of questions and which ones work best for you.

Question Strategies

✓ Read Carefully

Read the question and the answer choices carefully. Don't miss the question because you misread the terms. You have plenty of time to read each question thoroughly and make sure you understand what is being asked. Yet a happy medium must be attained, so don't waste too much time. You must read carefully and efficiently.

✓ Contextual Clues

Look for contextual clues. If the question includes a word you are not familiar with, look at the immediate context for some indication of what the word might mean. Contextual clues can often give you all the information you need to decipher the meaning of an unfamiliar word. Even if you can't determine the meaning, you may be able to narrow down the possibilities enough to make a solid guess at the answer to the question.

✓ Prefixes

If you're having trouble with a word in the question or answer choices, try dissecting it. Take advantage of every clue that the word might include. Prefixes can be a huge help. Usually, they allow you to determine a basic meaning. *Pre-* means before, *post-* means after, *pro-* is positive, *de-* is negative. From prefixes, you can get an idea of the general meaning of the word and try to put it into context.

✓ Hedge Words

Watch out for critical hedge words, such as *likely, may, can, sometimes, often, almost, mostly, usually, generally, rarely,* and *sometimes.* Question writers insert these hedge phrases to cover every possibility. Often an answer choice will be wrong simply because it leaves no room for exception. Be on guard for answer choices that have definitive words such as *exactly* and *always.*

✓ Switchback Words

Stay alert for *switchbacks.* These are the words and phrases frequently used to alert you to shifts in thought. The most common switchback words are *but, although,* and *however.* Others include *nevertheless, on the other hand, even though, while, in spite of, despite,* and *regardless of.* Switchback words are important to catch because they can change the direction of the question or an answer choice.

⊘ FACE VALUE

When in doubt, use common sense. Accept the situation in the problem at face value. Don't read too much into it. These problems will not require you to make wild assumptions. If you have to go beyond creativity and warp time or space in order to have an answer choice fit the question, then you should move on and consider the other answer choices. These are normal problems rooted in reality. The applicable relationship or explanation may not be readily apparent, but it is there for you to figure out. Use your common sense to interpret anything that isn't clear.

Answer Choice Strategies

⊘ ANSWER SELECTION

The most thorough way to pick an answer choice is to identify and eliminate wrong answers until only one is left, then confirm it is the correct answer. Sometimes an answer choice may immediately seem right, but be careful. The test writers will usually put more than one reasonable answer choice on each question, so take a second to read all of them and make sure that the other choices are not equally obvious. As long as you have time left, it is better to read every answer choice than to pick the first one that looks right without checking the others.

⊘ ANSWER CHOICE FAMILIES

An answer choice family consists of two (in rare cases, three) answer choices that are very similar in construction and cannot all be true at the same time. If you see two answer choices that are direct opposites or parallels, one of them is usually the correct answer. For instance, if one answer choice says that quantity x increases and another either says that quantity x decreases (opposite) or says that quantity y increases (parallel), then those answer choices would fall into the same family. An answer choice that doesn't match the construction of the answer choice family is more likely to be incorrect. Most questions will not have answer choice families, but when they do appear, you should be prepared to recognize them.

⊘ ELIMINATE ANSWERS

Eliminate answer choices as soon as you realize they are wrong, but make sure you consider all possibilities. If you are eliminating answer choices and realize that the last one you are left with is also wrong, don't panic. Start over and consider each choice again. There may be something you missed the first time that you will realize on the second pass.

⊘ AVOID FACT TRAPS

Don't be distracted by an answer choice that is factually true but doesn't answer the question. You are looking for the choice that answers the question. Stay focused on what the question is asking for so you don't accidentally pick an answer that is true but incorrect. Always go back to the question and make sure the answer choice you've selected actually answers the question and is not merely a true statement.

⊘ EXTREME STATEMENTS

In general, you should avoid answers that put forth extreme actions as standard practice or proclaim controversial ideas as established fact. An answer choice that states the "process should be used in certain situations, if…" is much more likely to be correct than one that states the "process should be discontinued completely." The first is a calm rational statement and doesn't even make a definitive, uncompromising stance, using a hedge word *if* to provide wiggle room, whereas the second choice is far more extreme.

✓ Benchmark

As you read through the answer choices and you come across one that seems to answer the question well, mentally select that answer choice. This is not your final answer, but it's the one that will help you evaluate the other answer choices. The one that you selected is your benchmark or standard for judging each of the other answer choices. Every other answer choice must be compared to your benchmark. That choice is correct until proven otherwise by another answer choice beating it. If you find a better answer, then that one becomes your new benchmark. Once you've decided that no other choice answers the question as well as your benchmark, you have your final answer.

✓ Predict the Answer

Before you even start looking at the answer choices, it is often best to try to predict the answer. When you come up with the answer on your own, it is easier to avoid distractions and traps because you will know exactly what to look for. The right answer choice is unlikely to be word-for-word what you came up with, but it should be a close match. Even if you are confident that you have the right answer, you should still take the time to read each option before moving on.

General Strategies

✓ Tough Questions

If you are stumped on a problem or it appears too hard or too difficult, don't waste time. Move on! Remember though, if you can quickly check for obviously incorrect answer choices, your chances of guessing correctly are greatly improved. Before you completely give up, at least try to knock out a couple of possible answers. Eliminate what you can and then guess at the remaining answer choices before moving on.

✓ Check Your Work

Since you will probably not know every term listed and the answer to every question, it is important that you get credit for the ones that you do know. Don't miss any questions through careless mistakes. If at all possible, try to take a second to look back over your answer selection and make sure you've selected the correct answer choice and haven't made a costly careless mistake (such as marking an answer choice that you didn't mean to mark). This quick double check should more than pay for itself in caught mistakes for the time it costs.

✓ Pace Yourself

It's easy to be overwhelmed when you're looking at a page full of questions; your mind is confused and full of random thoughts, and the clock is ticking down faster than you would like. Calm down and maintain the pace that you have set for yourself. Especially as you get down to the last few minutes of the test, don't let the small numbers on the clock make you panic. As long as you are on track by monitoring your pace, you are guaranteed to have time for each question.

✓ Don't Rush

It is very easy to make errors when you are in a hurry. Maintaining a fast pace in answering questions is pointless if it makes you miss questions that you would have gotten right otherwise. Test writers like to include distracting information and wrong answers that seem right. Taking a little extra time to avoid careless mistakes can make all the difference in your test score. Find a pace that allows you to be confident in the answers that you select.

✓ Keep Moving

Panicking will not help you pass the test, so do your best to stay calm and keep moving. Taking deep breaths and going through the answer elimination steps you practiced can help to break through a stress barrier and keep your pace.

Final Notes

The combination of a solid foundation of content knowledge and the confidence that comes from practicing your plan for applying that knowledge is the key to maximizing your performance on test day. As your foundation of content knowledge is built up and strengthened, you'll find that the strategies included in this chapter become more and more effective in helping you quickly sift through the distractions and traps of the test to isolate the correct answer.

Now that you're preparing to move forward into the test content chapters of this book, be sure to keep your goal in mind. As you read, think about how you will be able to apply this information on the test. If you've already seen sample questions for the test and you have an idea of the question format and style, try to come up with questions of your own that you can answer based on what you're reading. This will give you valuable practice applying your knowledge in the same ways you can expect to on test day.

Good luck and good studying!

Language, Linguistics, and Comparisons

Language Function, Variation, and Discourse

Sociolinguistics, Dialect, and Sociolect

Sociolinguistics is the study of the factors that lead to variation in language use, such as region, gender, class, ethnicity, age, occupation, or bilingual status. A **dialect** is a variation in one or more features of a language, such as spelling, pronunciation, or word choice. **Sociolect** refers to language variations shared by members of the same social class.

Sociolinguists also study how our language use varies depending on the **situation**—people have a tendency to adopt the dialect of those they are speaking to, especially after lengthy exposure. People often adopt shared language as a means of showing solidarity with one another, as in numerous examples of working class English. Many studies have shown, however, that people often adopt an **aspirational dialect**—in other words, they adopt the language patterns of a social or economic class they hope to join. Research has also suggested that women use higher-status language on average than men, perhaps to compensate for their perceived lower status in society.

Dialect vs. Language

A dialect is a variation in a spoken language that nevertheless is intelligible to the larger language community. (If the variation is so large as to prevent mutual intelligibility, it is considered to be a separate language.) .

Dialects naturally arise when a language is spread across a wide area. Often gradients emerge such that all of the members of a dialect community can understand the neighboring dialects, but the differences between the communities furthest apart are so great as to impede communication. While the linguistic distinction between language and dialect is clear, the reality in use is complicated by political and cultural interests—Hindi and Urdu, for example, are treated as separate languages even though they are mutually intelligible, whereas Chinese is, in fact, a collection of mutually-unintelligible dialects unified only by a written language and a national identity.

ELLs may bring varying dialects into the classroom, and teachers should be careful to appreciate legitimate variation rather than impose an arbitrary standard. Differences in dialect may also slow language comprehension and acquisition, though the overall effect is likely to be slight.

Social Language vs. Academic Language

Social language is language used in everyday communication. **Academic language** is used in the classroom and workplace, and on standardized assessments. Most students are exposed to social language earlier and more completely than they are exposed to academic language and become more proficient in social language as a consequence.

Social language often doesn't follow grammatical conventions—in casual settings, people often speak in phrases rather than complete sentences, use slang, repeat themselves, and use narrative strategies that favor expediency rather than economy or logic. In an academic setting, by contrast, people are expected to use full sentences linked by grammatical transitions. Academic language typically requires a specialized or higher-level vocabulary, and variety is expected instead of repetition.

It isn't uncommon for ESL students to be fluent in social language while struggling to achieve even minimal competence in academic language. The student's perceived mastery of the more common social language may lessen their motivation to improve their academic language performance.

Different Social Functions of Language

The primary purpose of language is to allow people to communicate with and understand one another. Linguists often distinguish between academic language and social language—the latter being the everyday language we use in informal settings—and classify various types of social language based on their function. For example, the linguist Geoffrey Leach identified five different functions of social language. First, language is **informational**: we use it to convey information, and in this form, we value its accuracy and relevance. Second, language may be **expressive**, as when we use it to convey feelings or attitudes. Third, language may be **directive**—we may use it to convey orders or exert influence. Fourth, language may be **aesthetic**, as when it is used creatively or artistically. Fifth, language may be **phatic**—that is, it may be used simply to sustain a social relationship, such as when we engage in small talk with a stranger.

Other linguists have classified social language in other ways—for example, many add a category of apologetic language. The importance of all this research is to draw attention to the various functions of everyday language.

Various Functions of Language

Language has a number of functions. The most obvious is to **communicate facts, thoughts, or opinions** to others. Linguists describe this function as referential in that the language we use refers to something that exists in our minds. We also use language to **express emotions**—often involuntarily, as when we cry out in alarm. Language has a social function beyond the expression of thought—as when we engage in ritualistic pleasantries with a neighbor as a way of cementing a social bond. We use language to **record information** for future use, usually in written form. We also use language to **influence reality**—what the philosopher J. L. Austin called perlocutionary acts, as when we christen a ship with the invocation "I hereby christen..." We also use language to **facilitate thought and memory**, as when we talk to ourselves to overcome a mental block. Finally, we use language to **express our personal or collective identity**, as when we join a cheer at a sports stadium.

Basic Interpersonal Communication Skills (BICS) and Cognitive Academic Language Proficiency (CALP)

The terms "BICS" and "CALP," coined by the educational psychologist Jim Cummins, correspond to the broader concepts of social and academic language. Social language, or **BICS**, is the language used in everyday life; while academic language, or **CALP**, is the language used in formal academic settings.

Cummins highlighted the importance of treating the two types of language as **separate systems**. An ESL student will typically become proficient in BICS in as little as six months, while proficiency in CALP may take seven to 10 years. Furthermore, many English language learners never achieve full facility in CALP, whereas failure to acquire BICS is rare. Cummins warned educators not to make the mistake of assuming that a student proficient in BICS was also proficient in CALP—rather, it is natural for students to master the two competencies at different rates.

Different Academic Functions of Language

Academic language is the language used in the classroom, the workplace, and on formal assessments. ESL students also need to become proficient in **academic language** in order to express, or demonstrate, their knowledge in various content areas of interest.

Whereas **social or everyday language** is used to convey information, express feelings, or simply to cement social bonds, **academic language** is used to achieve other functions. One classification suggests that academic language is used to "describe, define, explain, compare, contrast, make predictions, and persuade."

Most ESL students achieve proficiency in social language long before they achieve academic language proficiency. An ESL student is likely to be immersed in social language early in his or her language experience, but will need academic language to be expressly modeled, scaffolded, and reinforced through targeted practice.

World English

The term "World English" refers both to the spread of English as the global language of business and science and to the existence of many regional and national English dialects. Many of these dialects now count more speakers than those in Great Britain or the United States, leading some to hypothesize that one of these dialects may one day replace that of American English as the informal standard. Scholars of **World English** map its spread along the lines of colonial influence, through commercial and scientific hubs, among the world's educated and economic elite, and increasingly through the instruments of modern technology, such as the Internet or cell phone platforms.

Diglossia

Diglossia is the use of two different languages (or two forms of one language) by a single speech community. One form is usually distinguishable as a high form, which is taught in school, used in formal situations, associated with prestige, and has a written form. The low form, by contrast, is acquired rather than taught, is used in informal settings, is often considered to signal low status, and often lacks a written form. Individuals who speak both forms typically engage in code-switching or alternating between the two languages to fit the context.

Classic diglossia describes the situation in which a community speaks two forms of a single language. Extended diglossia occurs when the community alternates between two separate languages depending on context.

Accentedness

Accentedness refers to how an ELL's pronunciation differs from that of a native English speaker. **Accentedness** is a major factor in determining both the comprehensibility of speech, or how difficult it is to understand; and the intelligibility of speech, or whether it is, in fact, understood.

These definitions have led scholars to suggest that, given limited instructional time, English language teachers should prioritize improving the elements of accentedness that have the most effect on **comprehensibility and intelligibility**—in other words, not all irregular pronunciations are equal. Linguists have developed the concept of functional load to measure how important the proper pronunciation of a phoneme is for the production of intelligible speech. One pragmatic conclusion is for teachers to focus on correcting pronunciation errors that carry high functional loads and spend less or no time correcting those with low loads. Some educators argue that a student's accentedness should only be of concern if it affects intelligibility. Comprehensibility, while desirable, is not a priority when instruction time is limited.

Basil Bernstein's Theory of Language Codes

A language code is the way language is used by a particular social group, in part as an expression of social identity. In the 1970s, the linguist Basil Bernstein suggested that language could be described as either consisting of elaborated code or restricted code. Individuals use an **elaborate code** when they communicate with strangers or people who do not share a common experience. In these instances, they speak explicitly, at length, and with minimal colloquial or expressive language. When in the company of friends or members of a shared community, by contrast, people use a **restricted code**, which relies on implied meanings and references, thereby communicating a lot with few words. Only individuals with shared background knowledge and experiences could understand restricted code, whereas any listener could understand an elaborated utterance. Bernstein argued that restricted codes are used primarily in narrow, unchanging social contexts where shared values can be assumed, whereas elaborated codes are used for broader, unpredictable interactions. He also associated the use of restricted codes with the working class.

Respecting ELL's Home Language

Learning a second language can be an intimidating experience in any circumstance, but it is even more daunting for students who are adapting to life in a new country or attempting to gain social acceptance from their peers. ELLs often feel stressed and are wary of making errors, which can impede the learning process. Teachers should create a positive environment that recognizes student competence in their native language. Teachers should also ensure that all languages are treated equally and that one native language doesn't have priority over another. This is particularly important during group work, when cliques of like-language students might exclude others. Teachers should enforce rules about when students are allowed to speak in their native language. Teachers can also organize activities that invite translation of home languages, or presentations by students of elements of their home cultures. Finally, teachers should attempt to involve parents in their students' lessons to create continuities between home and classroom experiences.

Communicative Competence

Communicative competence, developed by the linguist Dell Hymes, refers to a language learner's ability to communicate effectively in various social settings. In order to succeed in communication, we need to know not only *how* to speak (or write), but *what* to say to *whom* and under *which circumstances*.

Later, Canale and Swain identified four components of communicative competence. **Linguistic competence** refers to proficiency in grammar, vocabulary, and orthography. **Sociolinguistic competence** is the understanding of how to vary language use depending on the context or audience. **Discourse competence** is the knowledge of how to produce cohesive and coherent written or oral texts. **Strategic competence** is the ability to avoid or repair communication breakdowns—for example, by paraphrasing or using gestures to overcome the lack of useful vocabulary.

The concept of communicative competence focuses attention on the fact that there is more to communicative success than mastery of syntax or acquisition of vocabulary. Effective ESL teachers implicitly or explicitly teach all of the component competencies.

Coherent Texts or Conversations

Discourse may be defined as a coherent sequence of written or spoken sentences. Linguists study the way in which competent language users connect individual sentences in order to create coherent wholes. Linguists may focus on small-scale (word- or phrase-based) connectors called **cohesive devices** or on broader, logical relations between sentences. For example, a sentence might *add information* to the broader text, perhaps through the use of a phrase like "In addition..." A sentence might illustrate the *effect* of a previous cause, using "Consequently..." Sentences might also *clarify* previous sentences ("That is to say..."), provide a *summary* ("In conclusion..."), establish a *logical or temporal order* ("First... second..."), furnish an *example* ("For example..."), or *qualify* or *contrast* a previous point ("However..."). Each of these ways of relating one sentence to another contributes to the overall **coherence** of a text or conversation.

Coherence vs. Cohesion

Coherence and cohesion are terms used in discourse analysis to describe written texts. A text is **cohesive** if its individual sentences are linked in ways that bring them together into a single whole. A text is **coherent** if its ideas, or content, belong together. While it is simplistic, cohesion can be thought of as an achievement of grammar or rhetoric, whereas coherence demands that the text corresponds to logic or reality.

Linguists have identified five cohesive devices that establish links among sentences. **Reference** occurs when a word in one sentence refers to a word in another, such as a pronoun to its antecedent. **Conjunction** occurs when a sentence begins with a word or phrase, such as "however" or "alternatively," that ties it to the previous sentence. **Substitution** occurs when a specific word is replaced with a general word in a subsequent sentence—for example, first writing "I doubt he will study," and then "But if he does..." Writers may also intentionally leave out parts of a phrase previously used, a technique called **ellipses**. Finally, writers may employ lexical cohesion by replacing a word with an appropriate **descriptor**, as when "Edison" is replaced with "the inventor."

Spoken vs. Written Language

Spoken and written language differ greatly in both form and purpose. The grammar of spoken language is less rigid, to the extent that many linguists believe that phrases are the fundamental units of speech, unlike the sentences used in writing. **Speech** tends to include many repetitions, ellipses, and self-corrections; and relies heavily on slang and first-person pronouns. Successful speech depends on paralanguage—the nonverbal features of conversation, such as tone, gesture, and facial expression—for successful communication.

Written communication, by contrast, is planned, uses formal (and often complex) grammatical structures, avoids repetition, and relies on orderly presentation and evidence in order to be persuasive. Whereas speech is reciprocal—that is, it can adapt to the reactions and emotions of its audience—writing is non-negotiable, and thus must be crafted to be comprehensive and complete.

English-language students have far more exposure to spoken English than to written English. Their natural tendency is often to write as they speak—that is, in phrases rather than sentences. Similarly, the argumentative forms typically used in writing—with ideas presented in a logical sequence, or with a thesis followed with evidence or examples—are not the same as those used in speech and need to be expressly taught.

Connected Speech

Connected speech refers to the way in which the pronunciation of a word can be changed by the words around it. **Catenation** is the joining of the last consonant sound of one word with the beginning vowel sound of the next, as when "an apple" sounds like "a napple." **Elision** occurs when a sound is left out of a word—often a sound in a consonant cluster, as when "sandwich" is pronounced "sanwich." **Assimilation** is the blending of two sounds to create a new sound, as when "don't you" sounds like "doan chu" when spoken rapidly. **Intrusion** refers to the insertion of an unwritten sound into a phrase, as when "do it" is pronounced "dewit."

Connected speech presents obvious listening comprehension challenges for ELLs. In addition, ELLs who rely heavily on reading to learn English (as with grammar-translation methods still in use overseas) may use connected speech far too often when speaking, and thus sound unnaturally formal or stilted.

Main Genres of Academic Writing

- **Expository writing** is used to inform the reader by presenting information in an objective manner. It is written almost exclusively in the third-person, uses complex sentences, and often utilizes the specialized vocabulary of an academic or technical field.
- **Descriptive writing** is used to portray an event, place, or person, usually with depth and detail. It may rely heavily on adjectives and adverbs to provide vivid descriptions of sensory images. Descriptive prose is common in fiction but may also be found in advertising and journalism.
- **Persuasive writing** is used to advance an argument or point of view. It often begins with the statement of a thesis, presentation of evidence, and a restatement of the thesis as a conclusion. The author may explicitly state his or her own opinions, and likely will not pretend to be offering a balanced account of the subject.
- **Narrative writing** is used to tell a story, either fictional or factual. Narrations usually proceed in chronological order, often use literary devices (metaphors, etc.), and may make heavy use of description and dialogue.

Some typologies of academic writing consider poetry and letter/journal writing to be separate genres.

Phonology

Phonetics vs. Phonology

Phonetics is the study of speech sounds in isolation, and phonology is the study of how speech sounds function in a context—in a syllable, a word, a sentence, or a language as a whole. The speech sounds that each discipline studies are called **phonemes**. English, for example, consists of approximately 44 unique phonemes, arising from the 26 letters of the alphabet used singly or in combination. A competent English speaker can distinguish between these phonemes. Substituting one for another will result in a change in meaning—for example, substituting /m/ for /b/ in the word "ball" results in "mall."

Phonetics considers how individual speech sounds are produced and perceived and might ask which sounds are present in a given language. **Phonology**, by contrast, would study the ways in which those sounds are used to create larger units of meaning. **Phonological rules** are the ways in which sounds change depending on where they occur and how they are used in speech. For example, the deletion rule states that an unstressed vowel is often deleted in rapid speech, as when the /o/ in "police" is dropped and the word is pronounced as /pleas/.

Phonemes, Graphemes, and Letters

A phoneme is the smallest unit of sound in a language that makes a difference in meaning.

Phonemes can be written in two different ways. Linguists commonly represent phonemes by using the **International Phonetic Alphabet**, which assigns a different symbol to each sound commonly found in languages around the world. A second way to represent a phoneme is by using **graphemes**, which are individual letters or groups of letters that depict how a sound is written in a given language. For example, in English, the sound /t/ is written either with a single "t" (as in "tall") or with two "t's" (as in the word "better,"). Thus, English has two graphemes, "t" and "tt," that correspond to the phoneme /t/. Linguists have a special term, digraph, to refer to any two-letter grapheme, such as "tt" or "ch."

Phonetic alphabets and graphemes are necessary because written alphabets do not by themselves provide language learners with knowledge of how to pronounce a given word. Many letters have more than one pronunciation, and often are silent. In other words, spelling is not a reliable guide to pronunciation.

How Phonemes Can Be Classified

Syllables typically have two components, an onset and a rime. The **onset** is the phoneme, or sound, that occurs at the beginning of the syllable. In English, only consonants can be onsets. If a syllable begins with a vowel sound, the syllable has no onset. The **rime** is the vowel and any consonants that follow the onset. Thus, every syllable has a rime, but not necessarily an onset. For example, the one-syllable word "and" has no onset, only a rime. In the word "bat," by contrast, the /b/ is the onset, and the /at/ is the rime.

A second way to classify phonemes is by their **order** in a word. The first phoneme in a word is called the **beginning phoneme**, the last phoneme is called the **end phoneme**, and any phonemes in the middle are called **medial phonemes**. Teachers often promote phonetic awareness in beginning readers using this classification. For example, the teacher might teach the word "bet" by highlighting the beginning /b/, the ending /t/, and the medial /e/.

IRREGULARITIES IN ENGLISH SPELLING

Students of any language benefit if that language has **predictable rules** of grammar, spelling, or pronunciation. Learning is made even easier if the student experiences **positive transfer**—that is, if features of their native language are similar to those in English, and thus reinforce the learning process.

The fact that the 26 letters of the English alphabet combine to form approximately 44 distinct phonemes will complicate the learning process for ELLs, as there is no one-to-one correspondence between spelling and pronunciation. For example, the sound /k/ can be written in many different ways in English, as in "cat," "kite," and "tack."

Other features of English violate a regular one-to-one correspondence of letters to sounds. **Digraphs**, for example, are combinations of two or more letters to produce a unique phoneme—such as the /ch/ sound in English. **Diphthongs** are combinations of two or more vowels in a single syllable, often resulting in an unpredictable sound—for example, the word "chair" is usually pronounced with an /ur/ sound that is not evident from its spelling. **Consonant clusters** occur when two or more consonants combine to form a single sound, as with the /wr/ sound in "wreck." These features render English more difficult for the ELL.

THE INTERNATIONAL PHONETIC ALPHABET (IPA)

No alphabet has a one-to-one correspondence between letters and sounds. In English, for example, 26 letters generate approximately 44 distinct phonemes. Nor do any two languages rely on the same system of sounds, even when they share an alphabet.

The **International Phonetic Alphabet (IPA)**, which was created in 1888 and revised repeatedly since, provides a standard system of symbols for all of the phonemes used in human languages. The existence of the IPA allows linguists to refer to sounds independently to how they are represented in a specific language.

The IPA uses many symbols derived from the Latin alphabet, but it includes symbols from other sources, such as the Greek alphabet and even the Icelandic alphabet.

By convention, when linguists want to refer to a phoneme, they place a symbol within slashes or brackets ("/a/" or "[a]") in order to distinguish it from a letter that might have different sounds in different languages or multiple sounds in a single language.

LINGUISTS SOUND FRAMEWORK

Linguists who study the physiology of sound production have classified the phonemes according to how they are **produced**. Each phoneme is articulated in a unique way. Consonant and vowel sounds have different classification systems.

Consonants are classified according to three criteria: (1) the location in the vocal tract where they are produced (the descriptive terms used are bilabial, labiodental, interdental, alveolar, alveopalatal, velar, and glottal); (2) the manner in which they are produced (stops, nasals, fricatives, affricates, approximants, and glides); and (3) whether they are voiced or unvoiced. For example, the [b] sound is described as a "voiced, bilabial stop," and the [f] sound is described as a "voiceless, labiodental fricative.".

All **vowels** are voiced, and so the classification of vowels occurs along two dimensions, both of which refer to the position and movement of the tongue during utterance: (1) high, mid, or low; and

(2) front, central, and back. Thus, the short vowel [u], as in the word "boot," is produced high and in the back of the mouth.

Improving Pronunciation Skills

Perhaps the best way to help ELLs monitor their **pronunciation skills** is by using audio recordings in which ELLs repeat a word or phrase after a native speaker and then replay the recording. It may be helpful as well to provide students with surveys or question prompts that encourage them to reflect on which aspects of their pronunciation they need to improve on. Class activities like singing and choral reading are low-stress ways to focus on pronunciation. Above all, students have to be exposed to **modeled speech** at an appropriate level of phonetic complexity and given opportunities to practice in an environment in which they can focus on pronunciation rather than syntax or the complexities of social discourse.

Pitch, Tone, Intonation, and Stress

Spoken language relies on differences in sound to create differences in meaning. The primary source of these sound differences is phonemes.

Differences in sound can affect meaning at a level above that of individual phonemes, however, by operating on syllables, words, or even sentences. Linguists refer to these as **prosodic features of language**. The two main prosodic features are **pitch** (which in turn is divided into *tone* and *intonation*) and **stress**.

Pitch, while technically a difference in the frequency of the vibration of the vocal cords, is recognized by listeners as a continuum between low and high. Many languages use pitch to distinguish between words, in which case it is referred to as **tone**. Cantonese, for example, is a tonal language. If the pitch rises or falls over the course of a sentence, it is referred to as **intonation**. In English, intonation is often used to distinguish a statement from a question.

Stress refers to a difference in force applied to an element of speech, usually a syllable. Multi-syllabic words in English have a standard pattern of stress. With some words, changing the pattern of stress may lead to a change of meaning, as between "con-VERT" and "CON-vert."

Segmentals vs. Suprasegmentals

A segmental is a discrete, identifiable speech segment that contributes sound in a sequential pattern. Examples include phonemes, syllables, diphthongs, and blends. **Suprasegmentals** occur when phonetic properties are spread over a broader range of speech segments, as occurs with pitch (tone or intonation) or stress. Suprasegmental properties are thus not *inherent* in the individual speech segments, but rather *supervene* on them, constituting an additional communicative tool. The term "prosodies" is often used as a synonym for "suprasegmentals." ELL students must master prosody in order to achieve full linguistic competency, as misplaced stress or tone can readily cause communicative failure.

Phonetic Interference

Language interference occurs when features of a speaker's native language affects his or her ability to learn a second language. **Phonetic interference** refers specifically to issues that arise when trying to learn the sound system of a new language. In general terms, phonetic interference occurs when a language learner attempts to speak the foreign language using familiar sounds from their own native tongue. For example, Spanish has far fewer phonemes than English, including just one sound associated with the letter "i," the sound English speakers learn as the short "i" sound.

Spanish-speaking ELLs, then, will tend to pronounce all "i's" in English as long e's, a common example of phonetic interference.

One way to reduce phonetic interference is to introduce a word in **speech** before introducing it in **writing**, thus reducing the likelihood that a student will pronounce it according to native language rules. A second tactic is to devote large blocks of early instruction to the repetition of unfamiliar sounds.

EXAMPLES OF THE INTERNATIONAL PHONETIC ALPHABET

ʧ	"ch" sound, as in "chore".
ə	"uh" sound, as in "campus," or "love".
	This symbol is called the "schwa" and represents a common English sound.
ʤ	"j" sound, as in "jelly".
ʃ	"sh" sound, as in "shoe".
θ	"th" sound, as in "think".
ð	"th" sound, as in "the".

Morphology

Morpheme vs. Phoneme

A morpheme is the smallest meaningful unit in a language. A morpheme functions as a **linguistic sign**—that is, it refers to something in reality. A **phoneme**, by contrast, is a unit of sound that can be put together with other sounds to form words.

All words are morphemes or combinations of more than one morpheme, but not all morphemes function as stand-alone words. A **free, or independent, morpheme** can occur by itself; a **bound morpheme** can only occur in combination with one or more additional morphemes. Prefixes and affixes are the most common types of bound morphemes—although they do have meaning and function to alter the meaning of the free morphemes to which they are joined, they cannot stand on their own in English usage.

Order of Morpheme Acquisition in English

Research has demonstrated that ELL students acquire English morphemes in a consistent order, regardless of their native language or the instructional context. The following are the **stages of morpheme acquisition**:

- **Stage 1**: the "-ing" of progressive verbs ("eating"); the plural "-s"; and the copula "to be" (is, am, are).
- **Stage 2**: the auxiliary verb "to be" ("He is eating"); articles (the, a).
- **Stage 3**: irregular past tense verbs ("He went out").
- **Stage 4**: regular past tense verbs ("-ed"); third-person singular ("-s"); possessives ('s).

Teachers should take these stages into consideration as they decide in which order to introduce these forms. Further, teachers may opt not to explicitly correct errors that this model will predict students to master at a later date, and instead focus on correcting errors that correspond to a student's present stage of acquisition.

Word Analysis

Word analysis is performed by breaking a complex word into its **constituent morphemes** in order to help students understand an unfamiliar word. Word analysis relies on the fact that many English words are composed of separate, frequently-used morphemes with identifiable meanings. For example, teaching ELLs the meaning of the prefixes "re-" (again) and "un-" (not), or the Greek roots "auto-" (self) or "chrono" (time) allows them to understand a wide range of words composed of these elements. Another morphological regularity that students can exploit when analyzing unfamiliar words is the fact that English adverbs are often formed by adding the suffix "-ly" to adjectives. Thus, an ELL who knew the adjective "easy" could deduce that "easily" was an adverb by using word analysis.

Affix vs. Root

An affix, or **bound morpheme**, is a morpheme that cannot occur independently, but must be joined to another morpheme. A **root** (also called a base, or a free morpheme), by contrast, can stand alone.

One way to classify affixes is by where they are joined to the root morpheme: if they occur before the root, they are called **prefixes**; if they occur after the root, they are called **suffixes**; and if they occur in the middle of the root, they are called **infixes**. Infixes are rare in English but common in many other languages.

A second way to classify affixes is by how they change the meaning of the base to which they are joined. **Inflectional affixes** may change the number, gender, case, or tense of the root, but they do not change its basic lexical meaning, nor its grammatical form. An example is the addition of "-s" to "student": the word becomes plural but remains a noun. A **derivational affix**, by contrast, may change the meaning of the base word and/or its grammatical form. For example, the addition of "un-" to "happy" changes its meaning, and the addition of "-ish" to "child" changes a noun into an adjective.

Compound Words

Compound words are words created by combining two separate words. The resulting word often has a meaning that is difficult to predict from the meaning of the combined words. Many languages, including English, make generous use of **compound words**, while they are virtually non-existent in other languages.

While the meaning of many compound words adheres closely to the meaning of its separate parts—for example, the logic of "crosswalk" is easy to understand—others have either figurative meanings ("brainstorm") or meanings derived from older forms of English ("cobweb"), and thus may be difficult for ESLs to understand.

However, many compound words make delightful combinations and thus may appeal to ELLs: "bookworm," for example, or "skyscraper." Learning these words may also stimulate ELLs to propose compound words of their own, thereby providing them with an early experience of creativity in English use.

Cognates

Cognates are words that have a common origin, and retain similarities in meaning, spelling, or pronunciation. **Cognates** exist within a single language (in English, the words "biology" and "biography" share a common origin in the Latin root "bio," meaning "life") and between two languages that share a common origin. For example, the Spanish words "biologia" and "biografia" are cognates to their English counterparts, reflecting the common origins of Spanish and English.

The existence of cognates makes learning a new language easier, especially for beginning learners in need of comprehension early on. However, not all words that appear similar between languages actually have similar origins and meanings. Linguists refer to these as **false cognates**, and they make second-language learning harder rather than easier. For example, when English speakers encounter the Spanish word "embarazada," they often assume it means "embarrassed," but in fact, the two words are false cognates: "embarazada" means "pregnant."

English Etymology

Etymology is the study of the origin of words. Many English words have **Greek or Latin roots and affixes**. Learning those roots and affixes gives ELLs the ability to recognize the basic meaning of multiple English words and provides them with the means of deciphering the meaning of unfamiliar words by breaking them into their component pieces, which may be familiar. For example, knowing that the Greek root "micro" means "small" makes the following words accessible to an ELL: microsecond, microbiology, and microbrew.

Many English words are also formed from common Greek or Latin prefixes. Examples of common prefixes include "pre-," meaning "before"; and "semi-," meaning "half." Common suffixes include "-er," meaning "more"; and "-est," meaning "most." Knowing the meanings of these affixes will allow an ELL to decipher the meaning of many unfamiliar words.

The term "**derivation**" refers to the formation of new words by adding a derivational affix to a root. (Derivational affixes are affixes that typically change the meaning or word class of the root.) For example, the word "thankful," an adjective, can be derived by adding "-ful" to the root "thank," a verb.

Cognates vs. Loanwords

A loanword is a word adopted from a foreign language without translation, though it may be modified in small ways to fit the adopting language. **Cognates** are words in separate languages that have common origins. Cognates lead to similarities between languages by *descent*, whereas loan words lead to similarities by *borrowing*.

The existence of cognates is of great help to English language earners (ELLs) who speak closely-related languages. ELLs can often use the existence of known cognates to deduce the meaning of other words and even entire sentences. They are occasionally misled, however, by **false cognates**—words in two languages that appear similar but in fact have different origins and meanings.

Different languages loaned words to English at different times in history, depending on forces of exploration, colonization, and war. The leading **sources of English loan words** are German; Danish; French; Greek; Latin; and, following the colonization of America, Spanish and Native American.

Morphological Interference

Morphological interference occurs when a student's ability to learn a second language is influenced by the morphology of their native language. Languages differ significantly in how words are formed and what type of information can be conveyed in a single word (as opposed to being conveyed in a second word or conveyed simply by context). For example, English nouns typically have single and plural forms ("one goose," "two geese"), and verbs typically change with tense ("I eat," "I ate"). By contrast, nouns in Mandarin Chinese do not change with number, and verbs do not change with tense; this additional information is provided by context. Even closely-related languages exhibit significant differences. English speakers, for example, are accustomed to verbs that have the same form in the first-person singular, first-person plural, and third-person plural, but a different form in the third-person singular ("I talk," "we talk," and "they talk" contrast with "he talks"). Spanish, however, utilizes a different verb form in each of these cases. Having a sense of the variations possible in language can help an ESL teacher understand the cause of a student's English errors.

Syntax

Parts of English Speech

- **Noun**—a word that names a person, place, idea, or thing. Nouns are often combined with determiners to form the subject of a sentence. They are often replaced by pronouns.
- **Verb**—a word that expresses an action or state of being. Verbs are typically the core of the predicate of a sentence. In English, verbs change to agree with the subject and reflect tense, voice, mood, and aspect.
- **Pronoun**—a word that replaces a noun or noun phrase (its antecedent) that was previously used or understood.
- **Adjective**—a word that modifies a noun, typically by describing the quantity, quality, or by distinguishing one noun from another.
- **Adverb**—a word that modifies a verb, adjective, or adverb and often shows degree, manner, place, or time.
- **Preposition**—a word (such as "in," "to," "on," "with") that is usually combined with a noun or pronoun to establish a relationship between that noun and another part of the sentence. The relationships include things such as location or time.
- **Interjection**—a word or phrase used to express emotion or surprise.
- **Conjunction**—a word that links sentences, clauses, phrases, or words. Examples include "and," "or" and "but."

Review Video: What is a Determiner in Grammar?
Visit mometrix.com/academy and enter code: 385229

Noun

A noun is a word that names a person, place, thing, quality, or action. **Common nouns** refer to types or classes of things that have more than one member—for example, "president" or "state." They are not capitalized unless they begin a sentence. Proper nouns refer to specific people or things—for example, "President Lincoln," or "Florida." They are capitalized wherever they occur in a sentence.

Countable nouns refer to things that can be counted. They have separate singular and plural forms (one egg, two eggs), and in the singular form can be preceded by "a" or "an." Uncountable nouns, often referred to as mass nouns, cannot be counted (milk, rice). They do not have plural forms and cannot be used with "a" and "an."

Concrete nouns refer to things that can be perceived by the senses. Abstract nouns refer to things that cannot be perceived by the senses—for example, ideas, concepts, or beliefs. Whether a noun is concrete or abstract makes no difference in how it is used.

Conjunction

A conjunction is a word that connects other words, phrases, clauses, or sentences. **Conjunctions** are one of the eight parts of speech, along with nouns, verbs, pronouns, adjectives, adverbs, prepositions, and interjections.

Coordinating conjunctions link together words or phrases that have the same grammatical function. For example: "I like to bike, *and* I like to run." There are seven coordinating conjunctions: for, and, not, but, or, yet, and so—these can be recalled using the acronym FANBOYS.

Correlative conjunctions appear in pairs and also join words or phrases with the same function. Examples of correlative conjunctions include "either... or," "both... and," and "no sooner... than." For example: "I am going to the game, *whether or not* you come with me.".

Subordinating conjunctions join unequal parts of a sentence. Specifically, they link adverbial clauses—a type of dependent clause that serves as an adverb—to an independent clause. There are many subordinate clauses, but some of the most common are "when," "because," "before," and "if." In the example "I will go to sleep *when* you come home," the conjunction "when" joins the independent clause "I will go to sleep" with the dependent clause "you come home."

Pronoun and Antecedent

A pronoun is a word that takes the place of a noun (or noun phrase), which is referred to as the pronoun's *antecedent*. There are three types of pronouns. **Personal pronouns** refer to a specific person (or persons) or an object. They include many of the most common words in English: I, me, you, he, she, etc. **Possessive pronouns** indicate ownership: my/mine, your/yours, its, their, etc. **Indefinite pronouns** refer to nonspecific persons or things: anybody, everything, no one, someone, etc.

Even native English speakers make frequent errors when using personal pronouns. These pronouns have two forms: the **subjective form**, to be used when the pronoun serves as a subject or complements a subject; and the **objective form**, to be used when the pronoun serves as an object. The subjective personal pronouns are I, you, he/she/it, we, you and they. The corresponding objective pronouns are me, you, him/her/it, us, you, and them.

Syntax vs. Grammar

Syntax is the way in which words are combined in a language to create phrases, clauses, and sentences. The word is often used synonymously with "**grammar**." However, "grammar" has a prescriptive sense that is often missing from "syntax"—the former describes the way words should be combined in order to be considered correct, whereas the latter describes the ways in which they are combined in reality to achieve effective communication. In common usage, "grammar" is a broader term than "syntax," referring not only to syntax, but also to phonology, semantics, and even punctuation.

The most common **syntactic form** of an English sentence is subject-verb-object, as in the sentence "The dog bit the man." While this may seem too obvious to a native English speaker to be noteworthy, it is important to understand for a few reasons. First, many languages are constructed differently—for example, the basic order in Japanese is subject-object-verb. Second, the order is altered in English when the passive voice is used. For example, "The man was bitten by the dog" yields the syntactic form object-verb-subject.

Transformational or Generative Grammar

Transformational grammar (or generative grammar) is an approach to syntax, developed by Noam Chomsky, that hypothesizes that the surface structure of any language can be explained as a transformation of an innate (or universal, or deep) structure of language which humans all share in common. The term "generative" refers to the idea that language learners learn to form (or generate) sentences by transforming the deep structures present in brains at birth. For example, Chomsky argued that declarative and interrogative sentences share a single deep structure, and linguists have established a set of rules by which the former can be transformed into the latter.

Subsequent proponents of generative grammar introduced the term "**principles**" to name the rules of the hypothesized universal grammar and the term "**parameters**" to name the constraints that any actual language places on the set of universal rules. For example, a parameter of English grammar is that, in a verb phrase, the verb must precede its object complements, as in "ate the cake.".

Subject and Predicate, Noun and Verb

Beginning students are often taught that English sentences need, at a minimum, a noun and a verb. In fact, many sentences contain nothing more than a **noun** and **verb**—for example, "John is running." However, this description of the *simplest* of English sentences does not describe the *entirety* of English sentences, most of which contain other parts of speech in addition to a noun and a verb. In contrast, the more formal terms subject and predicate are exhaustive: they refer to all the possible elements of an English sentence.

A **subject** is what or whom a sentence is talking about, and a **predicate** tells something about that subject. Everything in a sentence is either part of the subject or part of the predicate. Simple nouns or pronouns often serve as the subject of a sentence, but the role can also be filled by more complex structures. Some sentences have implied subjects, as in command: "Be quiet!" In addition to the verb, the predicate often includes an object (direct and/or indirect) and various compliments.

Review Video: What is a Complete Predicate?
Visit mometrix.com/academy and enter code: 293942

Tense

In grammar, **tense** refers to the location of events in time. In English, tense is expressed by changing the form of verbs. While linguists recognize only two tenses in English (past and present) and classify the other variations in verbs as changes of aspect or mood, non-specialists commonly recognize twelve different tenses, which we can order in a 3 x 4 chart:

	Simple	Progressive	Perfect	Perfect Progressive
Present	I walk	I am walking	I have walked	I have been walking
Past	I walked	I was walking	I had walked	I had been walking
Future	I will walk	I will be walking	I will have walked	I will have been walking

The progressive forms are also referred to as continuous forms, as they are used to describe actions or states that are ongoing at a certain point in time. These are fashioned by combining a form of the verb "to be" and "-ing." The perfect tenses are fashioned by combining a form of the verb "to have" and the past participle of the main verb. The perfect progressive tenses are built using features of both the progressive and perfect tenses.

Subject-Verb Agreement

The basic rule of subject-verb agreement is that a singular subject requires a singular verb, and a plural subject requires a plural verb.

One exception is in the **simple past**, in which a stand-alone main verb (one without an auxiliary verb) doesn't change when the noun changes: "The man gave me a box," and "The men gave me a box," use the same verb form. Many helping verbs, however, do function according to the rule in the simple past.

A second problem arises with **compound subjects**—two or more subjects joined by "and," "or," or "nor." If two subjects are joined by "and," they should be treated as a plural subject taking a plural verb. If they are joined by "or" or "nor," however, the subject nearest the verb should agree with the verb: "Neither the dog nor the cats like liver.".

A third common error arises when the subject of a sentence is separated from the verb by an **intervening phrase** that contains a noun. Correct usage requires that the verb agrees with the subject, not the nearby noun. Thus: "The students who pass the test receive a prize."

Classifying Verbs

A **transitive verb** requires an object in order to constitute a complete thought, whereas an **intransitive verb** does not. "Throw" is an example of a transitive verb: it is incorrect to simply say "I threw" without adding an object. "Jump," however, is intransitive: "I jumped," is an acceptable sentence. Some verbs are both transitive and intransitive, depending on context.

Linking verbs do not indicate action, but instead connect the subject to a word or phrase that describes the subject. The verb "to be" is the most common linking verb.

Verbs that are conjugated to agree with a subject are called **finite verbs**. The three main types of non-finite verbs are infinitives, gerunds, and participles. An **infinitive** is a verb with the word "to" in front of it: to eat, to read, etc. A **gerund** is an "-ing" verb functioning as a noun—as in the example "I like swimming." A **participle** is a word formed from a verb but used either as an adjective, adverb, noun, or as part of a compound verb. For example, the past participle "gone" forms a compound noun in the phrase "has gone."

Independent Clause vs. Dependent Clause

A **clause** is a group of words with a subject and a predicate. A **sentence** goes one step further: it is a group of words with a subject and predicate that expresses a complete thought. For example, "When I saw him," is a clause, but it is not a complete sentence.

An **independent clause** is a clause that can stand alone as a sentence but can also be joined with other clauses to make other sentences. A **dependent clause**, by contrast, cannot stand alone as a sentence, but must be combined with another clause or clauses to form a sentence.

A **simple sentence** is a single independent clause—in other words, a complete thought consisting of a subject and predicate. A **compound sentence** consists of two or more independent clauses, often joined by a conjunction, such as "and" or "or." A **complex sentence** consists of an independent clause and a dependent clause joined by a subordinating conjunction such as "when" or "because." A **complex-compound sentence** is one with two or more independent clauses joined to one or more dependent clauses.

Appositive

An appositive is a noun, noun phrase, or noun clause that serves to explain or identify another noun nearby in the sentence. In the sentence "Your brother Skip called me," "Skip" is an **appositive** identifying the noun phrase "your brother." "Skip" and "your brother" can be described as being in *apposition*. In the sentence "Carla—the only teacher to attend the training session—was well-prepared for the exercises," "the only teacher to attend the training session" is an appositive that provides information about the noun "Carla."

In general, appositives that are essential to the meaning of the sentence are not set off by punctuation marks, whereas those that are not are set off by commas, dashes, or parentheses. Knowing this usage pattern would allow an ELL to recognize, for example, that the author of the sentence "Your brother Skip called me" recognizes that the person he or she is writing to has more than one brother, and thus signaled that the appositive "Skip" was critical to the meaning of the sentence by declining to set it off by commas.

Classifying Sentences

Sentences can be classified in various ways—for example, the categories "compound sentences" and "complex sentences" classify sentences according to their *syntax*. Another common way to classify sentences is by their *purpose*, or what they are meant to achieve in a communicative setting. In this context, experts usually identify four different kinds of sentences. **Declarative sentences** make a statement: "Jodie is a tall woman." **Interrogative sentences** pose a question: "Is your mom home?" **Imperative sentences** give a command: "Please come here." And **exclamatory sentences** express strong feelings: "I can't wait for tomorrow!" .

Review Video: Intro to Sentence Types
Visit mometrix.com/academy and enter code: 953367

Phrasal Verb

A phrasal verb is an idiomatic combination of a verb with another word, usually a preposition or adverbs. Examples include "blow up," "break down," "chip in," "get away with," and "add up." These verbs pose unique difficulties for ELLs because the word combinations are idiomatic and yet fixed. Further, many **phrasal verbs** can be split when used in a sentence—for example, when referring to a column of numbers, we can ask "Can you *add* them *up*?", interposing the word "them" in the phrasal verb.

ELLs are likely to find three aspects of phrasal verbs challenging: their idiomatic meanings, their seemingly arbitrary choice of preposition or adverb to couple with the verb, and the contexts in which they can and cannot be split.

Tag Question

A tag question is a declarative statement turned into a question by the addition of an interrogative fragment, as in the example "Portland is the capital of Maine, isn't it?" **Tag questions** are often rhetorical—the speaker does not seek an answer—and they are also used to communicate a desired answer to the listener. Many languages utilize tag questions ("n'est ce pas" in French and "da" in Russian are two frequent examples), but those in English tend to be complex and varied, thus posing production if not reception challenges for ELLs.

Predicate Nominative and Predicate Adjective

A predicate nominative is a noun or noun phrase (thus making it nominative) that follows a linking verb (and thus is in the predicate of a sentence) and renames the subject. For example, in the sentence "John's favorite book is *War and Peace*," "War and Peace" is a **predicate nominative**.

A **predicate adjective** is a word or words that follows a linking verb and modifies the subject of a sentence. In the sentence "The dog is brown," "brown" is a predicate adjective. Predicate adjectives are distinguished from ordinary or attributive adjectives, which typically precede the noun that they modify. Instead, a predicate adjective follows the noun and is paired with a linking verb.

Gerunds vs. Present Participles

Gerunds and present participles are both formed using the "-ing" form of a verb, and both are often parts of a broader phrase. **Gerunds**, however, function as *nouns*, while **present participles** function either as progressing verbs (their most familiar use) or as *adjectives*. In the sentence "Hiking to the top of Mount Kilimanjaro is hard work," the word "hiking" is a gerund: it is a noun, the subject of the verb "is." In the sentence "Hiking to the top of Mount Kilimanjaro, John fell and sprained his ankle," "hiking" is a participle that initiates an adjectival phrase modifying the noun "John."

Modal Verb

A modal phrase is an auxiliary verb that adds shades of meaning to the main verb of a sentence by adding an opinion, attitude, or feeling. The most common **modal verbs** in English are "would, will, can, could, may, and must."

Modals present several challenges to ELLs. First, student L1s may not have corresponding forms: Spanish, for example, has no word for "will" or "would." Second, modals often have several unrelated meanings—"may," for example, can convey both possibility ("I may come") or permission ("May I go?"). Third, modals are irregular in their conjugation—for example, the verbs listed above do not add an "-s" in the third-person present. Finally, when a modal is combined with another verb, the second verb is not used in its infinitive form, as is generally the case when a sentence contains two verbs. Thus, native speakers say "I can go," not "I can to go," but would use the infinitive form "to go" in most instances, as in "I want to go."

Semantics

Semantics

Semantics is the study of the meaning of words, phrases, and sentences. The **denotation** of a word is its most literal definition, the one listed in a dictionary. The **connotation** of a word is the associations and emotions that a word evokes, either because of personal experience or shared cultural understandings. Connotations may change over time, and even if they are relatively stable, they will likely be difficult for an ESL student to understand. For example, "slender" and "skinny" have the same denotations, but for most native English speakers, the former has a positive connotation, while the latter has a negative connotation.

Literal and Figurative Language

Literal language is language that means exactly what it says—the meaning of a literal sentence can be understood simply by understanding its component words. **Figurative language** conveys a meaning different from the literal meaning of its component words. **Metaphors** compare, or equate, two unlike things without using the words "like" or "as"—for example, "love is war," or "this problem is a real bear." **Similes** do the same, but use "like" or "as"—for example, "my throat is as dry as a bone."

An **idiom** is a figurative expression that has gained widespread usage in a language community. Unlike a metaphor or simile, it doesn't necessarily make a comparison. Many idioms carried a literal meaning when they were first coined, but that meaning has since been forgotten or rendered obsolete. For example, the idiom "Don't beat around the bush," which is now used to exhort someone to speak clearly and directly, originally described the practice whereby a group of hunters would beat bushes with sticks in order to flush out their prey. Idioms are particularly difficult for ESL students to learn because they can't be understood simply through a study of their denotation.

Homonym

Homonyms are words that are spelled alike or sound alike but have different meanings and origins. If two words are spelled alike, they are called **homographs** ("graph" in Greek means "to write"). If the two words sound alike, they are called **homophones** ("phone" in Greek means "sound"). Examples of homographs include "entrance" (as a noun, it means "a door"; as a verb, it means "to captivate.") Examples of homophones include "bear" (an animal) and "bare" (as a verb, it means "to uncover.") ESL students should be shown the written form to help distinguish homophones, and the spoken form to help distinguish homographs.

Two words may share both spelling and pronunciation but differ in meaning and, critically, in origin. (If they don't differ in origin, then they are not two different words, but simply one word with two meanings.) These words are referred to simply as homonyms. An example is "saw," which is both a cutting tool the past tense of "to see."

Language Ambiguities

Language ambiguities arise when ELLs are confronted with a word that has multiple meanings (homograph) or multiple pronunciations (heteronyms) and they must rely on **context** to determine the actual usage.

For example, if presented with the sentence "Jack will lead the tour," an ELL could use his or her awareness of the basic English sentence structure subject-verb-object to realize that "lead" in this example (a homograph) is a verb and not a noun. Similarly, if presented with the sentence "Please don't tear the paper," an ELL can deduce from knowledge of syntax that "tear" is a verb rather than the heteronym "tear," a noun referring to moisture in the eye.

Deciphering language ambiguities is an example of the broader use of **context clues** to decipher the meaning of unknown words or phrases. ELLs can often use their knowledge of sentence structure to deduce at least what part of speech an unknown word might be. For example, an awareness that the verb "to give" is often followed by both a direct and an indirect object, and that the former is usually an object and the latter a person, will provide an ELL with clues about an unfamiliar word.

Pragmatics

Pragmatics

Pragmatics is the study of how meaning is affected by context—or, stated differently, how people may use shared understandings and implications to reach understandings that are not entailed by the literal meaning of their words. An **implication** is a conclusion that can be drawn even though it isn't stated.

We rely on **shared understandings** in order to carry out conversations. For example, if a person tells me that she has two daughters, I assume that she has *only* two, although logically, her statement is consistent with her having five. When I ask someone "Could you pass the salad?" we rely on the implied understanding that I want the salad, not a yes or no answer. Even the length or nature of our casual exchanges with strangers are driven by shared understandings: when the cashier in the supermarket asks how we are doing, we both know that he or she isn't asking for a detailed reply.

These examples help illustrate the broader point that communication always takes place in a context that creates implicit meaning in addition to the explicit meaning represented by the words themselves.

Paul Grice's Cooperative Principle

The philosopher Paul Grice's work focuses on how pragmatics function in language—that is, on how we rely on shared assumptions, background knowledge, and implied meanings to communicate more or more clearly than our stated words would seem to allow. Grice's **cooperative principle** can be paraphrased to state that, when we engage in conversation, we assume that our interlocutor will cooperate in achieving understanding by speaking truthfully, logically, and concisely. Grice emphasized that what we *mean* is often *implied* by what we *say* and that a competent member of our language community will grasp the implications of our speech.

We successfully communicate implied meanings, Grice argues, when we obey four maxims of conversation. The **maxim of quality** states that we speak the truth. The **maxim of quantity** states that we provide as much information or detail as is necessary to fulfill our conversational purpose. The **maxim of relevance** states that we will stay on topic. The **maxim of manner** suggests that we will avoid ambiguity, use language our interlocutor can understand, and organize our speech in a logical way. Grice argues that these assumptions allow us to communicate many implied meanings without resorting to explicit explanations.

Register, Eye Contact, Physical Proximity, and Gestures

Pragmatic features of communication are the non-linguistic factors that influence what and how effectively we communicate in a given language community. These features are particularly important to ELLs because the conventions of their adopted language community might differ from those of their native language community.

Register refers to the formality of language. By convention, English speakers will speak more formally in a professional setting than when talking to a close friend; ELLs may need instruction and practice to master these conventions. Students from different cultures may also have a different understanding of the significance of **eye contact** during the conversation: whereas in the United States, direct eye contact signals transparency, in many cultures it is seen as an aggressive assertion of status. Similarly, ELLs may have a different sense of appropriate **personal space** when conversing than their typical American interlocutor, which can interfere with effective communication. The use of **gestures** in communication also varies widely by culture, as well as by context within a culture, and ELLs will have to learn or acquire the conventions of the language community in order to communicate effectively.

Locution, Illocution, and Perlocution

The philosopher John L. Austin launched what came to be known as **speech act theory** in the 1970s by distinguishing between **locution** (what a person says), **illocution** (what a person means), and **perlocution** (the effect the person's utterance has). The classic example is the utterance at the dinner table of the locution "Is there any salt?" which has the illocutionary meaning of "Please pass the salt" and the perlocutionary effect of the salt being passed.

A **pragmatic failure** occurs when a person fails to understand what is *meant* even though he or she correctly understood what was *said*. For example, a teacher might call the fact that a student is late to class by asking him or her "What time is it?" A pragmatic failure would occur if the student took the question at face-value and failed to understand it as a reprimand.

Culture

Cultural Concepts and Perspectives

External and Internal Culture

Culture is an integrated pattern of knowledge, belief, and behavior, held by a particular human group, that is learned and transmitted through generations. The term is broad, but culture can be thought of as consisting of what people (a) do, (b) believe or know, and (c) make and use.

Another way to think about culture is to differentiate between external and internal culture. **External culture** (often called material culture) refers to the objects and physical space people use to express their shared culture. Elements of external culture include architecture, clothing, food, technology, the arts, and language. **Internal culture** (often called non-material culture) refers to the shared patterns of thought and social behavior that exist as collective beliefs and customs. Elements of internal culture include values, family structures, social roles, beliefs and expectations, and worldview. External cultural markers are easier to recognize, but with the exception of language, the elements of internal culture have a greater influence on how students learn.

The Sapir-Whorf Hypothesis

The Sapir-Whorf hypothesis, which combines the work of the linguistic anthropologists Edward Sapir (1884–1939) and Benjamin Whorf (1897–1941), is the assertion that **language** has a strong, constraining influence on **thought**—and thus that speakers of different languages have different **worldviews**. In other words, language doesn't only reflect reality, but influences our perception of reality.

The strongest form of the hypothesis is now discounted, leaving a consensus that language *influences* thought. For example, research shows that a person is more likely to remember something that they can name in their language with a single word, but does not *determine* or *constrain* it. The widespread possibility of translation counts against the strong form of the hypothesis: although translators often lack a single word in L2 to translate a word in L1, they can invariably achieve a translation through a circumlocution.

The Sapir-Whorf hypothesis is an example of a theory that posits that thought is dependent on language. The common-sense view holds the opposite: people have thoughts and put them into words when they wish to communicate. The consensus view is that both mental processes occur.

Hofstede's Cultural Dimensions Theory

Geete Hofstede's cultural dimensions theory is a useful tool for understanding cultural differences. In the late 1960s and early 1970s, Hofstede conducted a multinational survey of national values, and concluded that key differences could be explained along six dimensions: (A) *Individualism versus collectivism*, which is whether people think primarily in terms of "I" or "we." (B) *Uncertainty avoidance index*, or the degree to which people are uncomfortable with uncertainty and ambiguity. (C) *Power distance index*, which is the extent to which people expect hierarchy versus equality. (D) *Long-term versus short-term orientation*, which includes a measure of whether people are pragmatic toward change or prefer to preserve cultural values. (E) *Indulgence versus restraint*, or whether a culture promotes leisure and self-gratification. (F) *Masculinity versus femininity*, which, in Hofstede's theory, refers to masculinity as a preference for assertive behavior, achievement, and material success; whereas femininity refers to a preference for modesty, cooperation, and caring for others.

A teacher might use Hofstede's dimension of power distance index, for example, to understand a student's degree of comfort or formality in interacting with his or her teacher. Students with a sharp sense of hierarchy might be unlikely to speak to the teacher unless spoken to or offer an opinion different than the teacher's.

Individualist vs. Collectivist Cultures

The distinction between individualist and collectivist cultures is the element of Geete Hofstede's cultural dimensions theory that has had the most influence on educational psychology. **Individualistic cultures** are those that value individual achievement and development above those of group success or cohesion. Individualistic cultures (like mainstream American culture) value freedom and individual initiative and tend to ascribe success and failure to individual traits such as motivation or intelligence. Individualist cultures encourage students to stand out from the group and students who do not are often viewed as mediocre and underachieving. **Collectivist cultures**, on the other hand, value group harmony and social acceptance, and may see standing out as a cause for concern or stress. In a collectivist culture, education is less the means to individual achievement and fulfillment, and instead a means to social acceptance and fulfilling an expected role.

Teachers need to be aware of these differences in order to understand **student motivation** and also to understand the impact of classroom activities that emphasize **individual performance** or bestow **individual praise**. It may be particularly hard for teachers raised in an individualistic culture to understand that, for some students, public individual praise may be distinctly unwanted and a source of shame.

Speech Act

A speech act is an utterance aimed at achieving something (rather than describing something), such as requesting, promising, complaining, or apologizing. The form **speech acts** take in a given language and culture are often highly standardized and routinized. For example, a native English speaker will recognize the question "Do you have a dollar?" as a request, but it may appear as a simple and out-of-context question to a non-native speaker.

Speech acts perform a pragmatic function that cannot be understood by means of literal semantic analysis. The existence of language features such as speech acts makes it imperative that a language learner also develops **cultural competence** in order to become a full and effective member of the L2 culture.

Differentiating Between Authorized and Unauthorized Immigrants

Contrary to popular opinion, a majority of school-age ELLs were born in the United States. Approximately 75% have **legal status**. Of the 25% who do not, the majority entered the United States legally—usually with a nonimmigrant or visitor visa—and then failed to leave.

The centerpiece of US immigration policy is **family reunification**—the majority of immigrants qualify to come to the US by virtue of having a close family member who is a US citizen or permanent resident. **Refugees**—from war, discrimination, or natural disasters—are another significant class of immigrants. Fewer immigrants qualify by virtue of having high job skills in short supply or by investing money in job-creating businesses in the US. Finally, the United States administers a **diversity lottery program** through which a limited number of high school-educated people from underrepresented countries qualify to immigrate each year.

Since the 1982 Supreme Court case *Plyler v. Doe*, school districts cannot exclude students on the basis of **immigration status**. However, unauthorized immigrants are often afraid to enroll their students in school, or to engage with school officials, out of fear of being reported to immigration authorities.

Push and Pull Factors

Everett Lee coined the terms "push factors" and "pull factors" in a 1962 book in order to classify people's motives for **migrating** (moving from one area to another) or **immigrating** (migrating from one country to another). **Push factors** are the unattractive features of a home country that compel people to leave. The most common push factors are a lack of economic opportunities, war, natural disaster, and repression or discrimination. **Pull factors** are attractive features of the destination country. The most common pull factors are economic opportunity, the prospect of reuniting with family members, and social and political freedom.

Secondary Migration and Transnational Migration

Secondary migration is the entry of people into the US from a location other than their country of birth. There are two primary types of **secondary migrants** to the US: refugees who flee their home countries to neighboring countries and from there arrange legal entry into the US; and individuals who first immigrate to countries with more lenient immigration policies, such as Canada, and then stage economic or family-based immigration to the US. The term is also used to describe the movement of refugees within the US from their original point of resettlement to locations they find more attractive. ELLs who experience secondary migration are more likely to have experienced interrupted or uneven schooling, including potential instruction in a non-English foreign language.

The term "**transnational migration**" refers to the practice of immigrants to the US maintaining close ties to their country of origin. Common expressions of these ties include regular home visits (students may spend their summers in their countries of origin), sending money or remittances to family members abroad, or making plans to return to the home country for retirement or after achieving citizenship. Transnational migration is often seen as a challenge to assimilation, but ESL teachers can cultivate students' ongoing ties to their home countries as an educational resource.

Generation 1.5

The term "generation 1.5" refers to individuals who immigrated to the United States in their late childhood or early teen years, and thus are neither first generation (adult immigrants) nor second generation (born in the US). They are likely to have substantial remaining ties to their home countries and, unlike younger siblings born in the US, may lack citizenship and thus be vulnerable to deportation. As late arrivals to the US school system, they may resist being labeled ELLs and thus avoid integration into standard ELL programs. While many will have a basic proficiency in social English, they may lag in the acquisition of **academic language**—a deficiency they might be unwilling to address if they are out of step with their peers who immigrated earlier in life or were born in the US At the same time, as relatively mature ELLs, they are likely to have a very good grasp of the **social and pragmatic** aspects of communication, and to infer meaning readily from context.

Diversity and Cross-Cultural Interaction

Acculturation, Assimilation, Accommodation, and Biculturalism

In the context of cultural contact, **acculturation** is the adaptation of a person or group to another culture, often in the context of immigration. The terms "**assimilation**" and "**accommodation**" refer to how complete that adaptation is: assimilation occurs when the individual adapts fully to the new culture and largely abandons the cultural markers of his or her first culture; whereas accommodation occurs when an individual accepts certain elements of the new culture, especially those necessary for public life in school or at work, but retains many elements of the first culture, particularly when at home and with family. **Biculturalism** occurs when a person functions fully and simultaneously in both cultures, balancing each without a drive to either assimilate or exclude the new culture.

Accommodation and assimilation are defined and used differently in discussions of language development, derived largely from the work of Jean Piaget.

Cultural Universals, Cultural Generalities, and Cultural Particulars

Cultural universals are aspects of culture that are shared by all human societies. The comparative ethnologist George Murdock created a list of more than 70 **cultural universals** in 1945—for example, fire-making, incest taboos, and inheritance rules. Cultural generalities are cultural features that occur in many cultures, but not all. Nuclear families are an example. Cultural particulars are cultural traits that are unique to a single culture - specific recipes or celebrations are examples. Anthropologists distinguish between **cultural traits** that arise independently from those that are spread through contact, or **cultural diffusion**. Cultural traits are generally viewed as *adaptive*—as furthering the survival and success of the social group—but *nonadaptive* traits exist as well, including many modes of production that are harmful to the environment in the medium or long-term. The forces of globalization have rapidly increased the rate of cultural diffusion and, in many instances, the extinction of narrowly held cultural particulars.

Culture Shock

The term "culture shock" refers to the feelings of confusion or alienation a person may experience when first living, studying, or working in a new culture. In broad terms, a person experiences **culture shock** when he or she is taken out of a cultural context that provided them with reinforcement and a sense of control and is inserted into another that they don't fully understand or feel competent in.

Adler's model proposes that individuals progress through various stages of culture shock. In the first, which Adler calls *contact,* but is often referred to as the honeymoon stage, the individual feels excitement and tends to focus on similarities between the home and new cultures. In stage two, *disintegration*, the individual focuses on differences and may feel alienated. In stage three, *reintegration*, the individual rejects the new culture. As the individual becomes more competent in the new culture, he or she will experience *autonomy*, the fourth stage, and relax the previous defensiveness. In the final stage, *independence*, the individual feels comfortable in the new setting and is able to offer generalizations and perspectives on the process of cultural adaptation.

Adjustment of Newcomers

Individuals adapt to a new culture in different ways, at different rates, and to differing degrees. Research suggests that the most important factor leading to rapid and large-scale adjustment is **language proficiency**. A second factor is **personality type**—outgoing individuals who are comfortable interacting with others tend to adjust quickly. **Cultural intelligence** also plays a role: if an individual is conscious of cultural differences (perhaps due to prior travel), he or she is more likely to recognize differences for what they are and develop appropriate strategies in response. Individuals with strong **social and family support networks** tend to adjust better and more rapidly, though if the home-culture network is dominant, it may lead to an incomplete adjustment. An individual's **emotional intelligence** also plays a role—knowing the cause of one's emotions and how to regulate emotional responses is important. Finally, the **response of the host community**—in the classroom or the larger community—is important: whether diversity is tolerated or even championed will make a difference to the adjustment process.

Cultural Congruence

In the educational context, **cultural congruence** exists when classroom experiences and instruction reinforce, or are at least consistent with, student home cultures. A culturally congruent classroom acts as a bridge between a student's first and learned cultures. Proponents argue that students learn best in **culturally congruent classrooms**—in part by eliminating the perceived choice that students in minority cultures make between learning and maintaining a loyalty to their own cultural traditions. In order to promote cultural congruence, teachers can incorporate content from student cultures or adapt their teaching techniques to reflect student learning preferences or customary patterns of interaction.

Cultural Pluralism

Cultural pluralism occurs when several distinct cultural groups and traditions coexist in a single society without an impetus toward assimilation to the majority culture. A commitment to **cultural pluralism** implies that cultural and linguistic differences are not a problem to be overcome, but rather a resource to be utilized in the education process. Historically, and in line with broader societal views, teachers tended to minimize cultural differences and work toward rapid assimilation of immigrants, in part by fostering a new and single-group identity. While rapid assimilation still exists as the perceived ideal in the minds of many Americans—and for many immigrants as well—many curriculums now emphasize the celebration of cultural differences and the promotion of bilingualism as a language goal.

Prejudice, Stereotyping, and Ethnocentrism

Prejudice is a negative opinion formed about an individual or group without basis or sufficient knowledge. **Ethnocentrism** is the belief that one's own culture is superior to others. It is contrasted with cultural relativism—the recognition that every culture has value and may serve needs and interests different from those of one's own culture. To **stereotype** is to hold a simplified and overgeneralized view of a group, often with a critical or prejudiced view.

Teachers should find non-confrontational ways to address and discuss expressions of **cultural bias** when they occur. Teachers should emphasize the difference between recognizing legitimate cultural differences and stereotyping. Teachers often shy away from discussions of cultural bias in multicultural classrooms out of fear of offending students or initiating disagreements. Training, such as that offered by the National Association for Multicultural Education, can help teachers overcome these fears and facilitate useful discussions.

Implicit Bias

Implicit bias occurs when unconscious stereotypes or opinions influence our behavior, often in direct contradiction to our consciously held beliefs. Psychological research demonstrates that we all hold **implicit biases**. The vast majority of human cognitive and emotional processing occurs unconsciously, and the mind's tendency to generalize and simplify is a necessary cognitive adaptation to a complex world. Thus, biases should not be seen as a personal fault.

Teachers can become aware of their implicit biases through **diagnostic tools** such as the implicit association test. In order to overcome these biases, teachers should be self-reflective, reviewing their actions and interventions at the end of the day to assess their evenness. Research shows that decisions made hurriedly, under stress, or with incomplete information are more likely to be biased—thus, when possible, teachers should slow their reactive decision-making. The best way to overcome bias is to get to know students as individuals rather than simply as members of a group. Implicit biases are heuristic devices our minds employ in the absence of information.

SHAPING TEACHER PERCEPTIONS OF STUDENTS

Fundamental attribution error is the tendency to attribute the negative behavior of others to a personality flaw, while attributing one's own negative behavior (or the behavior of people like ourselves) to situational, environmental factors. **Confirmation bias** is the tendency to make quick first impressions about a person or situation, overvalue subsequent information that confirms that judgment, and undervalue subsequent information that discounts it. **In-group bias** is the tendency to attribute positive motivations and personality characteristics to people like ourselves and not to people we perceive as different.

Teachers can minimize the effect of these implicit biases by avoiding early judgments about student abilities or motivation, by charitably seeking situational explanations for poor performance or behavior, and by getting to know students and their life circumstances.

Family and Community Involvement

Family Involvement and Student Success

Decades of research has demonstrated the strong correlation between **family involvement** and **student success**. Securing ELL parental involvement is particularly important—ELLs are disproportionately at risk for academic failure, and thus in need of support—and difficult to achieve, given language differences and cultural differences that may discourage parents from actively involving themselves in their children's education.

In order to overcome these obstacles, teachers should get to know each student's **cultural background and family circumstances** relevant to building a home-school relationship. Teachers should introduce themselves to parents and guardians and invite them to both group meetings and to one-on-one conferences. Teachers should establish multiple means of communication (email, phone calls, office hours) and, where feasible, translate messages into frequent L1s. Parents should be encouraged to volunteer in the classroom or chaperone field trips. Teachers should establish certain periods when parents can visit and observe the classroom. ESL teachers with relatively homogenous student populations may wish to sponsor information sessions during which translators are made available, either to discuss concerns specific to the ESL classroom or to provide general school-related advice and information to interested parents.

Involving the Community

Both **non-profit organizations** and **local businesses** often have an interest in the success of local schools, even if their directors do not have children currently enrolled in those schools. For businesses, visible involvement in school projects is an effective and targeted form of advertising—a way of demonstrating their commitment to the community.

Schools may need to be proactive in seeking **business or non-profit engagement**. One way to do so is to organize an annual community appreciation event and invite local organizations. Another is to encourage students to get their parents involved. Schools can invite community leaders to events and include them on email distribution lists that include descriptions of school goals and needs. When businesses do engage, schools need to make sure their efforts are recognized, whether it be in the form of on-site advertising or being recognized in school newsletters and notices.

Overcoming Parental Communication Challenges

While the **parents and guardians** of students are one of the most important audiences to target with school outreach and communication strategies, they are also one of the most difficult to reach because of multiple factors. Language barriers are the most obvious, but ELL parents and guardians may also come from cultures that discourage parental involvement in schooling. ELL families are also disproportionately poor, and parents may work long hours or multiple jobs, preventing them attending scheduled school events.

ESL teachers should develop proactive and multi-pronged **outreach strategies** in order to overcome these obstacles. Teachers should disseminate information through multiple channels, such as emails, blogs, and newsletters sent home with students. Teachers should strive to make their students' daily activities and responsibilities visible to parents in some fashion.

Teachers should signal their availability and strive to be approachable. They might perform home visits if allowed. Teachers should schedule regular (monthly) meetings as well as repeatedly invite parents to attend one-on-one conferences. Teachers may consider communicating with parents through student homework folders. In all of these engagements, teachers should provide translations and interpretations when possible, and strive to use simple and clear language.

Second Language Acquisition and Instructional Practices

Language Development Theories and Stages

The Behaviorist Theory of First-Language Acquisition

Behaviorist theories of language learning propose that humans learn language through a process of **reinforcement**. In response to a stimulus, children offer a spoken response, usually a repetition of something they've just heard, and then receive either positive or negative feedback. This feedback creates what founder B.F. Skinner (1904–1990) termed **operant conditioning**—a change in behavior in response to feedback. (in contrast, his so-called classical conditioning involves learning to associate two events but does not entail any behavioral change.) Through this back-and-forth inductive process, children learn the rules and patterns of language.

The behaviorist theory has intuitive appeal, as we often use variations of the repetition/feedback model in teaching. However, critics point out that the model completely excludes any **theory of the mind**, reducing the complexity of language to a rudimentary input-output model. Critics also challenged the behaviorists to explain how children could produce novel, and often complex, utterances that they had never heard—these utterances could not have been acquired through imitation, repetition, or reinforcement.

The Innate or Universal Grammar Theory of First-Language Acquisition

The universal grammar theory, developed by the linguist Noam Chomsky in the 1960s, posits that humans are born with **innate language abilities**, which include general grammatical categories and constraints that can be adapted to or activated by any language a child is exposed to. Chomsky gave the name "**language activation device**" to this hypothetical region of the brain devoted to language acquisition and production. Chomsky developed his theory in response to the behaviorist's suggestion that language competence is built through a process of trial-and-error.

The **universal grammar theory** helps explain several key features of languages and language learning: that all languages share certain properties; that children who are exposed to a common language will all converge in their competence, despite receiving different input; and that children will learn linguistic forms for which they have received no specific input. Chomsky also turned theoretical attention to the brain and its adaptive capacities. Critics of innateness theories suggest that it privileges syntax over semantics, pragmatics, and discourse; further, it focuses on developmental aspects of language acquisition at the expense of social and psychological aspects.

The Cognitive Constructionist Model of First-Language Acquisition

The cognitive constructivist model of L1 acquisition derives from the work of the Swiss psychologist Jean Piaget (1896–1980). Piaget hypothesized that **cognitive development** (and thus language development) occurs in universal, identifiable stages. **Learning** occurs when a child's experiences challenge his or her current understanding of the world, driving the child to a new, more complex stage of cognitive/linguistic development. Thus, language learning is a form of adaptation to one's environment.

Proponents of cognitive models of language learning point to the fact that language learning does appear to proceed according to certain **stages of complexity**—for example, learners in all languages master functional morphemes in similar order. Critics argue that there is little merit in Piaget's four-stage model, as the stages themselves cannot be empirically identified. Further, critics argue that the theory undervalues the influence of both culture and social interaction on language development.

Cognitive constructionism differs from social constructivism in its suggestion that learners create representations of their world largely on their own inquiries and activities rather than through social interaction.

Social Constructivism Theory of First-Language Acquisition

The social constructivism theory, attributed to the Soviet psychologist Lev Vygotsky (1896–1934), emphasizes the importance of social interaction in language theory. According to this model, children learn primarily from adults ("more experienced others" to Vygotsky) who model new language patterns and also correct errors. Vygotsky coined the influential term "**zone of proximal development**" to explain how learning occurs: according to Vygotsky, children best learn when presented with tasks or challenges that they can accomplish with the help of others, but not alone. The set of challenges that a child can accomplish with assistance or scaffolding fall within his or her zone of proximal development.

Social constructivism theory is often credited with giving proper attention to **discourse**, or actual language use. In this view, language is developed in a specific context rather than in accordance with universal structures or dispositions. Critics point to the fact that not all cultures prioritize interaction between children and more experienced others, and yet children in these cultures still become competent language users.

Jerome Bruner vs. Jean Piaget and Noam Chomsky

Discovery learning theory posits that students learn best when they **construct their own knowledge** through a process of inquiry, investigation, and problem-solving ("discovery") rather than when a teacher or parent tells them explicitly what they are expected to know. Bruner's theory has been very influential in the modern movement away from lecture-based teaching and toward methods that guide students in various **inquiry-based activities**.

Like Piaget, Bruner argued that children learn in different ways as they develop, moving from mere physical manipulation of objects to the creation of mental images to the use of language. However, unlike Piaget, Bruner believed these stages to be continuous, and that children could speed up their progression through the stages. He also theorized that it is language that causes cognitive development rather than vice-versa. Like Piaget, Bruner is a **constructivist**, emphasizing the active role of the learner in building understanding through successively more complex engagements with the world. Chomsky, by contrast, prioritizes the importance of innate cognitive potentials.

The Critical Period Hypothesis

The critical period hypothesis argues that there is an **optimal age for learning a language** and that the ease with which a person can learn languages declines over time.

The hypothesis was first formulated by neurologist Wilbur Penfield and then elaborated by Eric Lenneberg, who argued that language learning is dependent on **brain plasticity**, which in humans is at an optimal level for learning during a critical period extending from roughly age two until puberty.

The hypothesis has been extended to L2 learning based on the claim that adults rarely achieve full fluency in a second language learned later in life, failing most often to master complex grammatical structures or achieve a native accent. Critics of the hypothesis point to the fact that some adult-learners do fully master a second language. They also point out that factors other than brain development could explain the difference in L2 learning, as adults and children learn in different motivational and social contexts.

The hypothesis privileges the explanatory framework of developmental biology by positing the existence of certain biological potentials for and limitations to language learning. It shares this orientation with Noam Chomsky and the universal grammar school of language acquisition.

Connectionist Theories of Language Acquisition

Connectionist theories attempt to apply insights from neuroscience and computer science to explain language acquisition. Proponents look to advances in knowledge of how neurons function in order to explain how learning occurs. For example, the more frequently a given set of neurons fires in tandem, the more established that neuron network becomes—a feature that helps explain memory and is seen as a mechanism by which a language learner comes to associate words with objects or events. In more general terms, learning is seen as the development of specific **connections** in an otherwise general network in response to environmental stimuli. Computer scientists working in the field of artificial intelligence attempt to build learning networks with silicon chips playing the role of simplified neurons. Computer scientists have built models that simulate many language-acquisition activities, including how to break a continuous auditory stream into words and how to correctly form both regular and irregular verbs. These models rely primarily on statistical, inferential learning rather than on the symbol and rule-based learning typically advanced by non-computational models. Critics of the existing computational models point to their unrealistic initial assumptions and abstractions from human reality, whereas proponents see these as weaknesses that can be overcome in time.

The Emergentist Theory of Language Acquisition

The emergentist theory suggests that children learn language by using a simple but adaptable set of **neural networks** to process and understand the complex linguistic environment they are immersed in. The theory differs from the innate theories of scholars such as Noam Chomsky in that it doesn't suggest that children are born with an expansive universal grammar hard-wired in the brain—rather, children are born with a **pattern extraction ability** that is effectuated by the growth and strengthening of neural networks. Emergentist theory shares with social constructionism the idea that social interaction is critical for language development but differs in its focus on the brain's ability to find patterns and extract meaning from what is potentially an overwhelming linguistic environment. The theory suggests that the brain narrows the field of possible meanings through the use of contextual, phonological, and morphological cues and by applying a type of statistical analysis of frequent language forms. While the brain is inherently capable of narrowing the field of possible meanings and finding patterns, parents and teachers can help the process by providing rich, structured, patterned linguistic input.

The Competition Model of Language Acquisition

The competition model of language learning/acquisition attributed to Brian MacWhinney and Elizabeth Bates argues that there is no fundamental difference in how people acquire a first language or learn subsequent languages—in both cases, various cognitive processes compete to offer the best **interpretation of the language cues** offered to the language learner by the surrounding environment. The cognitive processes that make the best interpretations of the language—those that lead to the learner having successful interactions and speech acts —are reinforced as neural networks eventually get consolidated as permanent features of the brain.

(With its focus on the development and consolidation of neural networks in the brain, the competition model is a type of connectionist theory of language learning.) .

The competition model rejects the idea of innate *linguistic* structures in the brain. Rather, it posits that language develops through the interaction of generalized *cognitive* structures in the brain (those responsible for all aspects of thought, not just language) with the environment.

Model of First-Language Acquisition

Developmental psychologists have created approximate timelines for both first-language acquisition and second-language learning. The following are typical stages and landmarks in first-language acquisition:

1. **Pre-speech stage (0-6 months)**: babies may produce what are called comfort signs (grunts and sighs) while paying attention to spoken language and beginning to distinguish phonemes.
2. **Babbling stage (6-8 months)**: babies begin to babble, or produce rhythmic sounds with syllable-like stops, often with repeated patterns. Babbling practices essential motor skills and allows infants to learn how to produce basic sounds.
3. **One-word stage (10-18 months)**: children produce their first words, usually in reference to people, objects, or actions that produce desired outcomes. Overextension and underextension (using words too broadly or too narrowly) are common.
4. **Two-word or telegraphic stage (18-24 months)**: children produce two-word phrases using lexical rather than functional or grammatical morphemes.
5. **Multiword stage (30 months)**: children speak in complete sentences, adding functional and grammatical elements, though often making errors.

Pivot Grammar

The cognitive psychologist Martin Braine created the **pivot grammar model** in the 1960s to explain how children first structure language when moving from the one-word to the two-word speaking phase. Braine noticed children create many utterances anchored by a single word (the **pivot**) used in combination with a larger variety of words (which he termed **open-class words**). For example, children commonly use the anchor "all" to create oft-repeated variations: "all gone," "all done," "all eat," etc. "More" is another typical anchor: "more milk," "more TV," etc. Researchers noticed that children use certain pivot words first and others second, suggesting that in this phase they have begun to understand differences in word class and function. While some scholars suggest that pivot grammar is compatible with universal grammar (UG) models, others argue that, with pivot grammars, children are not building upon *syntactic* regularities, but rather upon *lexical* regularities—a direct challenge to the UG model of how children acquire languages.

Holophrase

A holophrase is a single word used to express complex thought. For example, a toddler who utters the **holophrase** "up" may be intending the more complex thought "pick me up." Consistent with the idea that children understand more language than they can produce, holophrastic conversations with adults often consist of the adult trying to interpret the meaning of a holophrastic phrase, offering alternatives to which the child responds with body-language affirmations or rejections. For example, a toddler may say "mommy," leaving an adult to guess "where's mommy?" or "you want mommy's bag?", one of which will eventually trigger the toddler's assent.

Some holophrases may consist of unanalyzed combinations of two or more words—for example, "allgone." According to development theory, children pass into the subsequent, **telegraphic stage** of language development when they begin to produce two-word utterances, many of which are structured around pivot words as elaborated in the pivot grammar model.

Comprehension-Based Approaches to Second-Language Learning

Comprehension-based learning focuses on building students' **receptive skills** (listening and reading) before they are asked to produce the language (through speech or writing). Proponents of this theory argue that **listening comprehension** is the most fundamental linguistic skill and serves as a useful basis for the others. Listening is also viewed as the least stressful language skill, and thus the one most likely to engage and encourage early learners. Students should not be forced to speak until they are ready, and an early silent period in which students listen to meaningful speech is expected. Stephen Krashen and Tracy Terrell's natural way methodology is a leading example of a comprehension-based approach to second-language learning.

Communicative Approaches to Second-Language Learning

Communicative approaches to second-language learning focus on providing students genuine, meaningful, experience-based interactions in the target language. Teachers spend little time talking about the target language or teaching grammar and instead focus on facilitating **target-language**. Students often work in pairs or groups, role-playing or negotiating the transfer of information that one student has and another lacks. Unlike comprehension-based approaches, reading, writing, speaking, and listening are integrated from the beginning. Constructivist theories emphasize that learners don't acquire knowledge but construct it through their own experiences. Constructivists therefore seek to engage language students in as many reality-based participatory scenarios as possible.

As defined, communicative approaches are the most commonly used approaches in the modern classroom.

Grammar-Translation and Audio-Lingual Methods

The grammar-translation method relies on explanations in the students' native language of the grammatical structures of the target language. Students are challenged to read difficult texts in the target language and to translate sentences from L2 to L1. This model is based on the way Latin was traditionally taught, with a focus on verb declensions. Modern approaches focus on **communication** rather than explicit knowledge of grammatical structures and favor sustained use of L2.

The **audio-lingual method** relies heavily on repetition and drills, with language skills built systematically from simple to complex structures. The focus is on accurate pronunciation and the minimization of errors. Oral exercises are designed to control the vocabulary and grammar structures in use rather than to reflect real-world communication. This method dominated in the US immediately after WWII but has since been replaced by methods that encourage dialogue in realistic settings and trust that learners will overcome most of their early errors in later stages of speech development.

Silent Way, Suggestopedia, and Total Physical Response

In silent way classrooms, teacher speech is minimized: after initially modeling an expression, the teacher uses a series of props, such as Cuisenaire rods (rods of different lengths and colors that can model both vocabulary and syntax) to help the students learn basic structures.

Suggestopedia relies on music and rhythm to reinforce language patterns. Students are given scripts of L2 to read aloud with games and music. Later in the lesson, they might elaborate on the script with their own inventions or compare the L2 script to an L1 translation before moving on to another script.

The **total physical response method** begins with the teacher giving elementary commands in L2 ("stand up!"). As students progress, the commands become more complex. Eventually, the students begin to give one another commands. This technique is still used in ESL instruction today but is one of many teaching techniques rather than an exclusive approach to learning.

Krashen's Monitor Hypothesis

Stephen Krashen argues that individuals who acquire languages know inherently what is correct in that language, even if they have not formally studied the grammatical or syntactical rules of that language. However, learning plays a role even for individuals who have acquired a language: once they learn explicit rules, they can use them to **monitor** and correct their language use. Monitoring one's language, however, takes time and conscious attention, and thus is more feasible when writing than speaking. As Krashen points out, it is difficult to speak fluently and simultaneously attend to what one is saying—attempting to do so usually leads to interrupted speech. Critics of the monitor hypothesis include both those who argue that children may monitor their speech before they have learned language rules; and those who argue that, as defined, the hypothesis excludes use in the vast majority of speech and thus is of limited scope.

Krashen's Acquisition/Learning Hypothesis

Stephen Krashen distinguishes between acquiring a language and learning a language. **Acquisition** is an unconscious, natural process that occurs when a learner uses the language for a variety of real-life purposes and interacts extensively with native speakers. **Learning**, by contrast, is a conscious process during which a student is likely to study parts of a language in sequence, as when they study vocabulary lists or learn to conjugate verbs. Krashen argues that only acquisition leads to fluency, and he further claims that learning cannot be transformed into acquisition. Unlike some theorists, Krashen did not deny that adults can acquire (rather than learn) a new language but doing so would require an adult to immerse him or herself in that language. Krashen's distinction is widely used in language theory. Critics, however, have disputed his claim that learned languages cannot subsequently be acquired, and that the distinction is difficult to define in some contexts.

Krashen's Natural Order

Stephen Krashen argues that people acquire aspects of language in a **natural order**, regardless of which language they are acquiring or which language is their primary language. That is, certain grammatical structures are acquired early in the language process and others later. For example, research shows that individuals acquiring English will master the use of the "-ing" form of verbs before they learn to add an "-s" to the third person singular form of regular verbs. Research since Krashen's formulation of the hypothesis has weakened his findings, but not overturned them. Critics have argued that, in fact, one's first language does influence the order in which elements of a second language are acquired.

Krashen's Input Hypothesis

Stephen Krashen argues that language acquisition takes place most efficiently when students are presented with **input** that is slightly beyond their current mastery level. In other words, students should be able to understand most of what they hear or read, but not all. If used correctly, students will be able to understand this **comprehensible input** through the use of context, their background knowledge, or non-linguistic cues. If comprehensible input is used effectively, it eliminates the need for explicit explanation of new structures or meanings; students will be able to deduce the meaning without explanation. Merrill Swain answered one of the principal criticisms of this hypothesis—

that it only treated comprehension, not speech production—by coining the term "**output hypothesis**." In Swain's view, students will be motivated to improve their speech production when they notice, in conversation, that they are unable to express themselves fully.

Krashen's Affective Filter Hypothesis

Stephen Krashen's affective filter hypothesis states that students learn most effectively in **low-stress learning environments**. Affective factors such as boredom or anxiety, Krashen argues, create **affective filters** that interfere with the learning process. Krashen is co-credited with developing the natural approach to second-language learning around this idea. This approach emphasizes that students should not be forced to speak until they feel comfortable doing so in order to avoid affective interference in the learning process. Krashen argued that children are less affected by affective factors than adults, providing children with an advantage in language acquisition. This assertion has subsequently been challenged. Krashen's hypothesis remains useful, however, in drawing attention to the importance of non-linguistic factors in language acquisition.

Michael Long's Interaction Hypothesis

Michael Long's interaction hypothesis is similar to Stephen Krashen's input hypothesis in emphasizing the importance of **comprehensible input**—language just beyond an ELL's mastery level—for language learning. Long, however, adds an emphasis on conversational interaction, suggesting that advances in language learning will occur most readily when conversation partners have to negotiate meaning to be understood—by paraphrasing, restating, asking for clarification, using context clues, etc. Proponents of the hypothesis often add the qualification that it helps if the conversationalists are of equal status or social position (peer conversations, for example, rather than student-teacher conversations), so that the conversational queries and negotiations can occur freely. Critics have pointed out that conversational clarifications are not always successful, particularly when conducted by non-proficient language speakers.

Cognitive Strategies in Second-Language Acquisition

Students use a variety of strategies in learning a second language, including cognitive strategies, social strategies, and communication strategies. **Cognitive strategies** are those that students employ to understand a task at hand and include such activities as memorizing, categorizing, summarizing, generalizing, deducing, and using inductive reasoning. Research has shown that students who use a variety of cognitive strategies are more successful in learning a second language.

The term "**metacognitive strategies**" refers to strategies that students use to improve their own learning process. Planning, self-monitoring, prioritizing, and setting goals are all examples of metacognitive strategies. The use of metacognitive strategies is highly-correlated with language student success. Thus, an ESL teacher should monitor and encourage the use of these strategies.

Robert De Keyser's Skill Acquisition Theory

The skill acquisition theory posits that individuals learn skills by gradually transforming **declarative knowledge** into **procedural knowledge** through meaningful use and practice. In this model, students learn declarative knowledge about a language through classroom instruction or observation—for example, they might be taught a specific grammatical form. They then proceduralize it in use, ideally through contextualized practice. Repeated practice leads to automaticity marked by fluency and the absence of errors. The theory thus emphasizes that full competency requires processing of information by two representational systems of the mind—the declarative and the procedural—which reinforce one another in language learning. The distinction between declarative and procedural knowledge mirrors in some ways the distinction between learning and acquiring knowledge—the goal within De Keyser's framework is to move an ELL student toward further degrees of automaticity.

Model of Second-Language Acquisition

Researchers have found that second-language students progress through predictable stages as they advance from their first classroom encounters with a language to full proficiency. Recognizing which stage students are in will help ESL teachers design appropriate learning activities.

1. **Silent period** (also called the preproduction stage)—the learner knows around 500 words but is uncomfortable speaking. Teachers should allow the student to build receptive skills while gaining confidence.
2. **Private speech** (early production stage)—the learner creates one- and two-word phrases using 1,000 words. Teachers should pose questions that allow abbreviated answers and scaffold their instruction.
3. **Lexical chunks** (speech emergence stage)—the learner uses 3,000 words to form short phrases and sentences with frequent grammatical errors. Students are able to conduct short conversations with peers and read beginning stories.
4. **Formulaic speech** (intermediate language proficiency)—the learner uses 6,000 words to make complex sentences, state opinions, and share thoughts. Learners can study content subjects in English. Teachers may shift the instructional focus to writing.
5. **Experimental or simplified speech** (advanced language proficiency stage)—the learner approaches fluency and can make generalizations about grammar and semantics. The learner may exit the ESL program but continue to receive assistance with writing and in the content areas.

Silent Period of Second-Language Development

The term "silent period" refers to a common first stage in language acquisition, during which a student speaks little while he or she gains confidence and consolidates comprehension of the spoken language. Experts agree that students at this stage should not be forced to speak. Teachers might elicit "Yes" or "No" answers, or head nods and shakes. They can also ask students at this stage to draw pictures that demonstrate their understanding or draw connections between pre-printed images. If a student is hesitating to speak due to a lack of confidence, the teacher can interact first with him or her in a one-on-one, protected environment, and generally strive to create a low-risk classroom environment.

Acquisition of First and Second Languages

The following chart outlines some of the differences in the acquisition of first and second languages:

First Language	Second Language
Is acquired without conscious effort	Requires conscious effort
Is a natural, integrated part of daily life	May take place primarily in a classroom
Is based on a Universal Grammar	Is affected by first-language grammar
Doesn't require instruction	Requires instruction
Needed to function in life and satisfy desires	Learners may have varied motivations
Cognitive and affective factors are less important	These factors are central to the rate of progress

There are many similarities in the acquisition of L1 and L2: both occur in predictable stages, mistakes are normal, learners of both rely heavily on context and cues, production is more difficult than comprehension, and learning occurs most rapidly with interaction and task-based instructional scenarios.

Sequential Bilingualism, Simultaneous Bilingualism, and Multilingualism

Bilingualism is the ability to use two languages fluently, while **multilingualism** is the ability to use more than one language fluently. **Simultaneous bilingualism** occurs when a child is raised bilingually from birth or is introduced to the second language before the age of three. **Sequential bilingualism** occurs when a child obtains fluency in a second language after the first language is well established—usually around the age of three.

Recent research has demonstrated that children can readily learn more than one language at a time. This research overturns the limited capacity hypothesis—the assertion that children who were exposed to more than one language at a time would experience delayed and incomplete proficiency in either—that influenced the field for decades. Current research suggests bilingual learners may experience slight delays in speech production, but the variance is small and within the range of normal development. Further, bilingual children often possess smaller vocabularies in either language than their monolingual peers, but their combined vocabulary is on par with that of their peers.

Code-Switching

Code-switching is a phenomenon in which speakers switch from one language to another in the same conversation, often in the same sentence. **Code-switching** among bilingual Spanish-English speakers is so common that a name for it has been coined: "Spanglish." One reason people code-switch is that they are unable to think of a word in the language they are speaking, and so they resort to a word from their native language. However, in conversation with other bilinguals, code-switching may signal solidarity or familiarity, or it may be used to convey associative, technical, or figurative meanings not available in the primary language. Bilingual speakers often use their native language to talk about their daily life and use their learned language when discussing academic or job-related topics.

Code-switching can also refer to alterations in discourse undertaken in a single language—for example, when one speaker changes accent to match that of his or her interlocutor, or when an English speaker drops the final "-g" on progressive-tense verbs to project an informal, working-class form of speech.

Interlanguage

An interlanguage is the version of a learned language produced at any given moment by a language learner. An **interlanguage** contains elements and structures of both L1 and L2, but may differ substantially from either, leading some linguists to refer to the interlanguage as an entirely separate language. Interlanguage is often referred to as a strategy adopted by a learner to compensate for his or her limited proficiency in L2. While interlanguage is considered a normal part of language learning, it risks becoming **fossilized** if a learner lacks the opportunity or motivation to improve upon it. Fossilization often occurs when a learner achieves a level of proficiency that allows for effective, albeit limited, communication.

Various **cognitive tendencies** contribute to the formation of an interlanguage. The linguist Larry Selinker, who first developed the concept of interlanguage in the 1970s, identified five such tendencies, including language transfer, which occurs when a learner applies knowledge or rules from L1 to L2. A second tendency, overgeneralization, occurs when a learner extends a language rule beyond its actual scope—for example, when an ELL universally adds "-ed" to create a past-tense verb, resulting in errors like "swimmed.".

Language Transfer

Language transfer is the influence of a native language (L1) on a learner's ability to learn a new language (L2). This influence can have either positive or negative effects—for example, the existence of cognates can help a learner understand L2, whereas the existence of false cognates exerts a negative influence. The term "**language interference**" is often used synonymously with "language transfer," but is also used to refer specifically to cases of negative influence.

Linguists often use **contrastive analysis**, or the comparison of two languages to identify similarities and differences, in order to determine whether language transfer is likely, and in which forms. In general, the more similar two languages are, the greater the likelihood of positive transfer.

Positive transfers often raise the confidence and spur the interest of language learners. Teachers can lessen the impact of negative transfers by becoming familiar with those most likely to arise from a given L1, and then explicitly teach methods of overcoming those transfers.

Contrastive Analysis

Contrastive analysis is the study of the similarities and differences between languages. Teachers can use the results of **contrast analysis** to anticipate language transfer issues likely to be present in their student populations. One of the most common examples is the use in Spanish and French of the verb "to have" in many contexts in which English uses "to be"—for example, a literal translation of the English phrase "I am hungry" becomes "I have hunger" in Spanish and French. In many languages, including Arabic, adjectives typically follow nouns, whereas in English they usually precede them, resulting in many Arabic-speaking ELLs saying things like "She is a woman smart." Haitian Creole verbs do not change to indicate either tense or person, which might lead to a Creole-speaking ELL overusing a single present-tense form. As a final example, Russian speakers use the present tense to convey ongoing actions that in English require the present progressive—thus, rather than saying, "I am reading right now," a Russian-speaking ELL might say "I read right now."

The Basic Word Order of English

Nearly all languages have **subjects** (S), **verbs** (V), and **objects** (O). This is an example of a non-absolute language universal. Of the possible ordering of those three components in a standard sentence, only three are frequently found—S-V-O (as in English), S-O-V (as in Japanese), and V-S-O (as in Malagasy).

Both Spanish and English rely overwhelmingly on the **S-V-O ordering**, though Spanish does allow for frequent subject-verb inversion in cases where English does not. Many Spanish sentences do not have a stated subject at all—because Spanish verbs are conjugated differently for each person (unlike in English), the subject of a sentence can be inferred from the verb. In English, adjectives typically precede nouns; in Spanish, the opposite is more common. In Spanish, nouns cannot modify nouns, so possession is indicated after an object, contrary to English: "John's car" versus "el coche de John" ("the car of John").

Universals

A language universal is a characteristic that is shared by all the world's languages. In 1966, the linguist Joseph Greenberg published a list of 45 allegedly universal characteristics of language, but modern linguists, with much more language data and computer analysis available to them, are much more cautious. The few agreed-upon **absolute universals** (those that know of no exception) are relatively uninteresting—for example, all languages have syllables, consonants, and vowels. Linguists work more fruitfully with **non-absolute universals**—that is, features that are found with a high degree of statistical regularity but also have exceptions.

Implicational universals are language properties that occur together—in other words, they fit the logical form of "If a language has A, it will also have B." An example of a non-absolute implicational universal is "If Verb-Subject-Object is the dominant syntax form in a language, the adjective will follow the noun."

Jim Cummins' Common Underlying Proficiency Hypothesis

The common underlying proficiency (CUP) hypothesis states that a bilingual or emerging bilingual individual will draw on a **common pool** of cognitive and linguistic abilities to speak either language. Thus, his or her abilities and knowledge in L1 are available for and will facilitate L2 learning. Cummins' idea is often called the "**dual iceberg model**" because he used this image to illustrate his idea that two apparently distinct peaks of visible ice (L1 and L2) are actually connected below the surface in a vast, single iceberg (the CUP).

The CUP stands in contrast to the **separate underlying proficiency (SUP)**, which theorizes that each language a person uses is processed and stored separately in the brain, and thus there is no positive transfer between the two. Proponents of SUP often argue that ELLs should be enrolled in full English immersion programs because their use and development of L1 will only distract from and slow their English acquisition. The preponderance of the evidence, however, supports CUP, as it has frequently been demonstrated that the frequent use of L1 by students in bilingual programs does not slow their acquisition of English.

Rebecca Oxford's Strategies Inventory for Language Learning

Oxford developed a six-category classification of strategies students employ when learning a language:

1. **Memorization strategies**—techniques used to remember and retrieve information. Repetition and formulaic expressions are examples.
2. **Cognitive strategies**—strategies, such as analyzing or drawing conclusions, that allow students to manipulate the target language.
3. **Elaboration**—connecting information to what is already known. An example would be connecting something to an analogy or usage in a phrase.
4. **Compensation strategies**—strategies used when students lack vocabulary in L2. Code-switching, or the insertion of L1 into L2 utterances, is an example.
5. **Metacognitive strategies**—strategies used by students to improve their own learning habits. Self-monitoring is one example, planning is another.
6. **Affective strategies**—strategies students use to control their own emotions. Both appeals for assistance and requests for clarification might be examples of affective strategies, as students seek reassurance or reinforcement of what they already know.
7. **Social strategies**—strategies students use to employ language in social settings. Role-playing is one example. Requests for clarification could be another, as students often ask for clarification as a way of continuing a conversation.

The Strategic Inventory for Language Learning

The strategic inventory for language learning (**SILL**) examination, developed by Rebecca Oxford, is designed to identify the learning strategies used by foreign language students. A first version was developed for English speakers learning foreign languages, and a second version (v 7.0) was created for students learning English as a foreign language. The SILL examination is used both for research purposes and to give individual learners insight into their own learning profile.

Oxford's model is perhaps the most influential of several that have emerged from a research focus on language learning strategies. The latter concept grew out of an earlier (1970s) focus on the characteristics of a good language learner. This line of research aims at identifying the strategies used by successful language learners and promoting their widespread use. The **cognitive academic language learning approach (CALLA)** is another popular model based on the idea of language learning strategies. Oxford, in turn, updated her thinking with the **strategic self-regulation model (S^2R) of language learning**.

CALLA AND CALP

The **cognitive academic language learning approach (CALLA)**, developed in the 1980s by Anna Chamot and J. Michael O'Malley, is designed to help English language learners (ELLs) with limited English proficiency transition to mainstream content classrooms, usually in secondary school. CALLA emphasizes **cognitive and metacognitive approaches** to learning by explicitly teaching learning strategies and encouraging students to both plan and evaluate their undertakings in order to refine their use of these skills. Chamot and O'Malley developed a taxonomy of learning strategies based on three broad categories: metacognitive strategies, cognitive strategies, and social/affective strategies.

CALLA shares with CALP a focus on helping ELLs who are likely already proficient in social English (basic interpersonal communication skills, or BICS, in Cummins' terms) gain proficiency in academic English, in what is often a daunting environment of an English-only mainstream classroom.

Factors Affecting Language Development

Learning Styles Affect Language Development

A learning style is a general predisposition to learn or process information in a certain way. **Learning styles** are the most common examples of **cognitive factors** that affect language development.

Numerous taxonomies of learning styles have been developed. One common framework suggests that students vary in their preference for *visual, auditory, kinesthetic*, or *tactile* learning. For example, a student with a kinesthetic learning preference will best learn through activities that require movement, such as presentations or role-plays; whereas a student with a visual preference will prefer to learn through books or information presented on a Smartboard.

Research on learning styles has failed to confirm that students learn best when taught in a style that matches their **declared preference**. Critics suggest it is more useful for teachers to vary learning styles in accordance with a particular lesson or task rather than with a particular student. Critics also point out that tailoring instruction to match a student's preferred style is tantamount to reinforcing their strengths and ignoring their weaknesses.

One conclusion from this research is that teachers should provide students a variety of ways to learn. Another is that a student's affect may be influenced by choice of styles—an important consideration for early ELLs entering a new environment.

Lois Meyer's Four Barriers

Meyer identified four **loads**—or challenges requiring effort to overcome—facing ELLs in the classroom. The first is **cognitive load**—the number of unfamiliar or unpracticed concepts presented in a lesson. The second is **cultural load**—the untaught, assumed cultural references embedded in a lesson which may present impediments to an ELL. The third is the **language load**—the degree to which the lesson language is unfamiliar and stretches a student beyond the range of comprehensible input. Meyer's fourth category is **learning load**—the extent to which the classroom learning activity is unfamiliar or stressful to the ELL. (For example, if the ELL is asked to debate an issue with a classmate but has no prior experience with debating and is uncomfortable with the interpersonal dynamic, the activity would present a high learning load.).

Meyer's work reminds ESL teachers of the multiplicity of factors that need to be planned or controlled in order to create an optimal classroom learning environment.

The Theory of Multiple Intelligences

In 1983, Howard Gardner broadened the definition of intelligence beyond its traditional meaning as what was measured on an IQ test. Gardner argued that we all possess seven (or eight) **forms of intelligence**, reflecting different cognitive processes in the brain and individual learning preferences. Gardner defined seven **original intelligences** and subsequently added an eighth: visual/spatial, bodily/kinesthetic, musical, interpersonal, intrapersonal, linguistic, logical/mathematical, and naturalistic.

Educators have used the **multiple intelligences model** to inform second-language instruction. What scholars such as Mary Ann Christion emphasize is the need for ESL teachers to build a repertoire of instructional activities and techniques (and assessment types) that exercise each/all of the intelligences. A varied approach will reach a wider spectrum of learners; further, a skill or lesson taught in multiple forms is more likely to be understood and retained.

Student's Linguistic Background

A student's **relative proficiency in their native language** (L1) is a factor in L2 language development. Students proficient in L1 already possess the perceptual ability to distinguish sounds, words, and syntactical patterns. They will likely also possess certain useful cognitive skills, such as the ability to compare, generalize, and predict. In addition, there may be specific similarities between L1 and L2 that allow for positive transfer.

The **common underlying proficiency model** is based on these ideas—that the various skills and concepts developed during L1 acquisition are available for subsequent learning. The model hypothesized that all language learning draws upon a common core of cognitive-linguistic knowledge rather than knowledge segregated in the brain by language. This model has largely been confirmed by subsequent research.

Age and L2 Acquisition

The **critical period hypothesis (CPH)** argues that, due to brain development, there is an optimal age for learning a language (roughly from age 2 to puberty), and that a person's ability to learn languages declines over time.

While the CPH strikes many as intuitively true, subsequent research has rendered the issue more complex. There is no doubt that children and adults learn languages differently. Adults have cognitive and experiential advantages, and usually make more rapid progress in syntax and grammar than do children. Children tend to enjoy more exposure to the target language. In addition, they appear to have advantages in affect and motivation. For example, the fact that adults are conscious of the learning process and are aware of the difficulty of learning languages often reduces their motivation to learn. As implicit, intuitive learners, children are less likely to be discouraged by the difficulties of learning. Further, adults tend to be more self-conscious about making mistakes, a distinct disadvantage when learning a language.

A fair conclusion might be that, while adults have more disadvantages in learning languages, these can be overcome. The one exception appears to be accent: research does sustain the claim that children acquire a native accent more often than adults.

Disability Misdiagnoses

The **Individuals with Disabilities Education Act (IDEA)** of 1975 established the right of students with disabilities to receive appropriate education tailored to their individual needs. The legislation qualifies students for what is called **special education assistance** if they do not reach age-level benchmarks in several language and mathematical competencies, including oral expression, written expression, listening comprehension, reading comprehension, and reading skill. However, IDEA specifies that these deficiencies cannot arise from **environmental variables**, including limited English proficiency or cultural differences. As many researchers have pointed out, however, many of the characteristics ESL learners manifest during the normal L2 learning process resemble those of native-speakers with disabilities, leading to frequent misdiagnoses.

School districts in the United States are required to have a process in place to evaluate children with potential disabilities. Student assessments are made by a team of professionals. If the assessment team, in conjunction with the child's parents, determines that a child needs special education services, the team creates an **individualized education program (IEP)** that specifies, among other things, the program accommodations, testing modifications, and counseling the child will receive.

Individuals with Disabilities Education Act (IDEA)

The Individuals with Disabilities Education Act (IDEA) obligates schools to provide **special education and supportive services** to students with certain **disabilities**. The law covers thirteen conditions. The most commonly-encountered conditions include attention deficit hyperactivity disorder (ADHD), which is subsumed under:

- Other health impairment
- Specific learning disorders (which includes dyslexia, dysgraphia, dyscalculia, auditory processing disorder, and nonverbal learning disability).

The other categories covered by IDEA are:

- Autism
- Emotional conditions (such as anxiety and depression)
- Speech or language impairment (such as stuttering)
- Deafness
- Hearing impairments (other than deafness)
- Deaf-blindness
- Visual impairment
- Traumatic brain injury
- Orthopedic impairment
- Intellectual disability (such as Down syndrome)
- Multiple disabilities

Learning Disability Characteristics

The responsibility to diagnose **learning disabilities** rests with trained professionals. However, ESL teachers should have a basic understanding of how the manifestations of learning disabilities and **L2 learning complications** differ. The most important insight is that learning disabilities very rarely manifest in just one language, and so a teacher who witnesses the problematic performance in L2 can observe how that student interacts with colleagues in L1, or potentially ask his or her parents about L1 production at home. Another general indicator of a learning disability is a language deficit that doesn't improve over time, or after targeted intervention. A third is a language deficit that comes and goes—in most instances of normal L2 acquisition, once a deficit is overcome, a student will make fewer and fewer repeated errors over time. Another sign of a potential learning disability is a domain-specific deficiency—if an L2 learner performs as expected in writing exercises, for example, but lags in speech production, a disability is likely.

Instrumental/Integrative or Intrinsic/Extrinsic Motivation

According to Ron Gardner's original classification, students are **instrumentally motivated** if they are learning English to achieve a specific goal, such as acquiring a job or getting into college. By contrast, they possess **integrative motivation** if they have a positive view of their future L2 community and wish to fully join it. According to Gardner, integrative motivation is more reliable and durable.

Psychologists often distinguish between **extrinsic motivation**, which is a focus on rewards or punishments; and **intrinsic motivation**, which exists when an individual wants to do something for the sake of it without concern for reward and punishment. Research shows that intrinsic motivation is more reliable, as extrinsic motivation tends to be temporary, inflationary, and often shifts a learner's focus from the lesson to the reward itself.

People differ in the nature, sources, and degrees of motivation, and so it is valid to speak of motivation as a trait. However, human motivation is also heavily context- and situation-dependent, and thus motivation is also a state that can and does change.

Benjamin Bloom and the Affective Domain

Benjamin Bloom differentiated between three **learning domains**—the *cognitive* (thinking), *sensory* (doing), and *affective* (feeling)—and developed a **taxonomy of concepts** for each domain. His taxonomy of cognitive learning skills and associated action verbs (explain, describe, evaluate, etc.) has been widely influential. His taxonomy of the affective domain is also of interest.

Bloom identified five **processes that lead to student growth** in affective response and understanding. The first process, in order from simple to complex, is *receiving*—a passive condition that is necessary for learning but which does not by itself add value. The second process is *responding*, in which a student is attentive to learning and responds with positive emotion. Bloom's third process is *valuing*, in which a student develops preferences and commitments. In the fourth phase, *organization*, a student develops a value system, combining elements to create a logical relational framework. In the final, *characterizing* phase, the student internalizes what he or she has learned and acts in principled ways according to this knowledge.

Bloom's concept serves as a reminder that education concerns more than just cognitive development and that the experiences and valuations that students encounter early in life have a lasting impact on their affective outlook.

Zoltan Dornyei's L2 Motivational Self System

Zoltan Dornyei built on the broader theory of the ideal self in proposing that L2 students draw upon three different sources of motivation. The first is the **ideal L2 self**—the image the learner has of the person he or she would like to become through the process of language learning. The second source of motivation is the **ought-to L2 self**, which is an image driven by a sense of obligation, often one imposed by others' expectations. Finally, the **L2 learning experience** captures situational motivations, the types that arise daily in the classroom. Dornyei argues that teachers should find ways to appeal to a student's ideal L2 self in order to ensure persistent and consistent motivation.

Dornyei argues that teachers must attend to motivation in different ways. First, they must create the basic motivating conditions in the classroom. Second, they must generate initial, individualized motivation. Third, they must maintain and protect that motivation. And finally, because positive self-assessment is necessary for sustained motivation, teachers must encourage students to self-monitor.

Teacher Expectations Contribute to Success

Research has demonstrated the importance of **teacher expectations** in student performance. The core finding is that teacher expectations are, to a degree, **self-fulfilling**—high expectations lead to better results. Other prescriptions are also well-established: teachers should not create differential expectations based on demographic factors, they should form groups composed of all levels of language proficiency rather than marginalize low performers, they should call on low-proficiency students as often as high-proficiency ones, and they should foster a culture in which errors are seen as a normal part of the learning process.

ESL teachers should also use their knowledge of language development and communicative competence to shape their **error-correction strategies**. Certain types of errors are natural at a given stage of language learning and will likely disappear without explicit correction; teachers can thus afford to let these pass. As a general rule, corrections involving vocabulary are easier for students to learn than corrections of grammar. And finally, teachers should focus on correcting errors that impede communication. Experts agree that error correction is less important to student success than allowing abundant opportunities for language practice and authentic communication.

Self-Efficacy

Self-efficacy is the perception people have about their competence. **Self-esteem** is a broader concept—it refers to a person's overall sense of self-approval or self-disapproval.

Attribution theory, first applied to the academic domain by the psychologist Bernard Weiner, uses the concept of self-efficacy to analyze what students believe is the cause of their success or failure on an academic task. Research shows that students tend to attribute academic outcomes to one of four general causes: ability, effort, perceived difficulty, or luck. Students with low self-efficacy tend to attribute academic outcomes to causes outside of themselves (such as difficulty and luck) and are less likely to respond constructively to academic setbacks. Students with a high sense of self-efficacy, in contrast, tend to attribute outcomes to internal causes and are likely to respond to setbacks by working harder.

Educational psychologists studying the effects of **praise** on performance have demonstrated that students perform better, at least in the long run, if they are praised for their efforts or for a specific academic result rather than for their intrinsic ability. This finding reinforces the idea that students perform best when they focus on what they can control and when they believe they can influence the outcome.

Self-Esteem

Self-esteem is an attitude of approval or disapproval toward oneself. The psychologist Jonathon Brown has created a **typology of self-esteem** that is widely-used in ESL contexts. This typology differentiates between **general, or global self-esteem**, which is a person's broad sense of self-worth; **situational self-esteem**, which is specific to a certain domain, such as athletics or social skills or foreign language aptitude; and **task self-esteem**, which arises in the context of performing specific tasks or activities. Research suggests that, once formed by late childhood, global self-esteem changes little over a lifetime.

Self-esteem and academic success are linked in a chicken-or-egg type of cycle: high self-esteem is linked to better academic performance, and successful performance has been shown to be the most important factor in building situational self-esteem.

Learning a foreign language poses particular challenges to self-esteem. One reason is that students often feel the gap between what they can express in L2 and what they think or feel—or, in other words, they feel a large gap between their genuine self and the self they can communicate.

Anxiety

Anxiety is defined as an abnormal sense of apprehension, often accompanied by physiological signs of stress. As with many features of personality, anxiety can be thought of as both a trait, something which people experience in different degrees as a background feature of their personality; and as a state, in response to a particular event or experience.

Educational psychologists often differentiate between **three types of anxiety** experienced by the second-language learner: anxiety over one's ability to communicate in L2, anxiety that peers will view one's L2 communication in negative terms, and anxiety about evaluations and grades. Understanding the source of a student's anxiety will help the ESL teacher mitigate the anxiety's harmful effects.

In general, anxiety is **debilitative**—that is, it is something that detracts or distracts a student from learning. Research has shown, however, that anxiety can also be useful or **facilitative to the learning task**. Anxiety may lead to greater focus, greater effort, or a sense of competitiveness that can drive a student to mastery.

Inhibition

Inhibition is defined as the inner impediment to free expression or action. It is usually viewed in negative terms, often as a defense mechanism erected by individuals with low self-esteem. It is important to note, however, that the absence of inhibition can be pathological, as in the case of many mental illnesses.

Inhibition is a critical concept in language learning because of the importance of **performance** to language learning. Scholars agree that one's willingness to communicate—to seek out opportunities to communicate in L2—is a key factor in L2 learning success. Successful language learning also requires a measure of risk-taking—the willingness to make mistakes, often public ones, in learning a language.

Given the importance of production for language learning, good ESL teachers find ways to **reduce student inhibition**. Teachers should keep the classroom affective filter low; develop a classroom group identity conducive to risk-taking; allow inhibited students to proceed step-wise toward production, recognizing the necessity of a silent period; and ensure that inhibited students experience early success and ratification.

Language Ego

The psychologist Alexander Guiora asserted that individuals learning or using a second language experience widescale changes in their perceived identity, caused by what he referred to as the **language ego**. According to this theory, a person's original identity is closely tied to their L1 competency and mastery and is challenged or disrupted by an attempt to learn an L2. Guiora used this concept to explain why children acquire second languages more readily than adults—as their egos are less full-formed and less rigid, they suffer less from the feelings of incompetence or social embarrassment inevitable in the language learning process.

Subsequent theorists introduced the notion of **thick and thin language ego boundaries**, suggesting that students with thick boundaries feel fewer inhibitions in language learning and are more comfortable with the performance activities necessary for full linguistic competence.

Affective Filter

The concept of affective filter refers to the emotional response an ELL has to a language-learning environment. An ELL's emotional state can either hinder his or her learning (in which case he or she is described as having a **high affective filter**) or promote learning (a **low affective filter**). Factors that could contribute to a high affective filter include overcorrection of errors, fear of speech performance in front of peers, or test anxiety. Teachers can lower student affective filters by being cognizant of personality differences and language development differences, ensuring that peers are supportive, and errors are expected and considered to be routine, and limiting the number and significance of summative tests.

Lack of Formal School Experience

Students who lack prior formal education are likely to need additional support in the context of an ESL program. Students who have had their school interrupted by war or political upheaval (such as refugees) may suffer from trauma in addition to experiencing gaps in their education. Students who have never attended school are likely to completely lack **literacy skills**, putting them far behind their peers. They will also lack basic **learning and study skills**, which many students and teachers take for granted after a certain age. While students without educational experience are often highly motivated to attend school, they also have high drop-out rates, due in part to the demotivation they experience from lagging behind their age group in educational attainment. Even when such learners make dramatic progress, they often underestimate their achievement.

Acculturation Patterns

Acculturation is the adaptation of one person or group to the culture of another, often in the context of immigration. The term implies one-way adaptation of a minority group to the culture of a majority group. If the adaptation is complete and the minority comes to resemble the majority, it is termed "**assimilation**." If a minority community resists acculturation, we speak of **preservation** of their distinct culture. The term "**transculturation**" refers to the rare phenomenon of two equally dominant cultures mixing and each adopting elements of the other.

Linguist John Schumann's acculturation model argues that a person's **success in an L2** is directly related to his or her **acculturation into the L2 culture**. If a language learner joins the dominant-language culture, they will necessarily have more L2 language experiences, resulting in greater L2 competency. Schumann theorized that a number of factors could limit or even prevent an immigrant learner's acculturation, including his or her perceptions of the L2 language community, whether he or she lived in a cultural enclave or was geographically integrated, and whether the L1 and L2 languages were linguistically similar.

Elective Bilingualism vs. Circumstantial Bilingualism

The linguist Guadalupe Valdes draws a distinction between individuals who choose to study a second language (**elective bilingualism**), often for reasons of personal gain; and those who are forced to learn a second language (**circumstantial bilingualism**), as in the case of children immigrating to an L2 country.

Elective learners of a language, Valdez argued, usually learn the second language in an **artificial environment**, such as a classroom, rather than through immersion. Although they may eventually reach proficiency, their native language will usually remain dominant. Circumstantial learners, by contrast, do not learn a language because of an individual choice, but as a result of **new circumstances**, and in order to survive or succeed. They are likely to achieve greater mastery of L2 over time, and L1 and L2 are likely to assume complementary roles in their lives, with either dominant in a given situation.

The distinction between elective and circumstantial learners is likely to be most relevant in a class of **adult students**. Other conceptual categories may be more important when teaching children, such as their age when they immigrated, or whether they will remain resident in the US or return to a home country abroad.

Family Expectations

One of the mainstays of education research is that students are more likely to succeed if their parents hold them to **high academic expectations**. These expectations may manifest themselves in parental reinforcement and encouragement, parental involvement in school meetings and functions, or parental engagement with their child's homework. All three of these areas are potentially problematic in the case of ESLs. Setting aside the issue that cultures value education differently, especially for girls, families that seek to preserve their home cultures may inadvertently or purposefully limit a child's motivation to master L2—research clearly shows that language proficiency is affected by the degree of acculturation. More importantly, parents of ESL students may not involve themselves in school functions or even attend meetings with teachers, either because of different cultural understandings or because of their own limited English ability. Parents with limited English may not be able to help their children with their homework. And finally, research has revealed that a vicious cycle may develop in relationships in which a child's English proficiency far outstrips that of a parent—in these cases, the differential language abilities may lead to estrangement, conflict, and even withdrawal of parental support for language learning.

Political and Institutional Factors

The **educational policies** instituted at the federal, state, and local level influence the ways in which ESL programs are structured and administered in schools. Within the bounds of those laws, however, schools vary in their **initiatives** and **institutional approaches** to their ESL communities.

One way in which schools may differ is the degree to which their ESL students are **integrated** into the broader student community. Schools that celebrate diversity and promote the integration of different language communities achieve better language outcomes. Similarly, schools that **recognize and showcase minority languages and cultures** achieve greater buy-in from ESL students—if the value of their own cultures is recognized, they are more likely to embrace a new culture. Finally, school engagement with minority cultures should not stop with the students—successful schools also engage with the **community**, inviting parents and community organizations to participate in school activities and sponsor events that showcase minority cultures.

Impact of Poverty

The effects of poverty on student performance are numerous and well-documented: low-income students often lag behind their peers in cognitive abilities, experience emotional deficits (and thus fail to exhibit a full and appropriate range of emotional reactions), and experience ongoing stress, which substantially reduces their ability to learn. English language learners are disproportionately poor—by some estimates, more than 50% of ELLs come from low-income families—and thus ESL teachers need to understand how **poverty** influences learning and how to recognize students who may be at risk of failing academically or dropping out.

Many states or school districts have specific lists of **at-risk behaviors**, such as erratic attendance, behavioral issues, apathy, negative interaction with peers, and sudden changes in behavior. The at-risk concept is controversial because many believe it is applied wrongly to entire groups of students as a form of stereotyping rather than used constructively to identify students in need of additional support.

Effective Instructional Delivery

Jim Cummins and Cognitive Complexity

In 1981, Jim Cummins published a paper that modeled ELL communication experiences as falling in one of four quadrants created by sketching one axis measuring the **relative cognitive complexity** of the experience and the other measuring the **degree to which the experience occurred** in a context. Cummins outlined four resulting quadrants of experience: (I) cognitively undemanding, content-embedded; (II) cognitively undemanding, context-reduced; (III) cognitively demanding, context-embedded; and (IV) cognitively demanding, context-reduced.

This model built on his earlier distinction between **social (BICS)** and **academic (CALP) language**. Face-to-face social conversations generally fell in quadrant I, whereas learning activities with high academic language content fell in either quadrant III or quadrant IV. Cummins' main point was to underscore that ELLs needed more time to become proficient in academic-language activities, especially those largely free of context, such as standardized tests. Another insight to gain from the quadrants is that emerging ELLs need context support to learn academic language, at least early in their language development. ELL students who are challenged with cognitively-demanding tasks but given little or no support are unlikely to succeed and may become discouraged.

Vocabulary Acquisition Is Dynamic in Process

It is well known that language learners typically need to be exposed to a new word multiple times in order to learn it. This fact is particularly salient in the **acquisition of academic language** because, unlike common words in their social language vocabularies, students may rarely encounter academic language outside of the classroom. Thus, teachers should return repeatedly to academic vocabulary and attempt to situate new words in contexts which each add a new layer to student comprehension.

The idea that vocabulary acquisition is a **dynamic process** refers to the fact that student *understanding* of new words, and their ability to *use* those words, typically progresses over time—students seldom learn a word and then effectively use it as the result of a single encounter. When they encounter a word repeatedly, they might first simply be aware that they have heard the word before, then later have a vague sense of what *kind* of word it is ("I know we use it to describe people..."). They will likely *comprehend* it long before they learn to *use* it, let alone understand its related forms and how it fits in a network of synonyms, antonyms, and associated words.

Summary Frames

A summary frame is a series of questions, often provided in an outline form, that help students understand the way in which a reading passage is organized or the way their own writing should be organized. **Summary frames** can be created to illustrate a range of **rhetorical forms**. For example, to introduce students to reading or writing texts that compare and contrast, the teacher might provide this framework: "__ and __ are alike in some ways and different in others. They are alike because ___, ___, and ___. They are different because ___ and ___."

Summary frames are useful for teaching rhetorical forms, for illustrating how to combine sentences to form logical and orderly paragraphs, and for providing examples of transition words.

Activating Students' Prior Knowledge

Students learn new content most easily when it relates to the **knowledge they already have**. This is a central tenet of constructivist theories of learning and is widely accepted. Student background knowledge can range from isolated facts or impressions to full-blown **schema**—a mental framework for ordering and integrating knowledge. Background knowledge also has affective value—students who can relate what they are learning to their own past experiences are more enthusiastic and ultimately successful.

There are abundant techniques for **activating student prior knowledge**. One of the more common is an anticipation guide that poses a series of engaging questions to students about the unit to come. Good anticipation guides provide teachers with insight into student background knowledge and also stimulate students to think and talk about what they already know. Another common technique is to have the students fill out a know-want to know-learned (KWL) chart, which lists student prior knowledge explicitly in the first column.

Benjamin Bloom's Taxonomy of Educational Objectives

In 1956, the educational psychologist Benjamin Bloom created a **taxonomy of human cognitive skills** ranging from the concrete to the abstract and postulated that students progress in learning by mastering progressively more abstract cognitive skills. Bloom's original taxonomy included the following categories of cognitive skill, ranging from the most concrete to the most abstract: knowledge, comprehension, application, analysis, synthesis, and evaluation. Bloom also elaborated a **taxonomy of action verbs** that he argued were indicative of each of the cognitive activities—for example, when students *compare and contrast*, they are undertaking *analysis*.

Students of any language background need explicit instruction and practice in order to learn how to understand and produce academic language structured using cognitively complex verbs such as *analyze, persuade, differentiate*, or *evaluate*. Standardized exams typically test student familiarity with these concepts, increasing their importance for student success. However, research shows that classroom teachers typically prompt their students for responses on the lower end of the scale of cognitive demand—asking them to provide facts, for example, rather than analysis. ESL teachers must consciously frame their inquiries to spur their students to formulate cognitively complex responses.

Literal, Inferential, and Evaluative Comprehension

As ESL students progress in their language development, the ways in which they can respond to a written text will grow. At an early age, or at a beginning language level, students will strive for **literal comprehension**—an accurate understanding of the facts and events recounted in a text. By asking basic questions of early readers, teachers can check their understanding of vocabulary and syntax. Students with more reading experience achieve **inferential comprehension**—that is, using context clues and outside experiences to discover implied meanings in a text. Asking students about inferential meaning is a good way to bring their background knowledge into a classroom discussion and to get them to discuss ways in which the text relates to the real world. Students engage in **evaluative comprehension** when they offer an assessment of a claim in a text or use a text as a basis for expressing an opinion. Teachers can extend evaluative conversations by asking students for justifications or evidence for their claims and use them as a forum for putting targeted test vocabulary to use, such as *analyze, persuade*, and *contrast*.

Explicit Instruction

In order to effectively understand and use academic language, students must learn new, specialized vocabulary and develop strategies for deciphering complex and compound sentences. In addition to these basic skills, students also need to understand the different forms and functions of academic language and the basic conventions of each. Research suggests that students benefit from **explicit instruction** in these areas and benefit from repeated exposure to exemplary texts. Students will likely benefit from explicit instruction on how the form of a text follows its function, differences between persuasive and objective arguments, when to write from a third-person and a first-person point-of-view, and how to structure arguments with an appropriate balance of assertion and evidence.

Modify Rather Than Simplify

When teaching academic language to emerging ELLs, teachers should be careful not to **simplify** that language to the point where it ceases to be academic language at all. Given that ELLs develop proficiency in social language more rapidly than in academic language, resorting to restatements of essential ideas in social language might serve in the short-term to communicate a concept, but it will do nothing to advance the students' academic language proficiency. Instead, teachers should **repeat** their statements more slowly, and/or use **different intonations or stress** to call student attention to the aspects of the sentence that cause confusion or are critical to understanding. Teachers can **paraphrase** using synonyms for unknown words but should then revert to using the original word to demonstrate that the paraphrase was not for purposes of eliminating the new word from use. If teachers cannot help understanding by repeating their words more slowly or with indicative stress or tone changes, then they should aim at explanations that *elaborate* rather than *simplify* the original statement.

Promoting Language Acquisition and Literacy

The Matthew Effect

The Matthew effect was named after the biblical verse that spurred the saying "the rich get richer and the poor get poorer." It describes the well-verified educational observation that students who **learn to read** well and early experience wide and growing educational advantages over their peers who do not—even when other factors such as cognitive abilities are accounted for. Children who read slowly or poorly not only fail to understand other, content-area subject matter, but they are more likely to become discouraged and expend less effort. Critically, research shows that, in the aggregate, students do not overcome early reading lags later in their schooling; rather, the deficits and their consequences magnify over time. This research underscores the importance of **early phonetic instruction** and **interventions for students at risk**.

Balanced Literacy

Balanced literacy in its most basic form means combining **phonics instruction** with **whole language approaches**—those in which students are taught in the context of actual reading and writing exercises. Balanced literacy emerged in the 1990s as a corrective to instruction methods that relied too heavily on either phonics or whole language instruction.

Balanced literacy also refers to a more specific curriculum model that combines word work (phonics and vocabulary instruction) with a reading process and a writing process. In the balanced literacy reading process, teachers first **read aloud** to the students; then conduct **shared reading**, during which teacher and students read together; and finally provide **one-on-one help** to individuals or small groups reading on their own (these are typically called reading workshops.) The writing process is similar: at first, the teacher writes in a specific genre, articulating his or her reading to the class; then the teacher and students engage in interactive writing; and finally, the students write in small-group or individual writing workshops.

Language-Rich Classroom

A language-rich classroom is one in which students are continuously exposed to the language in many different forms. The concept includes ways in which the **classroom** is constructed—for example, teachers may build word walls (in which relevant spelling words, commonly-used words, or target vocabulary words are displayed), display student writing or other examples of written work in multiple genres, or label objects with various names or descriptive terms. The concept also refers to **student access to reading material**—for example, ensuring that students have access to the school library and that the classroom itself is stocked with level-appropriate books. The concept also includes **teaching activities**, including classroom reading in all of its forms (shared, guided, etc.), and questions and activities that call upon students to read outside of the classroom and report on how they have done so.

Schema

A schema is the **background knowledge** someone has about a certain topic. The knowledge might be information, associations, remembered life experiences, or even emotional responses. Research has demonstrated that background knowledge is essential to reading comprehension, as written texts invariably rely on implied meanings and a reader's background knowledge—only the simplest reading passages rely entirely on stated meaning.

Teachers can help **activate** student background knowledge by posing questions that help students relate the text to what they already know or that prompt them to involve their own experiences in their understandings of the text. Activating student background knowledge is important not only to enhance comprehension, it also raises student confidence by demonstrating that they have relevant experience and the tools to understand what they read, and it builds student enthusiasm for reading by connecting what they read to their broader lives.

Comprehensive Reading Program

The US National Reading Panel issued an influential report in 2000 calling for literacy teachers to create a **balanced reading curriculum**, incorporating a range of activities and reading skills: phonemic awareness, phonics (relating sounds to their written representations), fluency, vocabulary development, and comprehension. The panel built on the core insight that students with advanced phonics knowledge were not necessarily skilled readers: reading well is a multi-faceted skill that requires attention to context and the ways in which successful communications are structured.

A well-balanced reading program incorporates a **range of reading activities** to help students build literacy, from phonics activities to shared and guided reading, cloze activities, and teacher prompts that require students to draw connections between texts or search for implied meanings.

Purposeful Activities vs. Decontextualized Language

Meaningful and purposeful literacy activities are ones that engage the student in something beyond the text. For example, a text might engage the student with subject matter taught in a content classroom. Or the text might appeal to something of particular interest to a student, like a hobby or an aspect of their background or experience. A text might direct the student to accomplish something, as when they follow instructions or create a project based on a written description; or negotiate something, as when they follow up a reading passage with a small-group or peer-to-peer discussion.

Decontextualized language is language that addresses a subject that is unfamiliar to a student, and which offers few context clues that a student can use to aid comprehension. Reading and understanding decontextualized language is important for academic language fluency, but it is less appropriate for early learners. On the other hand, at appropriate levels of development, students should be challenged by inquiries that invite generalizations and abstractions rather than engage only with concrete and immediate things.

The Language Experience Approach

The key feature of the language experience approach to literacy development is the creation of a **class-specific text** based on a **shared student experience** (a field trip, for example). Typically, the teacher writes the first draft of the text, using student sentences and contributions, which can then be read for practice. The class revisits the text over time, adding new vocabulary, new syntax, and expanding the text to relate to new educational experiences. The text serves as a basis for both reading and writing instruction.

Proponents of this method of literacy development point to the strong association between student lives and the classroom text—of which they are, in essence, authors. The approach is not widely used, however, in part because of the near-universality of statewide or region-wide curricula planning, which leaves little room for a text that evolves in undefined directions.

Motivation to Read

A strong correlation exists between frequent reading, skilled reading, and academic success, and yet reading in the traditional sense—as a sustained engagement with a printed text—has declined significantly in the student population. Teachers can encourage student reading by strengthening their **intrinsic motivation**. One way to do this is to make sure that the books they read are relevant—to student interests, to contemporary events, to their different cultures. A second way is to engage in pre-reading activities that activate their background knowledge. A third is to allow students an element of ownership in the reading process, such as allowing them to choose which book to read, or when to read, or how they will be assessed on their reading. Choosing **level-appropriate books** is critical—students forced to read books that are either too hard or too easy quickly lose interest. Students should be allowed and encouraged to discuss what they read with their peers—not only does conversation aid comprehension, but it can also foster the sense that reading is worthwhile. Finally, teachers should make sure students are exposed to **reading role models**—be they parents, celebrities, or the teacher him or herself.

Kenneth Goodman

Goodman's 1967 research discounted the idea that students read by systematically processing and compiling sequential information. Rather, he argued, reading is a "psycholinguistic guessing game" in which students take rapid **surveys** of the written text and use it to make **predictions** on the basis of their background knowledge and assumptions of what is to come. Goodman argued that reading this way, with a constant interplay between thought and language, is actually more efficient and effective than is reading with careful and systematic attention to the text. In his view, the better a student is at reading, the less of a text they actually need to read in order to understand it. Goodman argued that many of the typical errors of early readers are in fact the manifestations of logical guesses that get refined through reading experience.

Appropriate Reading Materials

Extensive research, as well as common sense, attests to the importance of quality, age-appropriate **reading material** for the success of a literacy program. While ESL teachers often don't have a choice of which materials to use in their classes, whenever they do, they should select materials that (a) stimulate student interest, in part by including content and themes that are part of student background knowledge; (b) provide the proper conceptual load, or the amount of new versus familiar structures and vocabulary; (c) furnish sufficient contextual support for the narrative; (d) do not contain any culturally insensitive references; (e) are an appropriate length; (f) represent a diversity of genres; and (g) have a clear textual layout that enhances comprehension rather than impedes it.

Explicit vs. Implicit Instruction

Explicit instruction is when a teacher informs students of a specific lesson goal, provides an explanation of the important concepts, demonstrates their use, and then guides the students in practice. With **implicit instruction**, the teacher does not explicitly teach targeted concepts but instead relies on the students to learn them during the course of communication-based activities. In a rough sense, advocates of implicit instruction model language as something that is **acquired**, and advocates of explicit instruction see it as something that is **learned**. Modern research suggests that teachers need to use both strategies; however, a consensus has emerged that certain skills should be explicitly taught. In the reading domain, this includes the vocabulary and syntax of academic (as opposed to social) language and various comprehension strategies, such as how to infer meaning from a text or synthesize information from multiple texts. In the writing domain, the process of writing itself—proceeding from planning to drafting, evaluating, revising, and editing, with best practices for each—is thought to best be taught explicitly. At earlier stages of literacy, phonics instruction is often approached explicitly, as well as those grammatical structures that are least transparent or held in common with the students' native languages.

The Importance of Scaffolding

Scaffolding is a teacher's use of supports to help student understanding of concepts or mastery of skills. Well-chosen **literacy scaffolding techniques** allow students to engage with texts and writing projects just beyond their current proficiency levels, or in what Vygotsky referred to as their zones of proximal development.

Numerous scaffolding techniques exist to support both reading and writing instruction. For example, a teacher using the **directed listening and thinking activity (DLTA)** would pause a story frequently to ask students questions that led them to predict what might come next—and then eventually prompt the students to formulate their own questions and predicted answers. **Shared reading**—in which a teacher reads along with a class, modeling things like pronunciation and fluency - is another common scaffolding technique. For writing, an example is an **interactive dialogue journal**, in which a teacher and student pass a journal back and forth, each writing in response to the others' comments and prompts. **Mapping**, in which students brainstorm about the words and concepts that relate to a central theme, is a useful scaffolding technique to use in the planning stages of a writing activity.

Gail Tompkins' Five-Level Scaffolding Model

In an influential 2011 textbook, *Literacy in the Early Grades*, Gail Tompkins outlined a **five-stage model of scaffolding** conceived for widespread use in the classroom. The stages are designed to be used either successively—as a teacher gradually reduces the amount of support provided as students become more independent—or selected for use based on a given task or classroom composition. In the **stage of greatest support**, a teacher models the skill or task. In the second, **shared stage**, the students contribute to the task, but the teacher still performs the act or records the product. In the third, **interactive stage**, the students and teacher share in both the conceptualizing and the creation of the product. In the fourth stage, **guided practice**, the students undertake the task, either alone or in groups, with the teacher providing assistance as needed. In the final, **independent work stage**, the students perform the entire activity without significant teacher assistance.

Integrating the Four Basic Language Skills

The main reason to teach the four skills in conjunction is that they **reinforce** each other. All contribute, in a unique way, to a student's overall language knowledge and ability. Further, there is a *pragmatic* reason to teach all four: in the wider world (beginning in content classrooms) the students will need to use all four skills, often simultaneously, in actual communication contexts.

The ESL teacher who is tempted to privilege the teaching of oral skills over written skills should remember that second-language learning often follows a different **pattern** than first-language acquisition—while with L1, oral competency almost invariably precedes written competency, the sequencing is far more variable with L2. In particular, students with strong L1 literacy may progress more rapidly in L2 reading than in L2 speaking, and their reading skills will support and stimulate their speaking progress.

Teachers should find ways to combine the skills in **mutually-reinforcing ways** when designing learning activities. For example, students could read a text, discuss it, and then write about it, explicitly incorporating ideas that they heard in conversations with their peers.

Appropriate Cultural Content

Research demonstrates that students learn to read and write more effectively when texts activate their **background knowledge**. ELLs are likely to have acquired a substantial portion of that knowledge in a different cultural context.

Using **culture-specific content** accelerates language learning in at least two ways. First, students tend to be more interested in texts that relate to their culture. Second, when students read a text for comprehension, they are essentially using what they *already* understand as a means to grasp what they *don't* understand. A text that incorporates familiar cultural references will provide them with more point of comprehension with which to leverage meaning from the unfamiliar text.

In selecting culturally-specific texts or calling upon students to speak about their culture, teachers should be aware that not all students are experts on their native cultures. Nor should a teacher assume that a student wants to speak about their native culture or even be identified by cultural origin.

Integrating English Language Learning

Perhaps the stereotypical image of English language instruction is that of a full-time, separate program that focuses on English proficiency, developing everyday vocabulary and scenarios to build social language skills. While this model of instruction exists, it is increasingly rare, due primarily to the recognition that students benefit most when **language and content** are taught at the same time. One reason is that if students are not taught content until they are proficient in English, they will be significantly behind their peers in content knowledge. Furthermore, content classrooms put language in context, allowing students to build mental networks of related terms and concepts. Content classrooms also give students a setting in which to *apply* the English they learn - making it much less likely they will forget it.

School districts and states differ in *how* they integrate English and content instruction for second-language learners—there are many different program models based on variations of **three fundamental approaches**: having ESL-trained teachers incorporate content knowledge into their curriculums; having content-trained teachers incorporate English language instruction into their curriculums; and having ESL and content instructors work in tandem, either through co-teaching or via a pull-out or push-in model.

Application of Standards-Based Curriculum and Instruction

Teaching Listening and Speaking

Verbal Communication

The term "verbal communication" is usually contrasted with nonverbal communication, and in this sense, it simply means communication that occurs via words. In this sense, it can include all four **major language skills**: speaking, listening, reading, and writing. The term "**oral communication**" narrows this field of skills to two: speaking and listening.

One way to think about verbal communication is to consider the various aspects of spoken language *beyond word choice* that convey meaning in conversation. These **prosodic aspects of language** include pitch, stress, rhythm, length, and loudness.

A second way to think about verbal communication is to focus on the goals of the conversational interaction and the different skills required to achieve those goals. For example, ELLs must learn how to identify the main point of an utterance while setting aside details or irrelevant information; in another context, they may need to focus on the details. Similarly, the skills needed to recap an event or a conversation when speaking to a peer are very different from those needed to give an oral presentation. ESL teachers need to understand the range of necessary skills and provide instruction and practice in each.

Demonstrating Listening Comprehension

In the early stages of English learning, a student may only be able to signal understanding by nodding, smiling, or performing whatever action is being asked. At this point in language learning, a student's responses will be based heavily on **nonverbal signals** and reference to **illustrations or realia**. The student will then develop the capacity to signal comprehension by choosing between one of a pair or set of options ("Where did John go? Home, or to the store?") before developing the capacity to formulate **simple answers without scaffolds**. At a more developed level, students will be able to provide **full-sentence answers** to comprehension questions and eventually to provide **multi-sentence summaries** that reveal his or her comprehension of literal and implied meaning, central and supporting arguments, and connections to other texts and real-world experiences.

Discourse Markers

A discourse marker is a word or phrase used to organize speech, manage the flow of a conversation, or convey an emotional attitude. **Discourse markers** are often inessential to the literal semantic meaning of a sentence but can be critical in conveying the **attitude** of the speaker. Examples include "well," "um," "you know," "right," and "maybe." Research demonstrates that even proficient ELLs use fewer discourse markers than native speakers, and early ELLs misuse and misunderstand their pragmatic use in speech. Discourse markers are heavily bound to context and are thus difficult to teach in any systematic way; however, ESL teachers may illustrate some common forms, such as how the expression "Yeah, right" can signal either agreement or skepticism, depending on stress and tone.

Framing a Listening Comprehension Activity

Students who listen to audio or watch video files at their **zone of proximal development** are unlikely to be able to answer multiple questions about multiple levels of meaning—at least not without listening to or watching the file multiple times. Teachers can help **facilitate student listening comprehension** by identifying in advance what they are listening for: the main idea, details in support of an argument, or the attitude of one or more interlocutors toward a proposed idea. Teachers can also prime students to listen for implied meanings or idiomatic expressions by providing suggestive clues: "The narrator in this video uses an interesting expression that means 'to lose something forever'—let's see if we can find out what it is." Teachers might subdivide the class and have each group listen for a different aspect of comprehension, and then combine the elements in a subsequent discussion. Teachers should be aware that it is easy for students to understand almost nothing of what they hear—either because they panic when they can't understand and lose focus, or because they translate L2 into L1 and miss the overall meaning.

Frontloading/Pre-Teaching, Chunking of Information, and Debriefing

Teachers frontload or pre-teach when they explicitly teach vocabulary, rhetorical devices, sentence structures, or content that students will encounter in a subsequent lesson. This technique is particularly useful in preparing students for listening comprehension activities in order to ensure that the students don't disengage when they encounter unfamiliar words or forms.

Chunking refers to the practice of dividing a lesson or a text into mentally digestible parts, often by stopping and inviting the students to pose questions, draw connections to prior knowledge, or anticipate what is to come. Teachers often chunk a reading comprehension exercise in order to ensure that students understand the text well enough to understand what is to come, either by asking direct comprehension questions or inviting the students to predict what will come next.

Debriefing is a specific type of lesson summary or wrap-up, usually used to revisit a key point or reinforce a specific learning goal, and to assess how successfully the students mastered the lesson.

Initiating and Negotiating Conversations

Teaching students how to carry out successful conversations is one of the most important outcomes of any ELL program. Students who speak flawless English will nevertheless fail to achieve their communication objectives if they do not learn the patterns and conventions of conversational discourse. In order to become proficient in oral communication, students must learn how to **initiate a conversation** with greetings and formalities, using a register appropriate to the setting. Students must also learn how to **reinforce** their interlocutor's utterances, either through nonverbal cues (nodding, smiling) or appropriate and well-timed interjections. For social purposes, students should learn how to **alternate** conversation, ensuring that all parties are equal participants. Students should develop a repertoire of **active listening** techniques, and learn to extend the conversation with open, closed, and clarifying questions. These skills are particularly important when students have a specific conversational objective, such as achieving a consensus or securing specific information. Finally, students must learn the conventions of **closing a conversation**.

Retelling, Restating, and Summarizing

Real-world communication relies heavily on one person summarizing an idea, event, or encounter for the benefit of others. ELLs need to learn how to deliver concise and accurate **summaries** for purposes of work and school and need to learn how to accurately **paraphrase** conversations and **telescope** narrative events in order to sustain successful social conversations.

Learning how to use **reported speech**—retelling what someone said to an audience later in time, as when you report Joe's words "I am sick" as "Joe said that he was sick"—is a relatively advanced language skill. Even early ELLs, however, can practice retelling events and experiences, and more advanced students can practice narrating them in different registers, as they might do in talking to a teacher rather than a peer. One commonly used technique to practice this skill is to have students interview one another and then report their findings to the class. Another is to have the students summarize a story or video using a targeted number of sentences—with the target set to help the students approximate the amount of detail to provide when summarizing.

Purpose, Audience, and Subject Matter

The term "**register**" refers roughly to the degree of formality or informality of speech, but in a broader concept, it refers to the way in which a particular group speaks to one another—for example, a group of doctors will speak to one another in a medical register. In the rough sense of the word, scholars often speak of three distinct registers: **informal** (which students would use in casual conversation among themselves), **neutral** (which might govern most student/teacher interaction), and **formal** (which students would use in a presentation or when speaking to an unfamiliar adult). In transitioning from informal to neutral or formal conversational registers, students will need to learn to use complete sentences rather than rely on contextual meaning, eliminate slang and excessive discourse markers, and avoid hyperbole and repetition.

English language learners also need to learn the basic conventions of the various **academic disciplines**. For example, it may be appropriate to use figurative language when writing or speaking about the arts, but not when discussing math or logic. Language use also varies with purpose: the conventions that apply to speech intended to persuade are different than those that apply to exposition.

Review Video: Writing Purpose and Audience
Visit mometrix.com/academy and enter code: 146627

Teaching Reading and Writing

Decoding

Decoding is the practice of sounding out written words. In order to succeed at **decoding**, students need to understand the basics of **phonics**—how sounds correlate with letters—as well as how to blend sounds and segment words into **discrete sounds**. ELLs who successfully decode a written word may discover that they already know the word through speech—for this reason, decoding is often referred to as **word identification**.

Successful decoding reveals what the word is, but not what it means, either in isolation or in context. Therefore, decoding is an essential early reading skill.

Research suggests that phonics is best taught explicitly—teachers systematically teach letter/sound correspondence and advance through progressively more complex words by means of grouping words with shared sounds. Alternatively, phonics may be taught implicitly—teachers present whole words and then break them into sounds, inviting students to identify common, known sound patterns.

Approaches to Vocabulary Learning

The **definitional approach** to vocabulary learning is the most traditional. Students are either provided definitions of words or look them up in a dictionary, and they are drilled until they commit the meanings to memory.

A **structural approach** to vocabulary learning emphasizes the morphological features of a word—the root, prefixes, and suffixes. Once students learn the recurring morphemes in English, they can deduce the meaning of a word in isolation without relying on its context.

The **contextual approach** to vocabulary learning provides the student with multiple examples of the word used in a genuine context, allowing the student to infer the meaning without resorting to a dictionary or an explicit definition.

A **categorical approach** to vocabulary learning groups words into lists (categories) based on a semantic similarity. For example, a student might be given a list of words associated with driving a car: steering wheel, to brake, to accelerate, gear shift, etc.

A **mnemonic approach** to vocabulary learning works by building associations between target words and mental images so that when the student hears the target word, the image is also evoked, facilitating recall of the word itself.

Print Awareness

Print awareness refers to a child's recognition that the written symbols on a page represent letters and words and correspond to spoken language. The term also refers to the awareness that English text is read from left to right and pages are turned from right to left. **Print awareness** is an essential pre-reading skill which students must grasp before they learn how to read, spell, or practice handwriting.

Teachers can develop print awareness in early ELLs by modeling how a book is read, using a finger to trace the progression of reading from left to right and then wrapping around to the next line, showing how pictures are associated with parts of a story, explaining the role of title and author, and discussing how a book represents a complete narrative.

READING FLUENCY

Fluency in reading is the ability to read a text accurately, rapidly, and with feeling. The most important thing a teacher can do to promote fluency is to read aloud and often while taking care to read with expression and to model how words are not read one-by-one with equal spacing, but instead are read in groups with uneven pauses.

Students can practice reading a line of text after listening to the teacher read it or read the text in unison with the teacher—either one student at a time (**duet reading**) or the entire class (**choral reading**). Research suggests that **reading aloud** is more helpful to developing fluency than reading silently and that students can profit from reading the same passages repeatedly until they achieve fluency.

Fluency is highly correlated with **comprehension**. Jay Samuels developed the **automaticity theory** to explain this correlation. According to Samuels, students have limited mental attention, and the more reading functions they can accomplish automatically—such as decoding skills—the more attention they have to grasp the broader meanings of a text. In this view, fluency *is* automaticity.

PRE-READING, READING, AND POST-READING

Research demonstrates that students who approach a text with a purpose comprehend it better than students who simply read it passively without any expectations or goals.

Teachers can promote reading comprehension in the **pre-reading phase** by explaining the **purpose** of the exercise and what the students will be doing with the text once they finish reading it. They can preview the format of the text so that students know what to expect as they read. They can solicit student background knowledge to build context and stimulate interest.

Teachers should encourage students to monitor their comprehension while they read with a variety of **self-questioning strategies**. For example, when reading a text with headings, students can stop at the end of a section and verify that they grasped the point anticipated by said heading. If they are reading a persuasive essay, they can stop periodically and ask themselves if they are convinced by the writer's argument and evidence.

Finally, students should **assess and summarize** once they have finished reading. If they find that they don't understand part of the narrative or the author's argument, they should return to the text to improve their comprehension.

A TEXT'S FEATURES, STRUCTURES, AND RHETORICAL DEVICES

An essential element of reading comprehension is the ability to predict how a text will be structured and how its author will present information or construct a narrative. Students who can successfully anticipate and identify these aspects of a text will have an advantage in overall comprehension because they can use what they already know to infer further meanings and evaluate the credibility of the author or the quality of his or her argument.

Students can be taught the general **features** of fiction, non-fiction, and academic texts. Given the nature of the text, certain **structures** can be expected: fiction, for example, will likely contain a lot of dialogue composed of informal (social) language; academic texts, in contrast, will eschew dialogue and likely use only objective adjectives, such as those indicating size or number. Different types of texts incorporate different **rhetorical devices** as well: fiction may depend heavily on metaphor, while academic texts may rely on inductive and deductive arguments.

English Language Conventions

Modern approaches to writing treat the proper use of **English conventions** as one of several components of good writing, along with word choice, organization, voice, fluency, and message/content. Thus, while ESL teachers may choose to teach some conventions explicitly, they nevertheless take care to ensure not to let a focus on grammar, punctuation, or error correction impede the overall writing process in general.

Process writing breaks the writing task into **five phases**: prewriting, drafting, revising, editing, and publishing. In this framework, students focus on the correct use of conventions in the editing phase (though the teacher or peers may point out errors in the revising phase), well after the creative and expansive portions of the task.

Sheltered English Instruction (SEI)

In a **sheltered instruction program** (also called sheltered English instruction), intermediate English language learners are taught the full curriculum in English and are given appropriate support to further their content learning. SEI programs explicitly target **content knowledge** and only address English development indirectly by creating highly contextualized learning environments in which students can practice their English skills. Schools with large, homogenous ELL populations may have separate SEI content classes—sheltered 8th grade life science, for example—or a teacher may simply implement sheltering teaching techniques in a classroom of mixed native English speakers and ELLs.

SEI teachers deliver the same content as ordinary content instructors but attempt to communicate that content in ways that don't depend on **student English proficiency**. Thus, they often simplify, use demonstrations and realia, and allow students to use L1 resources to supplement their learning.

States and school districts use different variations of SEI. The most widely used include the sheltered instruction observation protocol (SIOP), the specially designed academic instruction in English (SDAIE) model, guided language acquisition design (GLAD), quality teaching for English learners (QTEL), and the cognitive academic language learning approach (CALLA).

Sheltered Instruction Observation Protocol (SIOP)

The sheltered instruction observation protocol (SIOP) was originally developed in the early 1990s as a 30-item **survey** to evaluate the effectiveness of a teacher's planning, implementation, and assessment of sheltered English instruction. The survey has been demonstrated to be valid and reliable and is still widely used to evaluate sheltered English programs, even those that do not follow SIOP as an **instructional model**.

The originators followed up on the success of SIOP as a survey tool by elaborating a full-scale approach to lesson planning and delivery, intended to give content instructors a systematic approach to teaching English language learners. SIOP divides the instructional process into **eight components**: lesson preparation, building background, comprehensible input, strategies, interaction, practice and application, lesson delivery, and review and assessment.

Content-Based Instruction

Content-based instruction (**CBI**) is a teaching method that teaches language indirectly by means of teaching **content in the target language**. CBI is an **umbrella term** that subsumes all teaching methods—such as sheltered instruction—that teach language and content simultaneously. In general, proponents of CBI argue that students can best learn languages indirectly, by focusing on (and being motivated by) interesting subject matter content. Some CBI programs carefully structure the subject matter content so that it systematically treats sequential features of the target language, while others are more immersive in the sense that they rely more heavily on the student's ability to infer meaning from a context-rich learning environment.

Task Complexity

Peter Skehan developed the concept of **task complexity** in the late 1990s as a framework for understanding the complexity of learning tasks in an L2 classroom. Skehan identified three factors that contribute to the complexity of a task: its **code complexity**, which is determined by language factors such as vocabulary and sentence complexity; its **cognitive complexity**, which is determined by the nature of cognitive processing required of the students and whether they are accustomed to that type of cognitive processing; and the amount of **communicative stress** involved in the task. Examples of communicative stress include time constraints or uncomfortable group dynamics. According to the theory, effective teachers will scale the scaffolding they provide to match the complexity of the task evaluated within this framework.

Task-Based Language Teaching

Task-based language teaching (**TBLT**) is a teaching method that promotes student language learning through the accomplishment of **real-world tasks**—for example, ordering a pizza or buying a phone. Proponents argue instruction organized this way teaches both the *formal aspects* of successful communication (linguistic competence) and the *social aspects* of communication. In some contexts, TBLT can resemble English for special purposes, in which advanced students are taught the vocabulary and rhetorical patterns particular to a given occupation or media.

While teachers implementing TBLT might pre-teach key vocabulary needed to perform a task, the method emphasizes student use of their whole repertoire of language skills, including the negotiation of meaning in situations where their formal knowledge of English is inadequate. Critics suggest that completion of a task is a poor measure of language improvement—once students reach a certain baseline competence, they can navigate a broad range of performative tasks, but may not be motivated or receive the instructional assistance to improve.

Creating Background Knowledge

Teaching is most effective when it builds upon what a student already knows in order to introduce something new. Teachers accordingly learn techniques for **activating student prior knowledge**, using techniques such as brainstorming on know-want to know-learned (KWL) charts. However, ELLs may have little or no knowledge to activate about certain topics (for example, US history). In these situations, teachers may need to *create* background knowledge before launching the core of a lesson.

In order to **create background knowledge**, teachers might use techniques such as anticipation guides, visuals, or parallels in the students' first culture or history. Teachers may also focus on key vocabulary through the use of techniques such as concept maps or word walls. If the new lesson depends on the students drawing connections with a previous lesson, the teacher may need to make that connection explicit—while native English speakers may pick up on a number of cues that suggest the connection, ELLs may not.

21st Century Learning

The 21st century learning initiative, launched in 2002, attempted to identify the most important skills students need to learn in order to succeed in the 21st century. The initiative's organizers strove to update the 20th-century's model of education based on the three R's (reading, writing, arithmetic) and the objective of providing students with content knowledge—to reflect the transformative effect of the Internet and the implication that the next generation would succeed not by *knowing* things, but by *knowing how to do* things. After multiple revisions, the organizers defined the key 21st-century skills as the **four C's**: communication, critical thinking, collaboration, and creativity. These skills have been increasingly incorporated into state standards.

Teachers may need to pay specific attention to ensure that ELLs engage in the four C's. When ELLs collaborate with native English speakers, they often get left out or left behind. In sheltered instruction content classrooms, ELLs may lack the English proficiency to easily express the higher order concepts required for critical thinking and may require specific prompts or scaffolding to engage effectively in communicative activities.

Modeling Tasks for ELLs

Teachers of English language learners (ELLs) should not rely entirely on verbal instructions when staging a classroom task or activity. Even if the ELLs understand enough to begin the activity, they may lack critical procedural understanding or the contextual understanding necessary to learn from the activity. In setting up such activities, teachers should **demonstrate** the key steps using both actions and words. When possible, verbal instructions should be supplemented with **visual displays**, such as flow charts, which divide the activity or process into identifiable stages. Teachers can also supplement verbal instructions with written summaries, ideally set out in brief, step-wise format. Finally, teachers might choose to **chunk** the instructions or stages in a task, pausing the students repeatedly to check their work and understanding before providing a demonstration of the next step.

Instructing ELLs in the Content Areas

Integrating English Instruction into Content Areas

In addition to learning to use the English language proficiently, ELLs are required to learn the same **content knowledge** as native English speakers. Usually, this is done in an **integrated classroom**, including both native and non-native English speakers, and not always with a teacher who is trained specifically for teaching English. Many times, a school or district has a specialist present to support English language learners and their teachers in **modifying** or **developing curriculum** and instruction. To succeed in teaching ELLs in content areas, the teacher must determine which language skills are necessary to learn and perform well in the content objectives. For instance, when teaching a physics lesson on kinetics, the language features of prepositions and sequencing may be necessary to understand object placement and order of events, but a student can still succeed if they make mistakes on plurals or struggle with their tense conjugations. In this content area, language-based corrective feedback may be counter-productive to the student learning the content knowledge. Focusing too much on unrelated language goals may take time away from the objectives at hand and may even artificially increase the students' cognitive load.

Specific Goals for Content-Area English Instruction

The primary goal for supporting ELLs in content areas is by making sure that the input they receive is **comprehensible**. The major factors of an ELL's ability to comprehend subject matter is that they have strong enough **general academic English fluency** for the level and have a strong enough foundation in the **content-specific vocabulary** and concepts involved. Specific objectives that a content teacher may employ to ensure their instruction is effective for ELLs in their class is to **pre-test** to determine students' current levels, **pre-teach vocabulary** to ensure students are primed for the focal points of lessons, and use frequent **comprehension checks** to ensure students are not lost. All students, and not ELLs alone need a certain level of academic knowledge before being able to learn new and more complex ideas. Pre-tests can give a teacher a strong baseline for where to begin instruction if students do not demonstrate readiness in the foundational knowledge. If a comprehension check shows that students are not sure of the material, the teacher should try rewording with simpler, but accurate language or try elaborating to clarify the point. Pre-teaching vocabulary is one of the most helpful ways of priming ELLs on new topics. Furthermore, cognates, or words that are shared between languages, are abundant in content areas and should be easy for the students to learn and retain with less effort.

Scaffolding Considerations for Content-Area Instruction

As with other types of English learning, employing a combination of instructional time and application time should help with retention of content knowledge. In instructional periods, the teacher should employ verbal scaffolding techniques, including prompting, questioning, and elaborating to ensure comprehension. Teaching should include **explicit teaching**, such as lecturing, but should also include modeling and opportunities for **practice and application** of ideas, especially discussion with classmates, as this helps with both expressive and receptive language skills. When using **modeling** to scaffold instruction, it is helpful to employ visuals and realia, or real-life objects, to help communicate ideas in a more concrete manner. In science, this may be a model or experiment. Mathematics instruction may benefit from using manipulatives or charts and graphs. In social science instruction, tables, timelines, and other types of visual representations of the information are helpful reinforcements of the concepts that may redirect the focus of the lesson on the visual and kinesthetic aspects of the materials, hopefully **reducing the language load** involved.

Discourse Complexity and Adaptation Techniques

It is important to note that different content areas may require distinct types and levels of scaffolding due to the language load involved in each subject. For instance, mathematics and science are inevitably going to have a lower **language-load** than history or theatre instruction, but they do have a higher load of **specialized vocabulary** and processes. For instance, laboratory equipment, such as beakers, goggles, and microscopes are all examples of specialized vocabulary that need to be understood to participate in activities safely. On the other hand, many history lessons may require reading passages that are several pages long to understand the narrative. The language may be less specialized, but the language load is certainly higher due to the volume of reading required. Depending on the circumstances, teachers may need to employ various types of adaptation techniques, including time extensions on work, allowing the use of extra resources, such as a bilingual glossary or dictionary, or excerpts from the reading instead of full-length passages.

Assessment

Standards-Based Assessment

Recent educational reform in the United States has focused on establishing grade-level content and skill **standards** to guide both instruction and assessment. This approach provides greater transparency—all stakeholders can view the learning objectives in advance—and gives teachers the means to develop integrated, proportional lesson plans.

One reason policymakers advocated for a **standards-based curriculum**, and in particular for standardized assessments, was to narrow the gap in academic achievement that exists between both states and the districts and schools within states. Standardized assessment rates would allow policymakers to identify districts and schools in need of more resources or educational reform.

Standards-based assessment is also popular among those who see the need for greater teacher accountability, as student performance on standardized assessments arguably serves as a basis for measuring teacher performance. Critics of standards-based assessment focused less on the *nature* of standards-based assessment than on the *number* and *assigned importance* of these assessments, arguing that these factors force teachers to teach toward the exam. In response to these undesired effects, the 2015 Every Student Succeeds Act (ESSA) scaled back the schedule of standardized exams prescribed by the previous No Child Left Behind (NCLB) legislation.

Backward Lesson Planning

Backwards lesson planning is a lesson planning process in which a teacher begins with a specific **learning objective**—often excerpted from the state learning standards—and then works backward to develop lesson plans and activities that will help students achieve that objective. The authors Grant Wiggins and Jay McTighe popularized the concept in their 1998 book *Understanding By Design*.

The **backwards lesson planning method** is meant to rationalize classroom activities to ensure that each makes a clear contribution to the learning process. In a common description, the process is meant to focus attention on *learning* rather than *teaching*. The method is associated with the focus on standardized testing that arose in the No Child Left Behind era, but it has broader application as a method of systematizing instruction and ensuring that the various elements in a lesson plan fit together and build on one another toward clearly articulated objectives.

Curriculum Mapping

Curriculum mapping is the process of ensuring that what is taught corresponds to the **expected learning standards**. In longer terms, it is a process that ensures that there are no gaps or redundancies in what is taught and that a course covers in a thorough and systematic way the corresponding learning objectives. **Curriculum mapping** usually involves allocating instructional time to the various topics to be taught, often in proportion to the topics' relative weight on standardized exams.

Curriculum mapping is used not only to align the content of a course to a set of standards, but also to ensure **consistency** in teaching from one grade to another, in multiple classrooms teaching the same grade-level subject, and to maximize the extent to which the curriculum in one course reinforces the curriculum in another. The latter aspect of curriculum mapping is particularly useful for ESL teachers who are striving to teach content (especially vocabulary) that their students will use in content classes.

The term "**curriculum calibration**" is also used to describe the process of aligning curriculum to standardized learning objectives.

Federal Requirements for ELL Participation

Federal law (Title VI of the Civil Rights Act of 1964 and the Equal Educational Opportunities Act of 1974) stipulates that public schools must provide the means for ELLs to **participate** "meaningfully and equally" in educational programs. The law requires that ELLs be provided **language services** to achieve English proficiency. States and school districts have measures in place to identify ELLs upon intake, they must monitor ELL progress toward achieving proficiency in English and content areas, and they must ensure that ELLs do not exit language service programs until they have demonstrated proficiency in reading, writing, speaking, and listening. The law also stipulates that ELLs be provided with needed **special education services**. Federal law does not prescribe what type of educational program be provided to ELLs—it leaves discretion to state and local authorities—but it does require the authorities to monitor the success of the programs and make adjustments if necessary. The **Every Student Succeeds Act (2015)** specified that ELL progress in English be assessed annually.

ELA vs. ELD

In 2010, a majority of states adopted a common set of standards (the Common Core) outlining what students should be expected to know in mathematics and language arts at each grade level. States that did not adopt the Common Core standards created their own standards designed to be comparable. The **ELA standards** set benchmarks for student literacy skills in the various subject matter areas.

English language development (ELD) programs utilize second-language instructional practices to assist students with limited English proficiency. When the Common Core was developed, many states with ELD programs, such as California, took steps to integrate the two sets of standards. In these settings, an ELD can be seen as a type of scaffolding program designed to help ELLs reach the same standards of literacy as native speakers. Other states and the WIDA (World-Class Instructional Design and Assessment) Consortium have also developed ELD programs to support ELA and similar standards.

Providing Differentiated Assessment and Instruction

ELD standards are designed to help educators identify and meet the specific needs of ELLs, recognizing that they are at a disadvantage in relation to native speakers in meeting the Common Core or other standardized benchmarks. ELD standards identify a range of **English proficiency levels**, such as beginner, intermediate, and advanced, thus providing a beginning framework for differentiation. Many ELD frameworks develop further categories that **subdivide** the primary proficiency levels—for example, California's ELD framework specifies learners in each of the three proficiency levels as needing substantial, moderate, or light support. The prescribed level of instructional support may vary by specific English skill, activity, or task. These categories provide teachers with a basis for providing differentiated instruction.

Many ELD frameworks, including California's, recognize long-term English learners (students who have been enrolled for more than six years and are not progressing toward proficiency) as a separate proficiency level and design differentiated lessons to meet their needs.

Reliability

An assessment is considered **reliable** if it yields similar results when retaken. Factors that affect reliability include the day-to-day wellbeing of the student (students can sometimes underperform), the physical environment of the test, the way it is administered, and the subjectivity of the scorer (with written-response assessments).

Perhaps the most important threat to assessment reliability is the nature of the **exam questions** themselves. An assessment question is designed to test student knowledge of a certain construct. A question is reliable in this sense if students who understand the content answer the question correctly. Statisticians look for patterns in student marks, both within the single test and over multiple tests, as a way of measuring reliability. Teachers should watch out for circumstances in which a student or students answer correctly a series of questions about a given concept (demonstrating their understanding) but then answer a related question incorrectly. The latter question may be an unreliable indicator of concept knowledge.

Validity

An assessment is considered **valid** if it measures what it is intended to measure. One common error that can reduce the validity of a test (or a question on a test) occurs if the instructions are written at a reading level the students can't understand. In this case, it is not valid to take the student's failed answer as a true indication of his or her knowledge of the subject. Factors internal to the student might also affect exam validity: anxiety and a lack of self-esteem often lower assessments results, reducing their validity of a measure of student knowledge.

An assessment has content validity if it includes all the **relevant aspects** of the subject being tested—if it is comprehensive, in other words. An assessment has **predictive validity** if a score on the test is an accurate predictor of future success in the same domain. For example, SAT exams purport to have validity in predicting student success in a college. An assessment has construct validity if it accurately measures student knowledge of the subject being tested.

Practicality

An assessment is **practical** if it uses an appropriate amount of human and budgetary resources. A practical exam doesn't take very long to design or score, nor does it take students very long to complete in relation to other learning objectives and priorities. Teachers often need to balance a desire to construct comprehensive or content-valid tests with a need for practicality: lengthy exams consume large amounts of instruction time and may return unreliable results if students become tired and lose focus.

Assessment Bias

An assessment is considered biased if it disadvantages a certain group of students, such as students of a certain gender, race, cultural background, or socioeconomic class. A **content bias** exists when the subject matter of a question or assessment is familiar to one group and not another—for example, a reading comprehension passage which discusses an event in American history would be biased against students new to the country. An **attitudinal bias** exists when a teacher has a pre-conceived idea about the likely success of an assessment of a particular individual or group. A **method bias** arises when the format of an assessment is unfamiliar to a given group of students. **Language bias** occurs when an assessment utilizes idioms, collocations, or cultural references unfamiliar to a group of students. Finally, **translation bias** may arise when educators attempt to translate content-area assessments into a student's native language—rough or hurried translations often result in a loss of nuance important for accurate assessment.

First, Second, and Third Generation Test Questions

Education theorists have identified three different types of test questions given historically to assess English language learner aptitude. Though each generation of test question has its strengths and drawbacks, the schema is meant to demonstrate a progression in the quality of assessment.

The **first-generation test question** was typically a single essay question which a teacher graded subjectively on a full spectrum of language criteria: syntax, content, organization, spelling, and penmanship. Alternatively, a series of unrelated short-answer questions were given without supporting context. The **second-generation test** was composed of multiple-choice or true/false questions, a format that solved the problem of subjective grading but left each question devoid of context. In addition, each question could only assess one skill or concept, necessitating long or incomplete exams. The **third-generation test** attempted to test language used in authentic contexts, often by having students analyze a real-life text or perform an authentic writing task. Though these tests were once again subjective in nature, teachers began to use rubrics to reduce the uncertainty involved in grading.

Portfolio Assessments

Portfolio assessments, in which either a student or a teacher collects a student's work over time for eventual formative or summative assessment, is a valuable assessment tool for ESL writing proficiency. Portfolios can be highly individualized or differentiated, allowing each student to be evaluated in terms of progress rather than by comparison with peers. By definition, a portfolio will contain a time-series of a student's work, making his or her progress over time evident. This quality is highly motivational. Finally, a well-constructed portfolio can help remind an ELL of the various *processes* involved in writing (by including various drafts) or the various traits of good writing (by including writing that focuses on vocabulary, voice, organization, etc.). **Portfolio assessments** share many of the weaknesses of other subjective assessments. To be effective, they should be accompanied by clear **rubrics** and frequent **student-teacher conversations** that clarify expectations.

Placement Tests

The purpose of a **placement test** is to identify a student's level of proficiency in the target language in order to guide his or her placement in a program or school. In order to be effective, a placement test should test an appropriate **range of language skills**—a multiple-choice test, for example, might offer insight into a student's knowledge of grammar or vocabulary, but will not test language production or reception. Ideally, a placement test will be tailored to a specific language program or school by including a sample of the actual material taught so that the results provide for unambiguous placements. However, programs can also adapt or interpret the results of standardized exams. Ideally, a placement exam will also offer an initial diagnosis of student strength or weakness in order to help teachers provide early efficacious instruction.

Identification Assessments

An identification assessment is used to identify students in need of **English language assistance**. By federal law (Title VI of the Civil Rights Act of 1964 and the Equal Educational Opportunities Act of 1974), school districts must have procedures in place to screen newly arriving students for potential language assistance. Districts typically begin this process by conducting a **home language survey**, a series of questions that seek to identify households in which a language other than English is spoken. In these cases, an expert will typically assess the student's educational history and, if there is little or no evidence of previous academic experience in English, refer him or her to take an identification assessment. Different states and consortia use different identification tests—in California, the ELPAC (English Language Proficiency Assessments for California) is used, whereas school districts in Texas may choose from a series of state-approved exams. A minority of states do not use an identification assessment at all but rely instead on a human screener to make ESL identifications.

Reclassification

Reclassification (or redesignation) assessments are used to determine whether an ESL student has reached sufficient proficiency to be classified as a fluent English speaker and effectively exit the ESL program.

Federal law requires that states assess ESL student proficiency every year, but it does not specify the criteria that a state must use in making reclassification decisions. Most states consider additional factors beyond test results, including teacher and parental input, when making reclassification decisions. However, overall **criteria for reclassification** differ widely by state—even states which use the same annual proficiency exam may set different thresholds for exit from an ESL program. Critics suggest that the reclassification process is often biased toward basic English proficiency but does not effectively measure student English proficiency in the content areas.

Diagnostic Assessments

A diagnostic assessment is designed to reveal a student's strengths and weaknesses. Unlike a placement exam, a **diagnostic exam** is not used to determine the appropriate level of instruction for a student, but the results can be used to tailor instruction or provide the student with an awareness of areas in need of improvement. Unlike an achievement test, a diagnostic test doesn't measure whether students have learned what has already been taught, but instead focuses on the direction of **future instruction**. Diagnostic tests are often detailed and comprehensive within a certain area of instruction (punctuation and capitalization, for example). ESL teachers often employ diagnostic exams at the beginning of an academic year, particularly if they have new or unfamiliar students in class, in order to get a sharper sense of what they should teach during the academic year.

Proficiency vs. Achievement Tests

Achievement tests are used to measure whether students have learned what has been taught—or, in other words, whether the student has gained the skills and knowledge targeted by instruction. **Achievement tests** are typically summative by nature, as they are usually administered at the end of a learning cycle.

Language proficiency tests are used to evaluate a student's overall language ability at a given moment in time rather than their mastery of recent classroom lessons. Proficiency tests (such as the TOEFL or IELTS exams) are often used to control access to schools or universities or to control the exit from ESL programs.

Using Assessment Results for Evaluation

ESL programs rely heavily on assessments to measure **individual student progress**. This same aggregated data can and should be used to evaluate the **overall ESL program** and to identify areas of improvement. It is important to remember, however, that not all measures of ESL program success are easily quantifiable—the degree to which ELLs are integrated socially at school is one example—and thus assessment results should not be the *only* basis for program evaluation.

Evaluators must be sure to use assessment data that pinpoints student success in both basic English proficiency and in use of English in the content areas. **Longitudinal (or historic) data** is also important: a school might be meeting regional or national benchmarks, but if its performance has declined over time, a responsible administrator will want to know why. Evaluators should also look at the assessment data from both **peer groups**—a school or district may be achieving consistent benchmarks but be lagging behind peers with similar students—and **high-performing groups**, which can serve as an inspiration for reform or renewal.

Formative vs. Summative Assessments

Formative assessments are conducted as part of an *ongoing* learning process. Their primary objective is to provide feedback that the students can use to improve their learning and teachers can use to improve their instruction. **Formative assessments** also contribute to student self-assessment by identifying areas of strength and weakness. Teachers should view formative assessments as a teaching tool—formative assessments should *contribute* to a student's knowledge in addition to *measuring* it. Formative assessments are also called **ongoing assessments**, a term that emphasizes the value of learning and having frequent, diverse, informal assessments.

Summative assessments are conducted at the end of a learning process. Summative assessments document a student's knowledge or learning, often by assigning a score or grade. They may identify student learning needs and are often used by teachers to plan and improve instruction for future use. However, the fact that they are conducted at the end of a learning process makes it more difficult for the student or teacher to make effective use of the feedback they provide.

Performance-Based Assessments

A performance-based assessment is one in which students demonstrate their learning by performing a **task** rather than by answering questions in a traditional test format. Proponents of **performance-based assessments** argue that they lead students to use **high-level cognitive skills** as they focus on how to put their knowledge to use and plan a sequence of stages in an activity or presentation. They also allow students more opportunities to individualize their presentations or responses based on preferred learning styles. Research suggests that students welcome the chance to put their knowledge to use in real-world scenarios.

In the ESL context, advocates suggest that performance assessments avoid many of the problems of language or cultural bias present in traditional assessments, and thus they allow more accurate assessment of how well students learned the underlying concepts. Proponents argue that performance assessments come closer to replicating what should be the true goal of language learning—the effective use of language in real contexts—than do more traditional exams. Critics point out that performance assessments are difficult and time-consuming for teachers to construct and for students to perform. Finally, performative assessments are difficult to grade in the absence of a well-constructed and detailed rubric.

Curriculum-Based Assessments

Curriculum-based assessments, also known as **curriculum-based measurements (CBM)**, are short, frequent assessments designed to measure student progress toward meeting curriculum **benchmarks**.

Teachers implement CBM by designing **probes**, or short assessments that target specific skills. For example, a teacher might design a spelling probe, administered weekly, that requires students to spell 10 unfamiliar but level-appropriate words. Teachers then track the data over time to measure student progress toward defined grade-level goals.

CBM has several clear advantages. If structured well, the probes have high reliability and validity. Furthermore, they provide clear and objective evidence of student progress—a welcome outcome for students and parents who often grapple with less-clear and subjective evidence. Used correctly, CBMs also motivate students and provide them with evidence of their own progress. However, while CBMs are helpful in identifying *areas* of student weaknesses, they do not identify the *causes* of those weaknesses or provide teachers with strategies for improving instruction.

Textbook Assessments

Textbook assessments are the assessments provided at the end of a chapter or unit in an approved textbook. **Textbook assessments** present several advantages for a teacher: they are already made; they are likely to be accurate representations of the chapter or unit materials; and, if the textbook has been prescribed or recommended by the state, it is likely to correspond closely to Common Core or other tested standards.

Textbook assessments can be limiting for students who lag in the comprehension of academic English, or whose preferred learning style is not verbal. While textbooks may come with DVDs or recommended audio links, ESL teachers will likely need to supplement these assessment materials with some of their own findings. Finally, textbook assessments are unlikely to represent the range of assessment types used in the modern classroom, such as a portfolio or performance-based assessments.

Portfolio Assessments

A **portfolio** is a collection of student work in multiple forms and media gathered over time. Teachers may assess the portfolio both for evidence of progress over time or in its end state as a demonstration of the achievement of certain proficiency levels.

One advantage of **portfolio assessments** is their breadth—unlike traditional assessments which focus on one or two language skills, portfolios may contain work in multiple forms—writing samples, pictures, and graphs designed for content courses, video and audio clips, student reflections, teacher observations, and student exams. A second advantage is that they allow a student to develop work in authentic contexts, including in other classrooms and at home.

In order for portfolios to function as an objective assessment tool, teachers should negotiate with students in advance of what genres of work will be included and outline a grading rubric that makes clear what will be assessed, such as linguistic proficiency, use of English in academic contexts, and demonstrated use of target cognitive skills.

Authentic Assessments

An authentic assessment is an assessment designed to closely resemble something that a student does, or will do, in the real world. Thus, for example, students will never encounter a multiple-choice test requiring them to choose the right tense of a verb, but they will encounter context in which they have to write a narration of an event that has antecedents and consequents spread out in time—for example, their version of what caused a traffic accident. The latter is an example of a potential **authentic assessment**.

Well-designed authentic assessments require a student to exercise **advanced cognitive skills** (e.g., solving problems, integrating information, performing deductions), integrate **background knowledge**, and confront **ambiguity**. Research has demonstrated that mere language proficiency is not predictive of future language success—learning how to utilize knowledge in a complex context is an essential additional skill.

The terms "authentic" and "performance-based" assessments are often used interchangeably. However, a performance-based assessment doesn't necessarily have to be grounded in a possible authentic experience.

Using Various Assessments

The goal of **assessment** in education is to gather data that, when evaluated, can be used to further student learning and achievement. **Standardized tests** are helpful for placement purposes and to reflect student progress toward goals set by a school district or state. If a textbook is chosen to align with district learning standards, the textbook assessments can provide teachers with convenient, small-scale, regular checks of student knowledge against the target standard.

In order be effective, teachers must know where their students are in the learning process. Teachers use a multitude of **formal and informal assessment methods** to do this. Posing differentiated discussion questions is an example of an informal assessment method that allows teachers to gauge individual student progress rather than their standing in relation to a universal benchmark.

Effective teachers employ a variety of assessments, as different formats assess different skills, promote different learning experiences, and appeal to different learners. A portfolio is an example of an assessment that gauges student progress in multiple skills and through multiple media. Teachers can use authentic or performance-based assessments to stimulate student interest and provide visible connections between language-learning and the real world.

Peer Assessment

A peer assessment is when students grade one another's work based on a teacher-provided framework. **Peer assessments** are promoted as a means of saving teacher time and building student metacognitive skills. They are typically used as **formative** rather than summative assessments, given concerns about the reliability of student scoring and the tensions that can result if student scores contribute to overall grades. Peer assessments are used most often to grade essay-type written work or presentations. Proponents point out that peer assessments require students to apply metacognition, builds cooperative work and interpersonal skills, and broadens the sense that the student is accountable to peers and not just the teacher. Even advocates of the practice agree that students need detailed rubrics in order to succeed. Critics often argue that low-performing students have little to offer high-performing students in terms of valuable feedback—and this disparity may be more pronounced in ESL classrooms than mainstream ones. One way to overcome this weakness is for the teacher to lead the evaluation exercise, guiding the students through a point-by-point framework of evaluation.

Differentiation

A teacher employs differentiation when he or she modifies instruction to meet individual student needs. Teachers may **differentiate** their instruction by (a) modifying the content of the lesson, (b) modifying how the lesson is taught or learned, or (c) modifying how students demonstrate their learning.

One way for teachers to think about differentiation in an ESL context is as the merger of a **content framework** (such as the Common Core) with an **ELD framework** (such as those developed by the WIDA Consortium or the state of California). ELD frameworks define proficiency levels for ELLs—for example, WIDA defines five levels, ranging from entering to bridging. The ELD framework also suggests ways in which teachers might differentiate various learning activities for students at different proficiency levels. For example, an entering student might follow an explicit, minimal writing model, and be given other activities to demonstrate the content knowledge, while a bridging student might be expected to organize his or her own lengthier, content-filled written response.

Using Student Assessment Results for Modification

Good teachers make a habit of **analyzing assessment results** in order to modify and differentiate their instruction. Teachers should attempt to determine whether cases of poor student performance were caused by language deficits or a lack of content understanding. Often teachers can determine this by looking at a student's response to other, similar questions, by assessing how well-written the student's responses are, or by consulting with a content instructor.

If the teacher discovers that a large number of students scored badly on a certain question or group of related questions, they should **reteach** that subject to the entire class. The teacher should try to identify the **core issue**—perhaps the lesson is too complex and needs to be divided into smaller, more manageable chunks; or perhaps success in the lesson was predicated on vocabulary that the students never grasped, in which case the teacher can begin anew with vocabulary instruction.

If the problem is a lack of content knowledge rather than language knowledge, an ESL teacher can plan more content-related tasks in consultation with the content instructor. If the problem is language related and affects only one student or a group of students, the teacher can use scaffolding and differentiated teaching to address the deficits.

Using Student Assessment Results for Reteaching

When assessment results show that a significant portion of the class lack specific knowledge or a specific skill, teachers should consider **reteaching** that subject. It is important to remember that assessment results might be as formal as student scores on an exam, or as informal as students signaling their understanding with a thumbs-up or thumbs-down gesture.

Reteaching strategies include re-explaining the subject more slowly and using simplified vocabulary; using visual aids; relying on students who understand the concept to peer coach the students who do not; providing more background knowledge or calling on student experience to situate the new material in context; and focusing instruction on the suspected problem area, such as new vocabulary or a particular grammatical form.

Granting ELLs Accommodations

The Every Student Succeeds Act (ESSA) of 2015 renewed the federal government's commitment to ensuring that states provide appropriate accommodation to ESL students taking state-level content exams. The ESSA leaves it to the states to define appropriate accommodation, and many variations exist. However, many states have joined multi-state consortia (the Partnership for Assessment of Reading of College and Careers and the Smarter Balanced Assessment Consortium are the two largest) for **assessment development**, leading to gradual harmonization of the accommodation standards.

Examples of the **accommodations** include allowing ESL students additional time to complete the tests, allowing the use of bilingual dictionaries, and allowing a native speaker to read a translated version of the test instructions.

Separate legislation (the Individuals with Disabilities Education Act) mandates accommodations for students (including ELLs) with **disabilities**.

ADAPTING CLASSROOM ASSESSMENTS ELLS

English language learners are at a disadvantage relative to their English-speaking peers when faced with **content assessments**. Researchers often say that they face doubling the cognitive load, as they must process both language and content in both their comprehension of the task and their production of a response. In order to get a clear sense of an ESL student's content knowledge, a teacher often must make adjustments to the test to render the language component more transparent and less taxing. Teachers can **modify** written exams by giving ESL students fewer questions; questions and/or instructions in simpler, more literal language; or questions with embedded cues and prompts. Teachers may also allow ESL students to exhibit their knowledge in different formats—for example, by means of an oral question-and-answer session, or by means of projects or presentations.

Professionalism

History of English Language Programs

Bilingual Education Before the 1960s

Scholars customarily speak of the **American approach to bilingual education** as one of neglectful tolerance from independence until approximately 1960. While the federal government provided no educational support to non-English speakers, individual schools with high immigrant populations often did on an *ad hoc* basis. In most schools, however, **English language learners** were given no instructional support and were expected to assimilate rapidly. While ELLs dropped out of school at higher rates than native English speakers, few attempts were made to determine why or offer remedies.

Several factors turned American opinion against bilingual education, beginning in the 1880s when an influx of non-English speaking immigrants raised worries that America might lose its identity—of which English was an important component. These concerns were exacerbated by the American experience in the two World Wars and the insecurities caused by the Great Depression. Restrictions were placed on immigration during this period, an English language requirement was added to the naturalization process, and bilingual education programs were scaled back in districts where they had previously existed.

Bilingual Approach and ESL Approach

Bilingual instructional programs begin instruction primarily or entirely in the student's **native language** and then transition to greater use of **English** over time. Most bilingual programs phase out classroom use of the native language over time, but some continue instruction in both languages, targeting full biliteracy as a goal.

ESL instructional programs, in contrast, provide **English-only** classroom instruction, with possible occasional use of a student's L1 in support. ESL programs include those that focus solely on developing English proficiency and those that focus on teaching ELLs academic content in ways that reinforce English language learning.

Research points to many benefits of bilingual instruction—perhaps most clearly, a student's literacy skills in L1 facilitate literacy in L2. However, a bilingual approach is often not feasible, as it requires a fairly homogenous L1 population (in the United States, this leads overwhelmingly to Spanish-English bilingual programs), a sufficient pool of bilingual teachers, and a legal framework that allows for non-English instruction.

Transitional Bilingual Education (TBE)

Transitional bilingual education (TBE) programs are one of the three main bilingual **language instruction education programs (LIEP)** in use in the United States. Students typically enter a TBE program as soon as they start school and initially receive all or most of their instruction in L1. The goal of a TBE is an early **transition to the mainstream curriculum**, and this typically happens after 2–3 years (another name for a TBE is an *early-exit program*). TBE programs do not target L1 proficiency as a goal, and seldom explicitly teach L1 literacy. Instead, L1 is used as a transition to L2. Students in TBE programs often experience difficulty transitioning to the mainstream curriculum, requiring additional support during their first years after exiting the TBE.

Developmental Bilingual Education (DBE)

Developmental bilingual education (DBE) programs are one of the three main bilingual **language instruction education programs (LIEP)** in use in the United States. Like transitional bilingual education (TBE) programs, DBE programs (also called *maintenance* and *late-exit programs*) begin with instruction in L1 as soon as students enter school, and gradually transition to instruction in English. Unlike in TBE programs, however, students never transition fully to English—DBE programs aim to develop **biliteracy** and to maintain a student's proficiency in L1 throughout the program—which typically lasts through 6th or perhaps 8th grade. Students in a typical DBE program might begin with 90% of their instruction in L1, and in their last year receive a 50/50 L1-L2 mix. DBE programs often evolve as an option in an already-established TBE program. DBE programs differ in how students learn in the two languages—L1 and L2 might be used in alternate periods, on alternate days, in alternate semesters, or to teach different subjects.

Dual Immersion

Dual immersion (**DI**) or **two-way immersion (TWI)** programs are one of the three main bilingual **language instruction education programs (LIEP)** in use in the United States. The defining feature of DI programs is that all students (both ELLs and English speakers) are taught in both languages, with the goal of **full bilingualism** for the entire school population. Some DI programs balance the two instructional languages equally, beginning with the earliest grades, but it is more common for DI students to begin with a higher proportion (80/20 or 90/10) of instruction in the non-English language, and transition gradually to equality. Even a 50/50 instructional balance, however, doesn't lead to equal language proficiency—research has demonstrated that native English speakers do not obtain the same level of L2 proficiency as non-native speakers obtain in English. This difference can be attributed both to motivation (learning English is more of a necessity than is learning a foreign language) and to the fact that the surrounding world provides far more opportunities to practice English than a foreign language. In addition to the language benefit, DI programs are credited with promoting biculturalism and tolerance.

Newcomer Programs

Newcomer programs are a type of **language instruction education program (LIEP)** developed specifically for immigrants who enter the United States between grades 6 and 12 and have experienced either **interrupted schooling or no schooling** in their home countries. These students often lack the basic literacy skills necessary to function in standard ELS classes, and almost invariably lack the academic English skills necessary to join their peers in content classrooms. School districts often create specific programs for these students, often off-site (thus the frequent term "newcomer centers"). A typical newcomer program provides separate, all-day instruction for a year, and may include after-school programs to help students and their families acculturate.

Heritage Language Programs

A heritage language is a language spoken in a student's home, or by his or her ancestors, which the student has a strong desire to learn or retain. In the United States, the term is used most often to refer to Native American languages, though not exclusively so: the term may refer to the home language of recent immigrants as well. The teaching of **heritage languages** became a public issue when Arizona passed **Proposition 203** in 2000, limiting ESL instruction to full immersion to last no longer than a year. The proposition was seen as threatening Native American language programs in schools on or near reservations. While Arizona addressed the issue in part by issuing waivers allowing for dual-language instruction, many heritage language communities have resorted to after-school and weekend instructional programs. Many colleges offer heritage language programs, including in Spanish for individuals whose Spanish proficiency may have eroded after transitioning in school to an English-only curriculum.

Structured English Immersion (SEI)

Structured English immersion (SEI) is an ESL instruction model designed to transition ELLs to mainstream classrooms quickly (usually after one year) by emphasizing **English-language instruction** and deferring **academic content instruction** until students transition to mainstream classrooms. Students in SEI classrooms are typically grouped by proficiency. SEI teachers do not simply teach *in* English but teach the *rules and forms* of English—proponents argue that explicit teaching of grammar facilitates the eventual transition of ELLs from intermediate to full fluency. SEI was one of two language models prescribed by California's Proposition 227 in 1997 (since repealed) and is the language model required under Arizona's Proposition 203. Critics argue that one year is not enough time to achieve the proficiency to succeed in academic subjects; further, SEI's focus on explicitly teaching challenging grammatical forms at a relatively early stage of instruction is controversial.

Types of Support

As an alternative to either a bilingual program or an English-immersion program, many districts place English language learners in **mainstream classes** and then use pull-out or push-in methods to provide them with additional English-language assistance.

In a **pull-out model**, language specialists pull ELL students out of the classrooms for short, individual or group English language instruction. Lessons are often tailored to reinforce what the ELL is learning in the content classroom. Critics argue that ELLs pulled out of class may suffer social stigma; further, it is disruptive.

In the **push-in model**, the language specialist joins the mainstream classroom in one of several ways. The language specialist and the classroom teacher may co-teach, coordinating and dividing the curriculum. Alternately, they might divide the classroom into ELLs and native speakers during some portion of the day and teach simultaneous lessons at different degrees of English proficiency. More commonly, the language specialist can work with individuals or small groups in succession and serve as a ready resource for ELL students in need of assistance.

Civil Rights Act of 1965

Title VI of the Civil Rights Act of 1965 prohibits **discrimination** on the basis of race, color, or national origin in any program that receives funding from the federal government. In May of 1970, the Department of Education wrote a memo to school districts with high concentrations of Spanish-language students, warning them that a number of common educational practices denied these students their rights to an equal education, and thus constituted discriminatory policy in violation of the Civil Rights Act. Specifically, the memo stated that (a) when a lack of English ability excludes students from effective participation, districts must take steps to rectify the language deficiency; (b) districts must not misclassify ELL students as having special needs; and (c) ESL programs must be designed to achieve proficiency rather than simply lead to academic dead ends.

The **May 25 Memorandum**, as it came to be known, helped define access to appropriate language education as a civil right, and it identified several broad areas in need of reform. However, as a cabinet-level memorandum, it did not have the status of law. The principles within it, however, were endorsed as law by the Supreme Court in the 1971 case *Lau v. Nichols*.

BILINGUAL EDUCATION ACT OF 1968

The Bilingual Education Act of 1968 is a descriptive name given to **Title VII of the Elementary and Secondary Education Act (ESEA)** originally passed in 1965. ESEA was a cornerstone of President Lyndon B. Johnson's War on Poverty, reflecting Johnson's view of the importance of education in overcoming poverty. ESEA redefined the federal government's role in education, providing for dramatic increases in federal funding, as well as standards for equal access, educational achievement, and accountability. ESEA has been periodically reauthorized ever since its enactment. The 2001 reauthorization is called the **No Child Left Behind Act (NCLB)**, and the 2015 reauthorization is termed the **Every Student Succeeds Act (ESSA)**.

The Bilingual Education Act provided federal funding for districts to develop bilingual programs but provided no guidelines on what those programs should look like. The Act did not require that schools adopt ESL programs, but it encouraged and funded district-led innovations and did much to elevate ELL rights as a concern separate from that of racial discrimination.

LAU V. NICHOLS

The *Lau v. Nichols* suit was brought by Chinese students in San Francisco, who argued that the fact that their classes were taught in English rather than Chinese violated their rights under the Equal Protection Clause of the Fourteenth Amendment.

In its unanimous decision in favor of the plaintiff, the Supreme Court ruled that schools receiving federal funding must provide **English-language instruction** to students who lack English proficiency. The Court based its decision on the Civil Rights Act of 1965 (rather than the Fourteenth Amendment), finding that the lack of appropriate language education represented a failure to grant **equal access to educational opportunities**. The Court's decision meant that schools could no longer allow students to succeed or fail in an English-only curriculum but had to actively help students overcome language deficiencies.

The **Lau Remedies** are guidelines issued by the Department of Education to help districts develop language policies in accordance with *Lau v. Nichols*. The Remedies stipulate that districts should develop the means to identify and evaluate ELLs, provide them with appropriate instruction, and evaluate their readiness to exit the ESL program.

NO CHILD LEFT BEHIND (NCLB)

The No Child Left Behind Act (NCLB) was based on the premise that setting and holding schools and students accountable to high standards would promote academic excellence. The act mandated that all schools receiving Title 1 funding adopt **annual standardized tests**. Schools that failed to demonstrate adequate yearly progress on test results were required to create improvement plans and faced escalating penalties if they failed to improve.

The NCLB established, for the first time, **accountability and funding provisions for ELL programs** (under Title 3) separate from those allocated for the entire spectrum of socio-economically disadvantaged students (under Title 1). This separate attention raised the profile of ELL education issues. It also obliged states to monitor ELL academic performance more closely, and most developed uniform metrics for doing so. The NCLB required that states track three **annual measurable achievement objectives (AMAO)**—two that measured ELL English proficiency, and a third that measured ELL progress toward *content* standards. The third element proved problematic—few states managed to provide full accommodations for ESL students taking content exams. A large percentage of schools serving ESL populations failed to meet these standards and, they often argued, failed to receive the resources or other federal assistance necessary for improvement.

Every Student Succeeds Act (ESSA)

In the broadest terms, the Every Student Succeeds Act (ESSA) represented a devolution of authority from the federal government to the states. While ESSA retains the No Child Left Behind Act's (NCLB) basic framework of standardized testing and school accountability, ESSA grants states more discretion in how to **measure school success** (for example, states may include measures of progress in addition to measures of attainment) and how to address low-performing schools.

ESSA incorporates a measure of **ELL progress**—the rate at which students achieve English proficiency – into the overall Title 1 measure of school effectiveness, raising the potential that states and schools will make English-language education a stronger priority. (Critics worry that, by contrast, the relatively small population of ELLs will be lost, for funding purposes, in the larger Title 1 population.) ESSA also requires states to develop uniform **standards** for identifying, placing, and exiting students from ESL programs (previously, districts and schools could develop separate standards). ESSA also allows the **content test results** of ESL students in their first two years of schooling to be exempted from a school's reported results, reducing what were perceived to be unrealistic pressures under NCLB to realize early ELL success on academic content exams.

Castaneda v. Pickard

In 1978, Roy Castaneda, the father of two Mexican-American students, sued the school district of Raymondville, Texas, arguing that his children had unlawfully been placed in a classroom segregated by language ability, and further that the school district had failed to establish an adequate bilingual education program that would allow ELLs to re-enter the mainstream curriculum. Castaneda's case effectively challenged the courts to enforce *Lau v. Nichols*, which dictated that school districts take the necessary steps to allow ELL students to overcome their English language deficiencies.

In 1981, the Fifth US Court of Appeals issued what came to be called the **Castaneda Test** to assess whether district bilingual education programs were meeting the standards of the right to equal education concept in the Civil Rights Act of 1964 and the Equal Education Opportunities Act of 1974. Specifically, bilingual programs (a) had to be based on sound theory and have a legitimate design, (b) had to be supported with appropriate resources and personnel, and (c) must be evaluated to determine if they are effective.

Plyler v. Doe

The Supreme Court ruled in *Plyler v. Doe* that children could not be denied education because of their **immigration status**. The case arose when the state of Texas passed a law that withheld funds to pay for the education of, and allowed districts to expel, students who lacked legal status. In 1982, the Supreme Court ruled that the Texas law violated the **Equal Protection Clause** of the Fourteenth Amendment. *Plyler v. Doe* only applies to K-12 education. Legal battles continue over the issues of whether college students without status can be denied in-state tuition benefits, and whether public schools can gather information about student legal status during the enrollment process for possible reporting to the immigration authorities.

Proposition 227 and Proposition 58

As the state with the largest number of English language learners, California's ESL policies and innovations are important for teachers in any state to understand.

In 1998, California voters approved **Proposition 227**, which effectively **ended bilingual education programs** in public schools, requiring that ESL students enroll in one-year English immersion programs and then transition to mainstream English content classrooms. Studies showed mixed results—while students achieved greater success on standardized tests following implementation, so did students who continued in bilingual programs, suggesting that other factors, such as teacher training or the accountability measures of No Child Left Behind, were driving the improvements.

In 2017, Californians passed **Proposition 58**, which repealed Proposition 227 and gave public school districts the right to decide the best way to teach ESL students while retaining the responsibility to ensure that students achieve English proficiency. Given the apparent success of the Proposition 227 framework in raising student scores, its repeal is best seen as the result of a growing awareness of the value of **multilingualism** in an interconnected world.

LULAC v. State Board of Education

A **consent decree** is a mutually-binding agreement enforced by a court. In 1990, the **League of United Latin American Citizens (LULAC)** filed a suit claiming that Florida was failing to provide English language learners with equitable and comprehensible education under the existing framework of federal laws.

The case was settled in US District Court according to the terms of the consent decree. The consent decree—which covers issues such as identification and assessment, equal access to programming, teacher qualifications and training, monitoring, and outcome measures—now serves as the framework for Florida's ESL programs. Within education circles, the agreement is simply known as the **Florida Consent Decree**.

Changing Public Views of Bilingualism

Public debate on bilingualism in society and in schools can be simplified into two pools of thought: one worries that bilingualism **erodes national unity and identity**, and thus the growing numbers of non-native speakers in schools is a problem to be overcome; the other views bilingualism as a **resource to be cultivated**, arguing that a child's L1 helps him or her acquire English—and further, that globalization proves the importance of multilingualism. This debate is also often framed as one between the prioritization of *assimilation* versus *multiculturalism*.

The **Bilingual Education Act (BEA)** of 1968 (Title VII of the broader Elementary and Secondary Education Act, or ESEA) provided federal funding for bilingual education programs and recognized, at least implicitly, the value of students retaining their native languages and cultures. The **No Child Left Behind Act (NCLB)**, which replaced ESEA in 2002, struck all mention of bilingualism and implicitly repealed the BEA, renaming it the English Language Acquisition, Language Enforcement, and Academic Achievement Act. The NCLB's focus on standardized test results and short-term, transitional ESL programs mirrored broader national trends promoting assimilation, including the adoption of Proposition 227 in California and Proposition 203 in Arizona. **ESSA**, while not explicitly promoting the benefits of bilingualism, grants greater policy latitude to the states—leading some to adopt bilingual education programs.

The English-Only Movement

The term "English-only movement" in a broad sense refers to efforts to establish English as the only official language in the United States (which currently has no official language) and prohibit the conduct of government business in other languages. Various initiatives to pass English-only legislation in Congress have failed—however, more than 20 states have ratified some form of English-only legislation.

English-only initiatives in education customarily take the form of prescribing English as the only language of instruction, eliminating bilingual education programs, and accelerating ESL transition programs. Proponents of English-language programs often argue that both the nation and recent immigrants are served by rapid assimilation and that the latter are best served by rapid transitions to mainstream classrooms. This sentiment led to the passage of several propositions **banning bilingual education** in the late 1990s and early 2000s, notably in Arizona, California, and Massachusetts. The latter two states subsequently repealed their propositions due to both popular pressure and growing recognition that L1 proficiency and use does not delay L2 acquisition and may accelerate it. While research supports the efficacy of bilingual education, the broader cultural debate continues about what constitutes national identity and whether that identity is threatened by the use of non-English languages in school and society.

Overrepresentation in Special Education Programs

Research demonstrates that English language learners are referred to **special education programs** more often than their native English-speaking peers. The issue arises primarily because normal second-language development patterns can resemble emerging special education issues, especially to non-specialists. For example, if an ESL student doesn't speak much or respond to questions, he or she might have a hearing impairment or processing deficit—or simply be in the silent period stage of language learning.

An accurate referral requires the ability to differentiate between the effects of a student's language ability, content knowledge, and cognitive abilities—a complex assessment that should only be made by a trained evaluator. The Department of Education recommends that, whenever feasible, disability assessments be done in the **student's native language** in order to avoid confounding disability and language issues.

Disparities in Teacher Qualifications and Retention

Nearly half of school funding in the United States comes from **local property taxes**, which leads to significant discrepancies in funding for schools located in wealthy and impoverished neighborhoods. While federal Title 1 funds and some state funds lessen that funding gap, it still exists, and in many states and school districts, it remains dramatic. Fewer funds result in fewer resources, larger classes, and lower teacher salaries—which deters more experienced and qualified teachers from taking these jobs. In turn, the less experienced teachers take these jobs due to their availability. Placing these under-equipped teachers in overcrowded classrooms contributes to **sub-par student performance** and **high teacher turnover**. A high percentage of ELLs live in low-income neighborhoods and thus experience these funding inequities.

Tracking

Tracking refers to the practice of placing students in separate academic tracks based on their academic or test performance at an early age. Tracking is closely related to **ability grouping**, the grouping of students with perceived similarities in academic ability to allow for efficient and targeted teaching. Critics of the practice argue that it is self-perpetuating—students in low-track courses receive instruction that is less cognitively-challenging and utilizes less academic language, all but ensuring that they will remain on that track. For example, ELLs enroll in high school college-preparatory classes at lower rates than their peers—and have lower rates of participation in post-secondary education as well.

The vast majority of high school students have access to at least some **advanced placement (AP) exams** due in part to federal funding of AP programs and teacher training, but the number of exams offered at a given school is directly correlated with socio-economic status, as is student participation in the AP program. AP classes, which are often writing-intensive and demand the use of academic English, are often seen as poor fits for ELLs.

Ability Groups

The separation of students into groups on the basis of their **perceived ability to understand a topic** is a long-standing teaching practice. It appeals to the parents of high-performing students who generally want their children to receive targeted, accelerated instruction; it often appeals to teachers as well, as it allows them to give specific instruction to different groups, avoiding unnecessary and redundant explanations. Research, however, suggests that the minimal advantages that ability grouping confers on high-performing students would better be gained by placing them in separate, gifted programs, while the negative effects of ability grouping on low-performing students are extensive and self-perpetuating—in other words, students who are placed in low-performing groups tend to fall further behind in their education. In-class ability grouping is thus looked upon with the same disfavor as its larger-scale counterpart, tracking.

Underrepresentation in GT Programs

ELLs remain underrepresented in GT programs, despite long-standing awareness of the deficits and of the fact that selection should be based on cognitive aptitudes independent of English language proficiency. Many explanations have been offered for the discrepancy, including (a) the challenge for teachers in recognizing giftedness through the filter of another language and culture, (b) a bias toward verbal aptitude in the definition and assessment of gifted students, (c) the lack of appropriate cognitive testing in students' native languages, (d) a lack of systematic communication between school ESL and gifted programs, and (e) an unspoken sense that ESL learners must become proficient in English before their cognitive skills can be recognized.

Though the US Department of Education offers **Jacob Javits grants** to help states identify and serve gifted ELLs, the bulk of funding and guidance for gifted programs comes from the individual states. As a consequence, states differ greatly in how they administer these programs and in the measures they take to identify gifted candidates among the ELL population.

Restorative Justice

Research shows that (a) in recent decades, schools have made dramatically more use of **harsh disciplinary measures**, such as suspensions, even for non-violent student offenses; (b) these disciplinary measures disproportionately affect ELLs beginning at the secondary-school level; and (c) students subjected to disciplinary actions are far less likely to succeed academically. The high correlation between disciplinary action and student socioeconomic status suggests that the problem has complex and deep-seated societal roots. **Lack of student engagement at school** is one often-cited factor for the increase of discipline incidents. Within the ELL context, this can arise if ELL students are unable to successfully join the mainstream curriculum or are tracked in marginal and unchallenging courses.

Restorative justice refers to actions that schools can take to address disciplinary problems without suspending or expelling students. Restorative justice programs emphasize mediation of conflicts, the creation of support groups composed of peers and adults for students at risk, and the creation of disciplinary practices that keep students in school or at least engaged in academic activities.

ESL Advocacy

ESL teachers today are expected to not only be effective teachers, but also to serve as advocates for the interests of their ELL students. The importance of **ESL teacher advocacy**—which has been codified as standard by bodies such as TESOL and NBPTS (National Board for Professional Teaching Standards)—stems from the idea that ELLs are often disadvantaged in the education system, and that ESL teachers are uniquely positioned to *understand* what actions are necessary to improve ELL education and to act to *effect* change. Advocacy includes a wide range of activities, such as ensuring ELLs have fair access to school resources and programs, engaging the parents of ELLs to make sure they are aware of educational opportunities for their children, helping educate peers who may not have received training in delivering content instruction to ELLs, and correcting misperceptions at the school and in the community about ELL aptitude and education.

Inclusive and Safe Learning Environments

Maintaining High Expectations

Educators have long recognized that **teacher expectations** are one of the key factors that contribute to the academic achievement gap that exists between minority and low-income groups on the one hand, and white and privileged students on the other. In a broad sense, students tend to do as well as teachers expect them to. Research shows that teachers are often unaware that they exhibit these biases—making it critical that teachers of diverse students consciously model **high expectations**. ESL teachers should ensure that they view and treat student backgrounds as an asset rather than an obstacle, that they maintain a clear distinction between student language proficiency and cognitive ability, and that they recognize that student progress may start slowly but accelerate once the student achieves a threshold level of proficiency and acculturation.

Social Distance

Social distance, and the related psychological distance, refers to the degree to which individuals accept those that they perceive to be different from them—whether due to differences in race, age, gender, religion, economic class, linguistic ability, or any other category of identity important to an individual or group. In a strong form, **social distance** is a form of prejudice—an unfavorable image formed without basis—but it can be present in a weak form even where there isn't animus, as individuals in new social settings tend to gravitate toward people they perceive as being like themselves.

Teachers can reduce the social distance by encouraging or requiring students to interact with one another, by reinforcing the concept of cultural relativism, and by staging interactions that demonstrate the positive contributions of student differences.

Promoting Multicultural Perspectives

Teachers can promote **multicultural awareness** in the classroom in many ways. One is by explicitly teaching students about prejudice, stereotypes, and ethnocentrism. A second is to establish and enforce clear classroom policies regarding tolerance and cultural sensitivity. Building on this, teachers might ask students to reflect on their own behavior and identify an occasion when they might have acted based on an unwarranted stereotype.

Teachers can also structure the curriculum around **multicultural themes or events**, drawing examples and information from the students' home cultures. They can also adopt **multicultural resources** for use in the classroom, such as books, films, or works of art. Teachers might encourage students to consider minority viewpoints when discussing topics in history or current events. And finally, teachers should encourage students to draw connections between classroom lessons and their experiences in, and knowledge of, their home countries.

James Banks

In a 1989 article, the educator James Banks identified four different **levels of commitment** that schools take toward multicultural education. At the first level, the *contributions approach*, schools simply add a few references to minority or female contributions to the existing curriculum. This is often called, derisively, the holidays and heroes approach to multiculturalism. Banks calls the second level of engagement the *additive approach*. At this level, teachers incorporate numerous multicultural themes and concepts into the curriculum, but do so in a superficial way, teaching the issues from a traditional perspective—i.e., from the perspective of the dominant majority. Schools using the third level, the *transformative approach*, incorporate first-person minority perspectives on key issues and use teaching methods to investigate key issues from those points of view. Banks calls the fourth approach *decision-making or social action*. Schools that adopt this model encourage students to use what they learn about societal inequities to become agents of social change.

Multicultural Education and Paolo Freire

The term "multicultural education" generally refers to the practice of adapting the curriculum and classroom environment to reflect or incorporate the viewpoints of multiple, minority, or non-dominant student groups. **Critical pedagogy** is a type of social action that calls upon teachers in multicultural classrooms to be agents of change in addressing societal and institutional inequalities. In this view, teachers should strive not for equality, or treating everyone the same or being color blind; but instead strive for equity, an outcome that can only be achieved by providing additional help to students disadvantaged by multiple factors outside of the classroom.

Paolo Friere, an educator best-known for his work *The Pedagogy of the Oppressed*, focused on the potential of education to **transform**: education, and in particular literacy, is an instrument of power, and traditionally has served as a means (or one of them) of disadvantaging the poor. Teachers must not only work to empower disadvantaged minorities, but also help these students develop a critical approach to understanding their own treatment by society.

Linguistic Imperialism

The term "linguistic imperialism," popularized in a 1992 book by Michael Phillipson, refers to the spread and domination of one language over others, often in association with acts of power or violence. The classic example of **linguistic imperialism** is the spread of European languages in association with colonial rule, but proponents of the concept argue that it is still ongoing, with the adoption of English increasingly necessary to function in a global economy or to understand a reality shaped by an English-dominated media and Internet. In its radical form, proponents use a biological analogy to argue that the spread of English causes the extinction of local languages. Others point out that the widespread use of English does cause resentments at times, and spurs movements to revitalize waning languages. The concept might be most useful, however, as a reminder of the extent to which learning a second language—often, but not always, English—is necessary for individuals seeking to participate in a globalized world, even if only via the Internet.

Deterring and Addressing Cultural Conflict

Teachers can best deter cultural conflict in the classroom by openly discussing and celebrating cultural differences. Teachers should also ensure that students from different cultures interact frequently in group settings—first with explicit roles and clearly-defined procedural rules, and then, once students are comfortable with one another, with fewer teacher supports. When misunderstandings occur, teachers might lead open discussions (at a level of generality that won't call attention to a specific conflict) that reveal different cultural interpretations and expectations of common events. A teacher's ability to **mediate cross-cultural conflicts** will depend in part on how well they understand the competing cultures, and it may be necessary and wise to talk to each party to the conflict separately in order to fully understand their interpretation of the conflict. Assuming that two students from different cultures are acting in good faith, a mediated solution might take some version of the form "s/he didn't intend it the way you perceived it."

Instructional Planning and Organization

Meeting ELA Standards

The Common Core State Standards hold ELLs to the same **standards of English language arts (ELA) proficiency** as native English speakers, while recognizing that ELLs may need more time and more support to reach those objectives. In response, both the WIDA consortium and several states (such as California) developed **English language development (ELD) frameworks** to give teachers and parents a detailed roadmap of how ELLs could meet the ELA standards.

The various ELD frameworks define **scales** of student English proficiency (for example, WIDA's ranges from entering to bridging). The frameworks then elaborate **benchmarks** by grade and proficiency level (e.g., in the third grade, a student at the developing stage of proficiency should be able to...) and offer teachers curriculum guidance and provide instructional suggestions for the various grade and English proficiency combinations. In circumstances where ELLs are grouped by language proficiency, teachers can use the ELD frameworks to guide their classroom-level plans and instructional delivery; when faced with a class composed of students with varying levels of proficiency, teachers can use the frameworks to plan differentiated lessons and activities.

Using Formative Assessments

Modern education theory recognizes the value of using **formative assessments** in every classroom context. Teachers achieve the best outcomes when they utilize frequent, varied, and non-intrusive assessments that address clearly-articulated learning objectives and transparent state standards. Modern theory also suggests that grades should primarily reflect whether a student has attained an educational objective and not whether he or she struggled along the way. This insight is particularly important when teaching ELLs: while under the **Common Core**, they are held to the same English language arts standards as native speakers, so they enter the school system at a language disadvantage. In this context, ESL teachers need to make maximal use of formative assessments to identify what needs to be taught (or re-taught) and how.

Teachers should use formative assessments prior to launching an instructional unit in order to gauge student knowledge and needs; during instruction to check for understanding, identify needed lesson modifications, and detect students in need of help; and after instruction to ensure student comprehension with an eye toward modifying subsequent instruction.

Classroom Resources

Selecting Materials and Resources

Teachers must take care that the **resources** they choose for the classroom are age-appropriate, culturally inclusive, language-accessible, affordable, varied, and easily accessible. One challenge ESL teachers face is that resources that are language-appropriate for older ELLs may not be age-appropriate—i.e., students may perceive them as childish or demeaning. When assigning **online language tasks**, teachers need to make sure students have time to complete the work in class rather than assume the students have access to technology or the Internet at home. Teachers should invite students to bring **realia and written texts** from their native cultures for discussion but shouldn't make the presentation of a home culture mandatory. Teachers should strive to provide resources in **different media** (audio, visual, performative guides, etc.) in order to appeal to different learning preferences and to provide reinforcement of learning through multiple media.

Use of Technology

The use of technology in the classroom—and indeed, to blur the line between the inside and outside of a classroom—is widespread, limited in most cases only by funding and teacher unfamiliarity with emerging platforms. The adoption of **technology** is leading to the growth of blended learning, in which online learning replaces a portion of the face-to-face instruction time. Technology plays a key role in many classroom differentiation strategies, as students using software can learn at their own pace and using different learning styles. Technologies that are of particular value in ESL classrooms include **document cameras**, which can easily provide a visual accompaniment to a spoken lesson; and **online voice recorders**, which allow teachers and students to record specific lessons for targeted speaking practice. Any technology that gives quick access to pictures provides essential scaffolding for early ELLs. Anonymous chat and collaboration sites are particularly useful for ELLs who are not comfortable participating in class.

ESL teachers need to be careful not to require technologies that their students cannot afford, or to assume that students have Internet connectivity at home.

Meaningful and Purposeful Communicative Interactions

Meaningful and purposeful classroom activities are those that achieve a specific learning goal while engaging the students with a topic or a process that is interesting to them. The phrase "**communicative interactions**" points to the sociocultural aspect of language learning—students learn best when they are engaged in authentic communicative acts rather than simply listening to a lecture or practicing repetitive worksheet exercises.

In order to make lessons meaningful, teachers should use **authentic texts and realia**, examples and scenarios from the students' original cultures, and scenarios that reproduce scenes and activities that the students actually experience. Texts should include sympathetic characters facing familiar challenges.

In order to promote communicative interactions, teachers should stage activities that draw students into **conversations**, such as small-group discussions, problem-solving tasks, skits, or dialogue journals. In guiding the conversation, teachers should ask open-ended, exploratory questions that avoid right/wrong answers and invite elaboration. Students should assess and discuss what they read and should write in order to be read—whether it be a product like a classroom newsletter or a journal to be read by a classmate or a parent.

David Ausubel's Subsumption Theory

The educational psychologist David Ausubel's work underscored the importance of **context** for learning. In his view, students learn best when the new material relates to what they already know. He labeled this kind of learning **meaningful**, and contrasted it with rote learning, in which students learn isolated information that they can only relate to other information in an arbitrary way. With meaningful learning, new information is **subsumed** under existing cognitive structures and knowledge. Ausubel suggested that the most important factor determining whether students will remember what they learn is not repetition, but rather the **integration** of that knowledge in a system of meaning. Even information earned by means of an artificial mnemonic device will eventually be lost, Ausubel argued, unless it is used and thus anchored in a broader network of meaning.

Many of Ausubel's insights are now accepted as givens, but his work is a useful reminder of the importance of activating student prior knowledge, pre-teaching concepts, and in general providing students with a context for what is to be taught.

Use vs. Usage

The linguist Henry Widdowson drew a distinction between **language usage**, or knowing how to construct words and sentences in accordance with formal rules; and **language use**, or knowing how to use language in order to achieve an objective. Widdowson used these terms to draw a sharp distinction between **linguistic competence** and **communicative competence** and argued that the latter took more time for second-language learners to achieve. Extending the same distinction, Widdowson argued that sentences have *significance* in isolation, but *value* when they are considered in the context of a communicative act. Widdowson's ideas influenced the communicative approaches to language learning, with their emphasis on authentic speech acts and the importance of pragmatic dimensions of communication.

Implicit vs. Explicit Strategies

Teachers should teach grammar both **implicitly** and **explicitly**, according to both the subject matter and student needs. In general, students whose L1 is grammatically very different from English will require more explicit instruction. Several aspects of English grammar are hard for even speakers of closely-related languages—for example, word order, prepositions, auxiliary verbs, and modal verbs—and thus should be taught explicitly.

The goal of language instruction is **effective communication**, and teachers who are tempted to explicitly correct a student error should first ask themselves whether the error prevented communication. There are many reasons not to explicitly correct a student's spoken errors. Doing so interrupts the conversational flow, it may embarrass the student or discourage them from speaking in the future, and it may not even help—research shows that certain types of errors appear during the normal process of language development and then disappear without explicit correction. Teachers should be more liberal when correcting written work, both because the affective consequences are fewer and because students need more explicit instruction when learning academic language.

Paraprofessional

"Paraprofessional" is another word for teacher's aide, or someone who plays a supportive role to a certified teacher in a classroom. **Paraprofessionals** often take responsibility for the logistics of the classroom or a lesson, give individual attention to students who need it, manage a group of students when the class is divided, and help the classroom teacher with assessments. ESL-trained paraprofessionals are also used in content classrooms. Many school districts hire paraprofessionals who speak the foreign language most widely represented in the student population; in these instances, he or she can provide interpretation when needed.

New Literacies of Online Research and Comprehension

The concept of new literacies of online research and comprehension (often called simply new literacies) is based on the assertion that online reading and research requires a different set of literacy skills than does traditional, paper-based reading and research. According to this still-emerging body of research, success in traditional reading does not automatically translate to success in online reading. Further, students are likely to have significant advantages in online literacy over their teachers. And online literacy is **deictic**, or ever-changing, in ways that traditional literacy is not, making online literacy an ongoing, dynamic engagement.

Donald Leu has outlined **five functions** critical to online literacy. The first is **identifying the problem**. Students must initiate online research by accurately formulating a question or a search phrase—a skill seldom, if ever, needed in traditional reading. Second, students must know how to **locate information online**, skimming and choosing from search engine results. Third, students must be able to **evaluate sources for reliability and bias**. Fourth, they must be able to **synthesize information drawn from different sources**—as the number of sources has grown, so has the likelihood that relevant information will be spread among multiple locations. Finally, students may be called upon to **communicate their results in multiple new formats**, requiring a different range of rhetorical skills.

Computer Assisted Language Learning (CALL)

Computer assisted language learning (CALL) is the use of computer technology to learn languages. Discussions of CALL often distinguish between the use of computers as a tutor and their use as a tool for communicating with others. The most commonly used tutoring applications in ESL classrooms include **pronunciation tutorials**, in which students listen to native English speakers and record their own speech; **reading tutorials**, in which electronic glossaries provide definitions and draw connections between related texts; and programs that provide outlines and graphic organizers to assist in the **writing process**.

The use of computers as a communication tool is often called **computer-mediated communication (CMC)**. CMC may either be synchronous (real-time interaction with a teacher or other students) or asynchronous (in which one student posts work for later review or augmentation by another user).

CALL is widely-used to differentiate instruction and learning, as individual students can use CALL to learn different lessons at different rates. When used responsibly by self-motivated learners, CALL can provide unique opportunities for self-guided learning. As a communication tool, CALL expands the possibilities for distance learning and collaboration beyond the physical classroom. And finally, computer-based assessments can automate much of the grading and feedback functions of teaching.

Technology and Differentiate Instruction

The single greatest advantage of technology use in the classroom is the opportunities it provides for **differentiated instruction**. Using computer technology, a teacher can differentiate a lesson by content and degree of difficulty, by the amount or nature of scaffolding provided, by learner-style preference, and by a student's preferred method of demonstrating learning. If students have access to the learning technologies at home, they can listen to or read a lesson multiple times, gaining the critical advantages of time and repetition. The same technologies can be used to **differentiate**

assessments. With the right technologies, students can listen to questions multiple times or access hyperlinks to contextual information.

School use of technology varies greatly, as does student access to technologies at home. Teachers must be cognizant of these limitations and careful not to disadvantage students who lack access. While technology-based learning is great for differentiation and for autonomous learning, students who lack direction may waste their time or pursue inappropriate goals. Finally, even a well-equipped classroom may lack bandwidth or suffer technology failures—teachers have to be prepared with alternative lesson plans.

Corpus and Concordance

A corpus (plural corpora) is a collection of texts gathered by linguists for purposes of **research**. Today, linguists use computers to search and analyze textual data for insights into language use. Corpora are used, for example, to compile dictionaries, and to juxtapose prescriptive and descriptive grammars.

A **concordance** is a list of the ways in which a word is used in **context**. It can be very useful for an ESL student trying to understand idiosyncratic constructions—for example, which prepositions go with which verbs—or to see how an unfamiliar word is actually used in discourse.

Simple search engines will return some of the information available from a concordance, but intermediate and advanced ESL students may benefit from a **concordance program** that provides more information than a dictionary about actual usage. Concordances can also show which words are typically used in association with one another—a useful tool when building subject-matter vocabulary.

Content Instructors and ESL Instructors

While content teachers in states with high numbers of ELLs are likely to receive **professional development courses** to help them understand how to work with ELLs, a minority of states mandate such training, even though a majority of content classrooms contain at least one ELL.

ESL teachers are often called upon—either formally or informally—to **help their colleagues** effectively reach their ELLs. ESL teachers might help by identifying an ELL's language proficiency level or go further to suggest appropriate teaching supports, reasonable expectations, and teaching methods. They might organize multi-teacher conferences to ensure that the student receives consistent instruction throughout the day. ESL teachers might usefully join parent-teacher conferences to address language concerns. Finally, ESL teachers might either recommend ESL-oriented professional development activities to their colleagues or, in the absence of such activities, volunteer to lead periodic training seminars.

Furthering Professional Development

The best professional development provides a teacher with new ideas and the knowledge of how to implement them in the classroom. The simplest—and likely most effective—form of professional development is **networking** with other experienced ESL teachers, either as a peer or as a mentee. **ESL conferences** provide the best intersection of networking with learning about ESL research. The latter can also be accessed through professional journals and the websites of informational clearinghouses such as the Center for Applied Linguistics or the Centre for Educational Research on Languages and Literacies. **Websites** such as Colorin Colorado! and Brown University's Educational Alliance can be invaluable, and ESL teachers have established numerous useful blogs, online discussion groups, and Twitter feeds. Though they are potentially expensive in terms of both cost and time, **summer workshops** often offer more systematic training and a resume credential.

Finally, committed career professionals should consider doing their own **research for publication**, particularly in an aspect of ESL that they are passionate about.

TESOL, CAL, ACTFL, NCELA, AND NABE

Teachers and prospective teachers of ESL have a number of organizations they can turn to for information and professional development.

- **TESOL (Teachers of English to Speakers of Other Languages)**—the preeminent organization in the field, TESOL offers virtual seminars, online courses, certificate programs, and meetings/conventions dedicated to the field. www.TESOL.org.
- **CAL (Center for Applied Linguistics)**—a non-profit that conducts research into language and culture, develops assessment and curriculum material, and offers training and educational resources for teachers. www.CAL.org.
- **ACTFL (American Council on the Teaching of Foreign Languages)**—a membership organization promoting language teaching, with particular expertise in language testing, including for teachers striving for bilingual certifications. www.ACTFL.org.
- **NCELA (National Clearinghouse for English Language Acquisition)**—a resource site run by the US Department of Education, providing data, research, and the English Learner Tool Kit, which provides guidance to state and local educators on how to fulfill federal civil rights mandates in the area of English language acquisition. www.ncela.ed.gov.
- **NABE (National Association for Bilingual Education)**—a non-profit that advocates for educational equity and provides professional development and instructional resources for ESL teachers. www.NABE.org.

MTTC Practice Test #1

1. Phonemic awareness is a type of:

a. Phonological awareness. Phonemic awareness is the ability to recognize sounds within words
b. Phonics. It is a teaching technique whereby readers learn the relationship between letters and sounds
c. Alphabetization. Unless a reader knows the alphabet, phonemic awareness is useless
d. Prosodic fluency. Producing accurate tempo, pitch, and stress in speech.

2. Which of the following classroom practices is least effective with regards to second language acquisition:

a. Presenting sufficient and meaningful reading and writing experiences for students to practice strategies.
b. Frequent reading and writing activities at the student's current reading level.
c. Reviewing and re-teaching as required to ensure that students have integrated essential content.
d. Daily introduction to new words or concepts.

3. Is acculturation or assimilation more likely to produce second language learners who are successful at both BICS and CALP thresholds?

a. Assimilation: when learners feel their own culture is respected, their affective filter will rise, motivating them to learn.
b. Acculturation: adapting to a new culture, which includes understanding cultural expectations, semiotics, values, and beliefs, is essential to second language acquisition in that it provides appropriate context.
c. Acculturation: when language learners prioritize the demands of their new culture over their culture of origin, with time they abandon their prior cultural values and expectations and become a tabula rasa upon which the adopted culture can more fully write itself.
d. Assimilation: when language learners prioritize the demands of their new culture over their culture of origin, with time they abandon their prior cultural values and expectations and become a tabula rasa upon which the adopted culture can more fully write itself.

4. That tiny red car is a <u>Smart car</u>. In this statement, the underlined words are:

a. A predicate adjective
b. Predicate adjectives
c. A predicate nominative
d. Predicate nominatives

5. My neighbor's pit bull puppy is <u>protective</u>. In this statement, the underlined word is:

a. A predicate adjective
b. A predicate nominative
c. A predictive phrase
d. The object of a preposition

6. The primary approach to teaching English to non-native speakers prior to 1960 was:

a. Two-way immersion
b. Sheltered English
c. Immersion
d. ESL

7. Lau v. Nichols (U.S. Supreme Court, 1974) determined that ELLs must be given what right?

a. To the same educational opportunities as all students
b. To receive private tutoring until they are working at grade level or above
c. To instruction that they have the skills to understand
d. To unbiased, fair grading practices

8. How can a teacher best simplify a text for ELLs at the beginning and intermediate stages?

a. Substitute one-syllable words for two-syllable words; delete as much text as possible and provide illustrations instead; have students keep reader response journals
b. Shorten the text by putting more words on each page; delete illustrations that will distract the reader; provide a glossary of terms at the end of the book
c. Shorten the text; abbreviate sentences; substitute simple, concrete language for more complex language; break complex sentences into two or three simpler, more direct sentences; omit detail that enhances the text but doesn't change or clarify meaning
d. Clarify the text by offering interpretations at the bottom of each page; provide a Spanish-English glossary of terms at the end of the book; omit illustrations that will distract the reader

9. How are traditional ESL programs and Content-Based ESL Curriculum (CBEC) different?

a. Traditional programs are immersion programs in which LEPs are taught only in L2, and must "sink or swim." CBEC offers instruction in a two-way immersion format, given in both L2 and L1.
b. Traditional ESL programs prioritize social language skills. CBEC offers instruction in content areas that are age-appropriate to the LEPs' mainstreamed peers.
c. Traditional ESL programs focus on grammar; CBEC focuses on phonetics.
d. Traditional ESL programs prioritize a high level of CALP and do not find BICS to be central to communication.

10. Which takes longer to develop, BICS or CALP?

a. BICS.
b. CALP.
c. They are interrelated and therefore develop at the same pace.
d. They are not interrelated, but they take approximately the same time to develop.

11. The new ESL teacher is compiling a file of information for each of her students. Her files include level of L1 education and literacy; level of L2 competency in the four modalities of speaking, writing, listening, and reading; the type of depth of English study the student has undertaken; the student's interests and personality type; and the most effective learning styles for the particular student. What does the teacher most likely intend to use these files for?

a. She will use the information they contain to vary her lessons to meet each student's specific needs.
b. She will send them home periodically so that parents can read her notes and sign off on them.
c. She will use the information to separate the students into their respective levels in future classes.
d. She will share the students' files with classmates so they can get to know one another on a more intimate, personal level.

12. A class is doing a project about a kitchen they have been in. The project can be based on a grandparent's kitchen or that of a friend; an outdoor "kitchen," such as at a campground or on a deck; a play kitchen that they recall from pre-school; or any other type of kitchen. The students can work individually or in a small group of their choosing. Some students are drawing and painting, while others are creating 3-dimensional models. One group is creating a play that takes place in a kitchen. One child is writing about her grandmother, who cooks tortillas on a hot rock. Another is creating a shoe-box diorama that depicts a fisherman smoking a fish in a temporary smoke-house. The teacher has reviewed vocabulary with the students, but a number of them approach her for help with English words. What has the teacher created this project to do?

a. Expand the vocabulary of her students. Many of her ESL students lack basic English vocabulary, and the teacher knows that kitchen items, such as knives, saucepans, and cups are very commonly-used words that the students need to know.
b. Determine each student's preferred learning style.
c. Encourage students to be curious about and respectful of differences in culture.
d. Teach students about different cooking methods.

13. Which of the following statements is true?

a. ELLs typically are better able to express themselves verbally than they are to listen and then interpret what is being said by someone else.
b. ELLs who are not literate in their first language have a better chance at becoming literate in their second language.
c. ELLs often understand more in terms of vocabulary and correct syntax than they demonstrate in their own speaking.
d. Once an ELL has achieved BICS competency, CALP competency will soon follow.

14. What is Krashen's Monitor Hypothesis concerned with?

a. The importance of frequent assessment and adjustment of teaching methods according to the results
b. The degree to which an ESL teacher is monitored and advised by a mentor
c. Monitoring learning by using computer programs specifically designed for ELLs to offer a stable and consistent model of learning achievement
d. The ways in which language learning influences acquisition

15. An approach to language learning that begins with practical communicative usage and that over time incorporates grammar, vocabulary, phonemic awareness, etc. is known as a(n) _____approach.

a. Top down
b. Functional
c. Total Physical Response
d. Natural Approach

16. Second language acquisition research suggests L2s tend to do what to acquire linguistic rules?

a. Integrate formulaic expressions and apply new uses to them
b. Learn grammar rules and progressively apply them
c. Learn words and phrases as chunks and use them in repetitive ways
d. Try to apply phrases from L1 and bridge them into L2

17. What is a possible outcome when teachers interpret oral language proficiency assessments, such as the Language Assessment Scales-Oral, the Woodcock-Muñoz Language Survey, and the IDEA Proficiency Test in terms of an ELL's general scholastic performance?

a. The student is more likely to receive the help she needs, both in terms of language learning and in terms of academic achievement.
b. The student is more likely to be held back a grade.
c. The student is more likely to be placed in a special education program.
d. The student is more likely to be placed at a level higher than her language abilities can support.

18. Cummins' Common Underlying Proficiency theory holds that using one language encourages proficiency in both L1 and L2. What is the opposing theory?

a. Opposing Underlying Proficiency
b. Separate Underlying Proficiency
c. Anti-Underlying Proficiency
d. Opposite Underlying Proficiency

19. A teacher has decided to incorporate Total Physical Response strategies into her classroom instruction. She will:

a. Break from academic instruction every hour for 10 minutes of organized exercise
b. Involve her students in a series of physical activities in response to her instructions and requests
c. Break for academic instruction every hour for 5 minutes of independent exercise
d. Break from academic instruction two times a day (excluding lunch) for guided meditation practice and Brilliant Mind exercises

20. In second language acquisition, what is Stage II also called?

a. Speech Emergence Stage
b. Receptive Stage
c. Intermediate Proficiency Stage
d. Early Production Stage

21. Who is required by law to follow a student's IEP?

a. The school nurse
b. All school staff
c. Teachers who work with the student
d. No one is strictly required; an IEP is considered a best practice and should be followed, but if a teacher feels it is in the student's best interest to modify or deviate from the plan, she can do so without penalty

22. Basic Interpersonal Communicative Skills (BICS) and Cognitive Academic Language Proficiency (CALP) describe two distinct thresholds of language proficiency attained by a language learner. What are these two thresholds?

a. BICS skills are necessary for academic communication, require content-specific vocabularies and more sophisticated syntax, and do not rely upon external contextual information, while CALP skills permit social communications that are face-to-face and include contextual information, informal vocabulary, and relatively simple syntax.
b. BICS skills are limited to single-word responses in oral communication, include a very limited vocabulary in L2, and permit some interface with L1, while CALP skills require external contextual clues in order to be interpreted.
c. CALP skills are limited to single-word responses in oral communication, include a very limited vocabulary in L2, and permit some interface with L1, while BICS skills depend heavily upon prior knowledge.
d. BICS skills permit social communications that are face-to-face and include contextual information, informal vocabulary, and relatively simple syntax, while CALP skills are necessary for academic communication, require content-specific vocabularies and more sophisticated syntax, and do not rely upon external contextual information.

23. An SDAIE approach can be problematic for an individual ESL teacher because it requires specialized training, and because it is most effective when the program is adopted system wide. What strategy can such a teacher use to provide CBEC to her students without receiving that specialized training or having system wide support?

a. Determine the content areas that ESL students will be taught in the following semester and begin preparing them well in advance through a variety of approaches
b. Teach concepts essential to a core understanding of the material that reach beyond just specialized vocabulary
c. Organize learning thematically, and teach a series of interrelated, in-depth lessons related to that theme
d. All the above

24. Because the United States began as a melting pot of people from many different nationalities and ethnic groups, bilingual communities and education were a matter of course. It was essential for business people who served members of a particular culture to know that language, and immigrant children who did not speak English were often taught in their language of origin. By WWI, the United States began to develop a strong sense of itself as a nation, and English emerged as the "national" language. Non-English-speaking children were no longer taught in any language other than English. When did this trend begin to reverse, and why?

a. After WWII; Americans began to see themselves as part of a "world nation" consisting of a vast and diverse group of individuals with cultural ties worthy of respect.
b. In the 1960s; Cuban immigrants established a successful bilingual program, and the Civil Rights movement put attention on correcting educational and social agendas that were prejudiced in favor of the white middle class.
c. The late 1950s; the influence of early hippies and beatniks, who preached the idea of loving one another and living in peace had a strong, immediate impact on the field of education.
d. The 1990s; with the Clinton administration, saw bilingual education as an essential step toward leading the nation into the 21st century.

25. A classroom teacher has a highly diverse classroom, with children from 11 different countries speaking 6 different languages. How can she encourage mutual cultural respect?

a. Label objects in the room with all six languages; invite speakers from each of the countries to visit the classroom and talk about one or two aspects of their cultures; break the class into culturally diverse smaller groups for class projects and study; invite students to teach the class songs from their cultures.
b. Organize field trips to local museums to view the works of painters from other lands; show students photographs of types of clothing from the various countries; announce a "language day" once a month, on which only the teacher is allowed to speak English, and everyone but the English speakers are allowed to speak in their native tongue.
c. Give each child a journal, and ask them to use it to write down memories and information about their countries of origin. They may show their journals to one another, but two rules apply: 1) If you share with one, you must share with all and 2) Anyone you show your journal to must, in turn, show you theirs.
d. Hang flags representing all the different cultures the classroom contains; teach the class to greet one another in all of the languages and require them to do so before class starts each day; group children by language/cultural group for projects and group study to strengthen their bond.

26. A classroom teacher with several mainstreamed ESL students is frustrated. She has noted that few of their parents come to parent-teacher conferences, and those who do, come inconsistently and have little to say. She is aware that many of them have limited English skills, and also that several have very young children at home. What can she do to encourage the parents to increase their participation in their children's education?

a. Drop in unexpectedly at their homes with a gift of freshly baked bread or cookies.
b. Send home an announcement about a Foreign Parents' night, in which foods from many lands will be featured and for which they will be the featured speakers.
c. Invite several parents from the same or similar cultures to work with their children, a translator if one is available, and herself to create a classroom presentation on some cultural aspect that will be of interest to the students. For example, Mexican and other Central American parents might present a slideshow on the Day of the Dead, followed by a show-and-tell of objects used in that celebration.
d. Nothing. They have made it clear to her that they have priorities that do not include the needs of her student, their child. It's best if she simply expects less of them and takes it upon herself to provide additional academic and emotional support to the poor child, who is clearly being neglected.

27. Two young women are at a coffee shop. They are having an animated conversation about three young men sitting at a table across the room. Much of their conversation seems cryptic, either because they do not want others to understand, or because most of what they are talking about is fully present in the room, allowing them to use a verbal shorthand—or both. They don't realize a linguist is sitting at the next table, observing them and noting the relationship between orally manifested meaning (language) and contextual information conveyed through gesture, facial expression, inference, etc. In what area of linguistic study is the eavesdropper engaging?

a. Pragmatics
b. Contextual linguistics
c. Social linguistics
d. Etiquette orality

28. Communicative competence consists of both organizational competence (requiring competence with grammar and discourse) and pragmatic competence (which involves sociolinguistic and speech acts) and is currently the objective of many language education programs. To whom can the spread of its ideas best be attributed?

a. Canale and Swain
b. Chomsky
c. Hull
d. Krashen

29. Which answer best describes the stages of language acquisition?

a. Letter recognition stage; vocabulary development stage; listening stage; contextually predictive stage
b. Recognition of primary syntactical patterning stage; articulation stage; contextual referencing stage; BICS stage; CALPS stage
c. Pre-production stage; early production stage; speech emergence stage; intermediate fluency stage
d. Listening stage; copying stage; single-word response stage; multiple-word response stage; confidence stage

30. How are language acquisition and language learning distinct?

a. Language learning refers to learning a second language, where language acquisition refers to a primary language.
b. Language acquisition develops unconsciously through use, while language learning requires instruction.
c. Language learning precedes and is required for language acquisition.
d. All the above.

31. Realia means:

a. Real-world experiences
b. Reliable and, therefore, trustworthy methods of instruction
c. Concrete objects used in demonstrations to develop vocabulary and encourage discourse
d. Manifested, or "realized," concepts.

32. Current research suggests that employing a student's L1 in support of his or her L2 is likely to:

a. Increase comprehensibility
b. Decrease comprehensibility
c. Increase cultural load
d. Decrease that student's willingness to learn a new language

33. Canale and Swain find communicative competence in the relationship of what four elements?

a. Competence in grammar, vocabulary, semantics, and phonetics
b. Reading, writing, listening, and speaking
c. Reading, writing, math, and science
d. Competence in grammar, sociolinguistics, discourse, and communication strategies

34. An ESL teacher offers her students the following question to test their understanding of proper English grammar. Which of the following sentences is correct?

a. Both my dog and my husband thinks I am a servant.
b. Both my dogs and my husbands think I am a servant.
c. Both my dogs and my husband thinks I am a servant.
d. Both my dog and my husband think I am a servant.

35. Ms. Perez wants to raise her students' competency in CALP. Her strategies include "thinking aloud" to demonstrate cognitive process, differentiating instruction by teaching explicitly, and

a. Asking "what if" questions
b. Expecting maximum performance from students
c. Teaching test-taking and study skills
d. All the above

36. In the Early Production Stage of language acquisition, an L2 learner typically:

a. Understands 1,000 words and can respond to instructions involving up to three requests
b. Begins to speak in sentences of one-to-two clauses
c. Understands up to 5,000 words, but uses only a handful
d. Understands and uses roughly 1,000 words

37. The parents of a first-grade LEP student do not want her placed in a special education classroom; they feel that she is better off in a regular classroom at her grade level. The classroom teacher, ESL teacher, school counselor, and diagnostician are all certain that she has several interrelated learning disabilities, as well as some emotional issues. Given that she is unlikely to thrive in a regular classroom, will cause an extra burden of work to the teacher, and will without doubt be disruptive and cause problems for other students, can she be placed in special education classes?

a. No; parental permission is required.
b. Yes; parental permission is required, but in its absence a building can, with requests from four or more professionals, be overridden.
c. Possibly; the school must refer the case to Children's Protective Services, which will make the final decision.
d. Temporarily, while the district takes the parents to court to force the issue. If the court rules in favor of the parents, the district must place the student in a regular classroom, pay the parents' legal costs, and pay a fine if the judge so orders. If the court rules in favor of the district, the parents must pay all court costs, but no fine can be assigned.

38. TPR stands for:

a. Teaching-Productive Resources
b. Total Physical Response
c. Typical Production Register
d. Theory of Psychological Reference

39. Which of the following are traditional methods of teaching English?

a. Drills
b. Teaching frequently-used phrases
c. Immersion
d. All of the above

40. What is the Language Experience Approach also known as?

a. LEA
b. Me, Myself, and Eye
c. Dictated Stories
d. Directed Stories

41. Who described the Acquisition-Learning, Monitor, Natural Order, Input, and Affective Filter hypotheses?

a. Swain
b. Cummins
c. Gregory
d. Krashen

42. In 1981 the United States Court of Appeals for the Fifth Circuit overturned a 1978 federal ruling in the case of Castaneda v. Pickard. As a result, a three-pronged assessment was established to ensure that bilingual programs met requirements established by what act?

a. No Child Left Behind (2001)
b. Equal Educational Opportunities Act (1974)
c. The Bilingual Language Act (1968)
d. The Civil Rights Act (1964)

43. What criteria would be assessed in the previous question?

a. Students must be taught by bilingual teachers; BICS must be strictly enforced; and textbooks must be bilingual.
b. The program must be based on current education theory; there must be a 1:5 teacher/student ratio; and it must serve only Stage I and II language learners.
c. The program must be based on sound educational theory; must be put into service with sufficient personnel, materials, and space; and must effectively overcome language barriers and handicaps.
d. The program must "teach to the test"; must serve the needs of the community as a whole; and must offer alternatives for home-school families.

44. A kindergarten student new to the United States speaks almost no English. His teacher, who is a fluent Spanish speaker, has noted that both his vocabulary and mastery of underlying grammatical rules in Spanish are also weak. The student depends upon a shared external context to convey a disproportionate amount of his intended meaning in oral communication, or he withdraws entirely. What should the teacher expect from this student in terms of his relative ability to learn English?

a. Because his first language is not developed, he will most likely obtain English vocabulary and skills more rapidly, both because he is hungry for language and because there are fewer prior linguistic assumptions that could impede L2 development.
b. Because his first language is not developed, he will most likely obtain English vocabulary and skills much more slowly; the speed with which L2 learners develop proficiency can be anticipated by the degree of richness L1 exhibits.
c. It is too early to anticipate; each child is a unique being and to base assumptions of future learning on evidence of past learning is a fallacy.
d. It is too early to anticipate; because the child is so young, is new to the United States, and must therefore be experiencing culture shock and because at this point little is known about his family/social situation, the teacher must remain open and curious about the student's ability to absorb L2, or the teacher will risk doing him an injustice by labeling him and teaching him accordingly.

45. The Cognitive Academic Language Learning Approach and Specially Designed Academic English are examples of:

a. Sheltered English programs.
b. Content-based ESL models.
c. Nothing; both terms are invented.
d. Both A and B.

46. According to many researchers, a student's mastery of English is a(n)________ indicator of that student's cognitive abilities.

a. Clear
b. Accurate
c. Inaccurate
d. Partial

47. An ESL student at the intermediate level depends upon which skills to improve understanding and verbal ability?

a. Reading and writing
b. Writing and speaking
c. Reading and listening
d. Listening and speaking

48. Ricardo is in fourth grade and new to the school. His English vocabulary is quite strong, both in terms of social communication and in the sciences content area. He also has a solid basic understanding of grammatical structure, which is apparent in his writing skills. However, he is very shy and does not like to communicate verbally. On the rare occasion he does speak, it is either laborious as he reviews and practices mentally to make sure that what he's about to say will be correct, or he becomes anxious and his speech is peppered with errors in grammar and pronunciation. Several members of the class have begun to tease him. He reacts to teasing by blushing, exhibiting confused movements, and on occasion, by crying. How can this teacher support Ricardo's oral communication skills?

a. Shame the bullies by making them stand in corners and miss recess until they apologize to Ricardo in front of the entire class.
b. Assign an oral report to each member of the class. Encourage Ricardo, but do not baby him; he needs to develop a backbone.
c. Give Ricardo many opportunities during the day by inviting him to answer a question even if he hasn't volunteered by raising his hand; pairing him with one of the bullies, so they can begin to bond; and asking him to act as "teacher's helper" and co-teach a topic he enjoys.
d. Privately meet with the bullies and explain that it's important to welcome Ricardo; ask for their help in doing so. Pair Ricardo with class members who have a gentle, accepting nature to do projects that do not need to be orally presented. Do not force Ricardo to speak publicly, but do find opportunities for private, relaxed conversations about topics of interest to him. Do not correct errors; instead, model correct usage (lower his affective filter).

49. What is the BSM, and what is it designed to establish?

a. The Bilingual Strategies Method establishes effective instructional methods for mainstreamed bilingual students.
b. The Bilingual Syntax Measure is a tool designed to assess bilingual students for both native and L2 (English) proficiency.
c. The Burke-Stanley Milestone establishes points along the continuum from little English to full fluency.
d. The Babcock Statistical Model establishes a measurable baseline for bilingual educators.

50. In terms of models, which bilingual approach does research indicate is least effective?

a. Two-way immersion
b. Sheltered English
c. Mainstreamed classes
d. Pull-out ESL classes

51. ESL requires students "to listen attentively and engage actively in a variety of oral language experiences." Specifically, second language learners are, at the appropriate English proficiency level, expected to know whether to listen for information, understanding, or enjoyment; respond to questions and directions; participate in classroom discussions, songs, rhymes, and other language play; and:

a. Apply critical listening skills to deduce and evaluate ideas that may not be directly stated
b. Be willing to risk shame or embarrassment caused by errors in speaking, in order to learn
c. Listen closely and imitate precisely in order to absorb proper pronunciation
d. Learn the cultural values and expectations of their adopted country

52. A teacher is having fun with her students. She has created numerous sentences that are ridiculous in their "meaning." She has asked her students to tell her which of the sentences are possible in English, regardless of how odd the meaning is, and which sentences cannot make any sense whatsoever. An example of one of these possible sentences is: The grandfather clock and my grandmother are secretly in love. An impossible sentence might be: The shy giggling would not choo-choo the quickly goose. What is the teacher using the assignment to evaluate?

a. Students' semantic understanding
b. Students' syntactic understanding
c. Students' phonemic understanding
d. Students' morphemic understanding

53. According to Cummins' Threshold Hypothesis, cognitive and academic growth in L2 is largely dependent upon:

a. Development of CALP in L1
b. Research-based, high quality instruction
c. Development of BICS
d. L2 immersion

54. When does special education law apply to LEPs?

a. Never; the two are distinct and share no overlap.
b. Only when an LEP student also has learning, emotional, or physical handicaps as well.
c. Always.
d. It has not been definitively decided. The Supreme Court will hear Chin v. Battleridge District later this year.

55. Research indicates that the Silent/Receptive stage of second language acquisition typically lasts up to ______, during which time a learner understands and can respond to roughly ________ words.

a. Two years; 1,000
b. Six months; 500
c. One month; 100
d. 18 months; 1,000

56. CBEC stands for:

a. Collaborative Bilingual Education Center
b. Cooperative Basic English Continuum
c. Content-Based ESL Curriculum
d. Cognitive Bilingual Effort Council

57. A student is capable of speaking relatively easily, but slowly and makes periodic errors in speech. Which level of capability is the student most likely in?

a. Intermediate Fluency
b. Advanced Fluency
c. Early Production
d. Speech Emergence

58. Which of the following presents effective ways a third-grade teacher can help students expand their vocabularies?

a. Give them a word-a-day to memorize. They must use the word five times in conversation and once in writing. Then at the end of the week, give them the opportunity to write a creative story or poem using all five of the week's words.
b. Play a game in which one student selects a word from the dictionary that is complex and unknown. Next, singly or in groups, have students take a risk and try to guess the definition.
c. Teach a unit on prefixes and suffixes. Offer some examples of each. Next, group the students into teams and see which team comes up with the most words that use prefixes and suffixes. Challenge them by asking for a word with both a prefix and a suffix.
d. Have students find words in newspapers, magazines, and elsewhere that they do not understand. Give them the definitions, and have them write them down in a word book or put them on the word wall.

59. Krashen's Affective Filter Hypothesis theorizes that L2 acquisition can be supported or harmed by:

a. The effects of overwhelming media exposure
b. Classroom instruction that immerses the student in effective L2 instruction
c. The learner's family and community
d. The learner's positive or negative level of emotional comfort in L2

60. Two teachers are discussing a student with whom they both work. The term "communicative competence" comes up. What aspect of the student's development are the teachers discussing?

a. Her willingness to listen to another speaker's message and respond kindly and appropriately.
b. Her ability to use the elements of language (syntax, phonology, morphology, semantics) together with an understanding of social expectations and to use spoken messages that are appropriate in terms of how they are manifested and when, in the course of conversation, they are used.
c. Communicative competence is transparently interchangeable with CALP; the teachers are discussing her social language skills.
d. Communicative competence is transparently interchangeable with BICS; the teachers are discussing her academic language skills.

61. The ESL teacher has several students with little knowledge of English. How can she develop competency?

a. Drill verb cases; build vocabulary with a word wall; read the same books repeatedly to build their semantic understanding
b. Incorporate extra-linguistic materials into instruction, such as realia, gestures, and enactments (increased comprehensibility, contextual clues)
c. Have them listen and repeat exercises from a language CD; teach them a "word of the day" and ask them to use it five times in oral or written communication; praise them when they are successful
d. Invite members of a mainstreamed age-appropriate class to visit, and assign each child to a mainstreamed "mentor" to share conversations on topics the ESL children offer

62. The students in the above example have learned well; both they and their teacher are pleased with their increased competency. Which strategies should the teacher now employ?

a. Employ vocabulary the students understand and use it to teach new vocabulary; offer hands-on instruction; invite members of a mainstreamed class for peer tutoring
b. Incorporate extra-linguistic materials into instruction, such as realia, gestures, and enactments (increased comprehensibility, contextual clues)
c. Have them listen and repeat exercises from a language CD; teach them a "word of the day," and ask them to use it five times in oral or written communication; praise them when they are successful
d. Drill vocabulary and grammar daily; post new words on a word wall; assign independent reading and oral reports

63. A teacher asks her students to consider the following subject/verb and pronoun/antecedent relationships. Which of the following is correct?

a. Neither Eric nor Tim admits he made a mistake.
b. Neither Eric nor Tim admit they made a mistake.
c. Neither Eric nor Tim admits they made a mistake.
d. Neither Eric nor Tim admit he made a mistake.

64. An ESL teacher is using dialogue journals with her students. The students write in the journals three times a week on any subject they choose. What is the purpose of such journals?

a. The teacher will discover what is important to her students and can modify her instruction accordingly.
b. To give students ample time to practice writing dialogue, including grammatical practice, such as use of quotation marks, and content practice, such as writing dialogue that is dynamic, interesting, and characterizes the speakers.
c. The teacher will use these journals to correct student misconceptions about rules of grammar and semantics. Because the students are invested in their own words, they will be more open to such correction than in highly-systematized classroom instruction.
d. The teacher will write comments and questions in response, modeling correct English usage.

65. A teacher is having difficulty with her fifth grade ESL students. She pre-teaches lessons by giving students specialized vocabulary they will need, reminds them of prior knowledge, and writes important information on the board in her clearest cursive handwriting. She asks the ESL students if they understand; the students nearly always nod and smile in agreement. She speaks very slowly and loudly and is careful to use a few of the most current slang expressions to make the students feel that she "speaks their language." Nonetheless, the students demonstrate little understanding of the material when tested in an essay format. They do only a little better when asked to choose the correct answer on tests. What is the teacher doing wrong?

a. Some ESL students may not be able to interpret cursive handwriting.
b. When asked a question directly, many students will agree whether or not they understand what is being asked. Moreover, students may agree in order to avoid the embarrassment of admitting in public that they do not understand.
c. The teacher's use of slang that has not been taught as idiom is more likely to confuse the students than to clarify their English.
d. All the above.

66. In order to develop CALP, which of the following methods is most likely to succeed?

a. Give students a variety of communication experiences. Informal conversation with a peer, formal presentation before a class, personal journal writing, and reports will all contribute to the development of a student's CALP.
b. Group students homogeneously so that they can work on projects with a variety of different individuals and learn flexibility in learning styles.
c. Building literacy skills in all content areas will improve CALP and increase language and abstract thinking skills across the board.
d. No methods will work; CALP is a subconscious, natural process that develops in its own time and at its own speed. Attempting to streamline the process is likely to backfire, producing a speaker who is hesitant and insecure.

67. What criticism has been leveled at oral proficiency assessments, such as the Language Assessment Scales-Oral, the Woodcock-Muñoz Language Survey, and the IDEA Proficiency Test?

a. They are biased toward native English speakers.
b. They are biased toward non-native English speakers.
c. They do not accurately reflect native speakers' academic performance and therefore cannot accurately reflect non-native speakers' performance.
d. They do not accurately reflect native speakers' proficiency and therefore cannot accurately reflect non-native speakers' proficiency.

68. The degree to which an L1 learner is successful in acquiring a second language is determined by numerous aspects. Contributing factors include the learner's age, degree of instruction, opportunities to practice, willingness to practice, working and long-term memory, ability to process information, and:

a. Socioeconomic level
b. Degree of L1 development
c. Psychological health
d. Motivation

69. The Reading Proficiency Tests in English (RPTE) is used for _____ students in grades__________

a. All students; 1st-4th
b. LEP students; 3rd-12th
c. LEP students; all grades
d. All students; all grades.

70. A teacher's third grade class includes students from Costa Rica, Chile, Peru, Mexico, Korea, Vietnam, India, Iraq, and the United States. Over the course of several months, the class has explored the cultures of each country. The teacher has been careful to include lessons that demonstrate how different cultures have different values and beliefs about behavior, relationships, religion, and education. She has placed each of her students in small, homogeneous groups and asked them to create some kind of presentation that will teach the class about different cultural expectations and the emotions that can arise when there is cultural confusion. Of the following presentations, which is most likely to be the most effective?

a. A game the group creates that explores the foods of various cultures
b. Oral reports given by group members on how they celebrate Christmas.
c. A play in which a Korean student, a Hispanic student, and an American-born student perform a series of skits demonstrating how different cultures greet acquaintances and the confusion that can arise when people from two distinct cultures meet
d. A fairy tale orally presented in English, Spanish, and Korean

71. Developing a student's capacity for independent academic study and task completion through an approach known as __________ is achieved through the combined efforts of strategies, such as hands-on activities, accessing prior knowledge, pre-teaching content-area vocabulary, and putting the lesson into context with visual aids and modeling.

a. Native Language Support
b. ESL
c. Scaffolding
d. Direct Experience

72. The ESL teacher is fit to be tied. At the first parent-teacher conference, she clearly informed Hector's mother that her son lacked manners and was lazy and self-centered. She gave his mother the assignment of reviewing all school work to make certain it had been done—and done correctly. She conducted the conference in Spanish, because she wanted to be certain Hector's mother, who is Venezuelan, understood her. Hector continues to arrive at school with an empty book bag or with homework that has been incorrectly and hastily done. Furthermore, Hector's mother failed to show up at the last conference, calling to say she had to take an extra shift at work. What should the teacher do about this frustrating situation?

a. Separate Hector from the rest of the students by placing his desk in the hall. He needs to learn to be responsible for himself.
b. Ask that Hector be mainstreamed. He isn't doing the work, so ESL can't help him.
c. Try to reestablish positive communication with his family, stressing the importance of the teacher and parents working as a team to find real-life solutions that can be consistently implemented at home and at school.
d. Give up; Hector must remain in her class, but if no one else is trying, it's hopeless. Hector should be given only the time and energy the teacher has left after tending to the needs of other, more cooperative students in her class.

73. A teacher wants to encourage her first graders to have compassion for people from other cultures. She is writing and illustrating a story book about fictional children from all of the countries her students are from. Some of the characters come from wealthy countries and own many things. Others come from poor countries, wear cast-offs, and often go hungry. The story ends as one of the poor children dies of starvation, following which the narrator explains that had she not died, her family would have come to the United States, and she would be a member of this very classroom. The teacher believes this story will effectively portray the concept of compassion and the importance of taking care of one another. Is sharing this book with her students a good idea?

a. No. The students may believe that the character that dies was literally real rather than figuratively symbolic. Children from the countries the teacher has depicted as poor may feel shamed by their apparent poverty or frightened that they, too, might starve to death. Children from countries depicted as wealthy might either feel cheated, not being themselves wealthy, or entitled to the biggest and best of everything.
b. Yes. Children are innocent and open; they will be very moved by the idea of a friend they never got to know. It will encourage a great deal of loving compassion for others.
c. Yes. The students will likely have many questions, especially so because their teacher is the author. After the book has been read, the teacher can address some of these questions, being careful to call on students from all cultures.
d. No. It's likely that the students in the class who identify with the book characters from poor countries will become resentful of the U.S. citizens and try to harm them by forming a gang and waiting in the bathrooms to beat them up.

74. An ESL teacher has asked a group of high school students to visit her classroom and work individually with her students. The teacher has given the high school volunteers tape recorders, paper, and pencils and asked them to begin with a brief conversation with their respective L2s that will lead the L2s to a memory of a personal experience. The volunteers then take dictation, writing down exactly what the non-native speakers say. Next, the volunteers read their stories back to the authors. Following that, the authors read their own stories silently or aloud. This method is designed to simultaneously model encoding, develop sight word vocabulary, and motivate the ESL students to work toward fluency. This approach is known as:

a. Two-way immersion
b. Language Experience Approach
c. The Silent Way
d. Audiolingual Approach

75. An age equivalent score is used to tell whether a student is:

a. Working at an appropriate grade level in a particular content area
b. Working at an IQ level normal for equal aged students
c. Working at a level that is below or above others her age
d. Working at a specific standard level for a subject

76. An ESL teacher has several students who have attained BICS fluency. What must she do to help the students achieve CALP?

a. Develop tier 2 vocabulary; teach specialized vocabulary essential to a particular subject area; teach, offer ample practice opportunities, monitor, and re-teach more complex syntactical structures; offer instruction and practice in organizing ideas in terms of text.
b. Nothing; by definition, a student who is in control of BICS has already mastered CALP.
c. Nothing; there is no relationship between the two.
d. Continue instruction as she has been doing; BICS is the first milestone on the way to CALP. The teacher should continue to differentiate learning, provide ample opportunity for classroom face-to-face communication, provide meaningful texts, monitor students' progress, and adjust her instruction accordingly.

77. What 1982 Supreme Court case established for undocumented immigrant children the right to a free education?

a. Plyer v. Doe; 14th amendment
b. Lau v. Nichols
c. Meyer v. Nebraska
d. Castaneda v. Pickard

78. According to Krashen, people who overuse the monitor are typically:

a. Introverts who lack confidence
b. People with poor vision who require enlarged computer monitors
c. First-year teachers with less ESL experience
d. Extroverts with a high degree of confidence

79. Tea/tee, stair/stare, and shoe/shoo are:

a. Homophones
b. Synonyms
c. Homographs
d. Homonyms

80. What should a teacher working with an ESL student who is at the preproduction stage do?

a. Devise role-playing games and activities
b. Offer ample opportunity for face-to-face dialogue
c. Encourage silent students to speak; this is especially important for introverted students
d. Incorporate gesture, pictures, manipulatives, and other extra-verbal tools into her teaching

81. What are the characteristics of an additive educational program?

a. It works with students who come from families with a history of drug or alcohol abuse. By starting therapy at a young age, the hope is that these children won't grow up to become addicts as well.
b. It is a math and social studies program that focuses exclusively on the positive. In math, that means everything is described in terms of addition; for example, subtraction is negative addition. In social studies, it means that only those characteristics of a social group that are joyful, exuberant, or peace-loving will be taught.
c. It is a program that uses a student's culture of origin as a scaffold to teach her about her new culture.
d. It is a program that explores all the ways advertisements exploit cultures by furthering stereotypes and prejudices.

82. L2 development can be hindered by which of the following?

a. Idiomatic expressions
b. Vocabulary words that have multiple meanings
c. Carrying grammatical rules, vocabulary, and pronunciation from L1 and applying them to L2.
d. all of the above

83. The teacher is working with a group of ESL students who are at the Speech Emergence stage. She is careful to speak slowly and repeat essential vocabulary, uses gesture to reinforce her instruction, and gives students questions to use when interviewing one another for a writing project. The likely outcome is:

a. The students will respond well to the variety of strategies as their language skills continue to grow.
b. The students will become bored.
c. The students will become anxious and insecure.
d. The students' decoding skills will be enhanced.

84. A student who is new to the United States understands some English, but his vocabulary is limited, and his grasp of syntax is weak. Although he is 11, his previous education was very limited, so he has been placed in a 4th grade classroom. For the first few weeks, he was very quiet and kept to himself. In an effort to bring him out of his shell, his teacher put him into a pod with several highly social students whose first language is English. The students tried to draw him in, talking loudly and gesturing to make him understand. When he ignored them, they left him alone. To her dismay, the teacher's previously quiet student grew sullen and very angry. He hit a child during recess one day and stormed out of class in the middle of a lesson the next day. What is most likely the problem with the boy?

a. Since he started out quiet and rapidly became angry, it's probable that he is undergoing some kind of trauma at home.
b. He is experiencing a high affective filter due possibly to culture shock, which is heightened by being placed with younger students, as well as by his inability to freely communicate. He may feel shame, insecurity, embarrassment, frustration, or a combination of these, which he compensates for and covers up with anger.
c. He is simply undisciplined. Because he has spent little time in a school, he doesn't clearly understand the dynamics, rules, and regulations, and he must be treated with firm kindness.
d. He is simply undisciplined. He has probably gotten away with this type of behavior before, and he likely feels that it is a normal way to express pent-up frustration. The teacher must move swiftly to punish him for outbursts or striking others, as such behavior cannot be allowed.

85. Which of the following describes the Self-Contained Model for teaching?

a. Emphasis on technological aids and a single teacher who provides support as issues come up.
b. Students attend typical coursework with the general population of a school and receive adaptive help from a specialist at the end of the day
c. A single teacher has students in a self-contained classroom and is responsible for both language and academic performance
d. Students are given one day out of their five-day week to spend in an ESL class while the rest of the days, they attend traditional classes.

86. A previously happy and affectionate ELL has suddenly become tearful and withdrawn. She reacts very strongly to any kind of unexpected touch, and she has abruptly stopped giving hugs to the teacher or to her friends. She will not tell the teacher what is causing her sadness or hurt, but the teacher is aware that the girl's mother has a new boyfriend who has recently moved in with the family. The student, who used to love writing in her journal both in Spanish and in English, now uses it only for drawings. The teacher has not violated the student's privacy by looking at the journal without permission, but she has noticed that during journal time the girl angrily scribbles what appear to be pictures of a man (or someone wearing a hat and pants) being shot, stabbed, or otherwise tortured. What should the teacher do?

a. Read the journal without permission; the girl is obviously disturbed, and if she is being abused in some way, the teacher has the responsibility to find out in any way possible.
b. Nothing at the moment; she should continue to observe the student and offer her an ear. Until the girl asks for help, she can legally do nothing.
c. Refer the student to the school counselor, who is trained to help in situations such as this.
d. Get the mother's permission to refer the student to the school counselor. She cannot be referred without parental permission.

87. A student whose L1 is Basque is displaying certain problems. The ESL teacher is uncertain whether he has one or more learning disabilities or if it could be a problem with his language development. She is uncertain what to do. She knows that if she refers him for assessment, he might be inaccurately labeled as learning impaired and placed in a special education class. If his problems are language-based, such a move could be detrimental. She knows that there are no assessments available in Basque in her district, and she feels strongly that he needs to be presented with certain questions and allowed to answer in his own words before a decision is made. The boy's adult aunt, a fluent English speaker and the teacher's neighbor and friend, has offered to help as an informal translator. Is this a suitable fix?

a. No. The friendship between the teacher and aunt precludes using her as a translator. Both her friendship with the teacher and her familial relationship with the student could affect her objectivity.
b. No. She is not a trained translator, and, for this reason alone, the aunt is not suitable for this task. The school is legally responsible for providing a trained translator or materials in Basque, if they are available. The teacher must advocate on behalf of the student and try to find a trained translator or the materials in Basque.
c. Yes. The student needs to be assessed one way or another to determine whether he has learning disabilities or whether his problem is in the area of language development. It is unreasonable for the school to expect the teacher to devote hours to tracking down a translator, and the aunt will do the job for free. There's really no reason not to take her up on it!
d. Yes. The student will likely feel very comfortable with his aunt translating. There is the added bonus that if he doesn't understand a question or wants to ask what the purpose of it is, they can privately share a conversation about the test out loud, while simultaneously protecting the student's privacy.

88. Cooperative Learning is a teaching approach that combines students at varying scholastic levels and with various learning styles into small groups for learning activities that encourage interaction. All students have ample opportunity to speak, and groups foster a sense of mutual respect. Additionally, students at different levels and with different learning styles observe one another and expand their learning skills and strategies. This approach is most effective when:

a. The small groups are observed and monitored.
b. The groups are organized homogeneously.
c. Students work with the same classmates over the course of an entire school year.
d. Learning tasks are authentic, challenging, and meaningful.

89. The ESL teacher has a goal of increasing interaction among her students. She has studied Swain's theory of comprehensible output, and is basing her instruction accordingly. Which of the following would be an appropriate strategy for her to employ?

a. Project-based learning
b. Manipulatives
c. Rubrics
d. All the above

90. What is one difference between ESL and bilingual models?

a. ESL models are pull-out or push-in. Bilingual models are self-contained.
b. ESL models are English-only and employ a specific methodology to teach English and continue to develop L1. Bilingual models introduce instruction concepts first in L1 and over time transfer them into English
c. Bilingual models are pull-out or push-in; ESL models are self-contained.
d. Bilingual models are English-only and employ specific methodology to teach English and continue to develop L1. ESL models introduce instruction concepts first in L1 and over time transfer them into English

91. Which is more abstract, BICS or CALP?

a. Neither; both are concrete, hands-on teaching methods.
b. BICS; academic language requires abstract thinking.
c. CALP; social language requires abstract thinking.
d. CALP; academic language requires abstract thinking.

92. Which of the following is NOT required for an LEP's permanent record?

a. The student's level of language proficiency designated
b. A writing sample
c. Parental approval
d. Program entry and exit dates and notification of same to parents

93. Many times, ESL teachers must simplify a text so that students will be able to understand the ideas. Why is it important that the language be simplified by substituting common words for more abstract ones, by shortening sentences or turning a long sentence into two or three simple ones, or by deleting unnecessary information while modifying the concepts and ideas as little as possible?

a. ESL students generally are not at the same grade level as their English-speaking peers; therefore, they cannot understand texts that are too difficult.
b. Grade level content is essential. Simplifying language without simplifying content will help ESL students remain at grade level.
c. The statement is incorrect. It is essential to modify both language and ideas by stripping them of detail, clarifying language, and making ideas as simple as possible.
d. It's important to simplify texts by reducing and eliminating content to make it more understandable and, at the same time, retaining as much of the original language as possible. This is to challenge LEPs to reach the highest linguistic goal they can achieve; if language is stripped of meaning, it is more transparent and carries less cultural weight.

94. Many linguistics subscribe to the theory that a second language is both acquired and learned. Describe the distinctions between the two:

a. Acquiring simply requires exposure and is required for learning. When an aspect of a second language is "learned," it is fully absorbed and understood.
b. Acquisitioned language is specific to a particular field of study; learned language is general and required for all types of discourse.
c. Language acquisition is natural, subconscious, and concerned with message content. Language learning is formal, concerned with grammatical rules, and conscious.
d. Acquired language is that which is mimicked first, prior to understanding. With use comes comprehension of meaning. Learned language is the result of directed instruction and intervention.

95. A new middle school English language learner from South Africa is often late for class and seems to think this is acceptable. He is hardworking otherwise. The teacher is frustrated but considers why this may be the case. Which is the MOST likely reason for this behavior?

a. The student doesn't value school and doesn't care about being late.
b. The student comes from a culture in which a strict schedule is not valued as highly as in American culture.
c. The student doesn't know the time that the class begins.
d. The student focuses on his friendships more than his schoolwork because of his age and maturity.

96. Students in a third-grade intermediate-level English Language Development (ELD) class are developing their classroom presentation registers. Which activity would best help them?

a. Writing out their presentations on index cards
b. Practicing pronouncing different key vocabulary words for the presentation
c. Explicit teaching and modeling of how to deliver a class presentation
d. Editing each other's work and slides for grammatical errors

97. A high school art teacher has assigned biographical readings on different artists to her students, including several beginning-level English learners. Which assignment is MOST appropriate for her English learners to complete to help them comprehend the texts?

a. Assigning an alternative activity in which they look at artwork created by the artists
b. Using an organizer with fill in the blanks for key words to aid comprehension
c. Scrambling the text and asking students to put the biographical information in order
d. Asking students to paraphrase and summarize what they have read

98. A sixth-grade English language arts teacher is considering how to scaffold a reading activity with several short stories. Which of the following would be an appropriate pre-reading scaffolding activity to support her early-advanced English learners?

a. Activating prior knowledge through writing a creative piece in the perspective of one of the characters once the teacher has read the story aloud
b. Creating or selecting visuals to go along with the short stories to aid comprehension
c. Using a video to summarize what the story is about before reading the text
d. Selecting short passages from the reading to build student interest and have them predict what will happen in the text

99. What are ways that teachers can build rapport with families to increase family involvement in the school?

a. Learn the languages spoken by students, and greet parents in their native tongue.
b. Home visits to understand the student's culture, and get a sense of the student's life.
c. Read about the culture that the student comes from in ethnographic and anthropological studies.
d. Send newsletters home in English with the child.

100. According to Banks, which of the following describes an additive multicultural education approach?

a. Including new novels with diverse writers
b. Celebrating Black History Month with posters on the walls
c. Discussing racial injustices throughout American history
d. Having students create a petition to support equity in the community

Answer Key and Explanations

1. A: Phonological awareness. Phonemic awareness is the ability to recognize individual sounds within words. Segmenting words and blending sounds are components of phonemic awareness. Phonological awareness includes an understanding of multiple components of spoken language. Ability to hear individual words within a vocalized stream and ability to identify spoken syllables are types of phonological awareness.

2. B: Presenting sufficient and meaningful reading and writing experiences for students to practice strategies and reviewing and re-teaching as required to ensure that students have integrated essential content are part of scientifically-based, quality classroom instruction. Daily introduction to new concepts, words, and materials can be okay as long as they are integrated a little at a time. Students require multiple exposures to a word before recognition begins to happen automatically. This relies on Krashen's input hypothesis, that learners benefit from exposure to slightly more difficult language than their current level. This renders answer choice B as the least effective, since it implies only using a level of language that the student is comfortable with.

3. B: Acculturation; adapting to a new culture, which includes understanding cultural expectations, semiotics, values, and beliefs, is essential to second language acquisition in that it provides appropriate context. Acculturation permits ELLs to adapt to new cultural expectations without the loss of the culture of origin. Success with BICS and CALP in L2 is dependent on a degree of success in L1.

4. C: A predicate nominative. A predicate nominative is a noun phrase which defines or clarifies the subject, but is not interchangeable with it. Multiple words do not make multiple predicate nominatives, however; together they create a predicate nominative. It is not correct in English to state "A Smart car is that tiny red car," because Smart cars are multiple and not singular, and because Smart cars come in many colors besides red.

5. A: A predicate adjective. A predicate adjective is an adjective that comes after a linking verb (such as the verb "to be") and modifies or describes the subject. In this example, "puppy" is the subject, "is" is the linking verb, and "protective" is the adjective.

6. C: Immersion. Until the late 1960s, immersion was the primary language instruction model. Typically, immigrant students—many of whom had little or no English—were mainstreamed into a classroom where they received language and content instruction in English only. Immersion is also called the "sink or swim" approach. Research has shown that this method is not efficient or effective.

7. C: To instruction that they have the skills to understand. The 1974 Supreme Court decision as a result of Lau v. Nichols established that school districts must provide ELL students the tools necessary to understand instruction.

8. C: Shorten the text; abbreviate sentences; substitute simple, concrete language for more complex language; break complex sentences into two or three simpler, more direct sentences; omit detail that enhances the text but doesn't change or clarify meaning. Beginning/intermediate stage ELLs will be able to understand ideas, theories, and other forms of meaning when they are offered in the context of a language the ELL can understand.

9. B: Traditional ESL programs prioritize social language skills. CBEC offers instruction in content areas that are age-appropriate to the LEPs' mainstreamed peers. Traditional ESL programs make the rapid absorption of social language skills a priority and, to that end, teach streamlined, socially necessary vocabulary and simple syntactical structures that enable students to communicate their basic needs. CBEC instruction is more deeply grounded in the same content that non-ESL students receive in order to prepare them for mainstreaming.

10. B: CALP. On average, research shows that it takes five years or more from first exposure to gain grade-level Cognitive Academic Language Proficiency (CALP). Basic Interpersonal Communication Skills (BICS) can be achieved within two years of first exposure.

11. A: She will use the information they contain to vary her lessons to meet each student's specific needs. Because all students are individuals with unique abilities, experiences, and personalities, the most effective teaching methods must allow for modifying lessons to specific, individual needs. Parent's don't benefit from having these notes sent home to them. Separating the students into groups based on language levels is ineffective, since students benefit from interaction with others at various levels. Finally, it would be unethical to share a student's files with their classmates.

12. C: Encourage students to be curious about and respectful of differences in culture. For many people, the memory of a kitchen is especially evocative and suggests warmth, love, and nurturing. As the place where meals are prepared, kitchens are also very much cultural reflections—from the food chosen to the methods used to prepare it. By encouraging each student to share a memory of a particular kitchen, the teacher is encouraging wide cultural respect.

13. C: ELLs often understand more in terms of vocabulary and correct syntax than they demonstrate in their own speaking. The other statements contain information that is false.

14. D: The ways in which language learning influences acquisition. The Monitor hypothesis examines how language acquisition and language learning are related. Krashen sees acquisition as the utterance initiator, while learning is the monitor/editor. The monitor plans, edits, and corrects language acts when the ELL is not rushed. It also follows the rules of the language and fully integrates the rule under consideration. The monitor role should be a minor one, since it is conscious of itself and, therefore, is not intuitive. Interestingly, research indicates that extroverts tend to be under-users who are much more concerned with the immediacy of communication in the moment; introverts and perfectionists are over-users and are determined to speak correctly or not speak at all. Optimal users apply the monitor in a limited but appropriate way and exhibit a balanced personality that is neither extroverted nor introverted.

15. A: Top down. A Top down approach to language learning begins with practical communicative usage that, over time, incorporates grammar, vocabulary, phonemic awareness, and other essential elements of speech. The top-down approach emphasizes meaningful use of language over accurate use of language elements. The functional approach also emphasizes practical use of language, but emphasizes spoken language over written language, whereas the top-down method may use both written and spoken language together. Total physical response pairs physical action with learning to build solid associations with concepts. The natural approach tends to follow the pattern of first language acquisition, giving learners time to listen without speaking and slowly emerge into speech.

16. A: Second language acquisition research suggests that L2s tend to integrate formulaic expressions and then apply them to understand linguistic rules. Research shows early second language learners integrate a limited number of formulaic expressions that are perceived less as individual words than as functional phrases. These phrases are memorized as global wholes. Phrases such as "Where is the library?" or "Would you like to go with me?" later become templates for discovering the rules of the language. "Where is the library?" becomes the formula for "Where is the airport (Laundromat, etc.)?" "Would you like to go with me?" becomes the template for "Would you like to eat dinner with me (like to see a movie with me, etc.)?" Over time, the learner realizes that the subject can change, and that the verb must then change to be in agreement.

17. C: The student is more likely to be placed in a special education program. Oral-language proficiency assessments should not be used as an overall indicator of a student's academic performance, as research has demonstrated that ELLs with little English are very likely to be inappropriately placed in special education classes.

18. B: Separate Underlying Proficiency. According to the Separate Underlying Proficiency theory (SUP), no relationship between L1 and L2 language acquisition exists, because each language is retained by a distinct area of the brain that is in no way connected to an area reserved for another language. Currently this theory is generally disregarded.

19. B: Involve her students in a series of physical activities in response to her instructions and requests. Total Physical Response (TPR) employs physical involvement to make learning more meaningful and easier to retain. A sequence of instructions given by the teacher prompts a succession of detailed actions. Advocates recommend special hands-on training with a trained senior instructor.

20. D: Early Production Stage. In this stage, ELLs begin to use words that they learned in the Pre-production Stage. One word and yes/no responses are common. Conversation is initiated with gesture or one or two words. Children in this stage will verbally respond to an increasingly wider variety of linguistic stimulus.

21. C: Teachers who work with the student. By law, all teachers working with a particular student must follow that student's Individualized Education Plan.

22. D: BICS skills permit social communications that are face-to-face and include contextual information, informal vocabulary, and relatively simple syntax, while CALP skills are necessary for academic communication, require content-specific vocabularies and more sophisticated syntax, and do not rely upon external contextual information.

23. D: All the above. By consulting with mainstream teachers to determine what content the students will be learning in upcoming months, she can choose or modify appropriate and understandable texts. The ESL teacher should only teach the content that she feels confident with, and she should emphasize deeper understanding of limited content over a glancing familiarity with a wider range of content.

24. B: In the 1960s; Cuban immigrants established a successful bilingual program, and the Civil Rights movement put attention on correcting educational and social agendas that were prejudiced in favor of the white middle class.

25. A: Label objects in the room with all six languages; invite speakers from each of the countries to visit the classroom and talk about one or two aspects of their cultures; break the class into culturally-diverse, smaller groups for class projects and study; invite students to teach the class songs from their cultures.

26. C: Invite several parents from the same or similar cultures to work with their children, a translator if one is available, and herself to create a classroom presentation on some cultural aspect that will be of interest to the students. For example, Mexican and other Central American parents might present a slideshow on the Day of the Dead, followed by a show-and-tell of objects used in that celebration.

27. A: Pragmatics. Pragmatics examines how speakers' linguistic understanding depends upon external context, how meaning can be found in the confluence of the rules of a language—its grammar, vocabulary, idioms, and so forth—and contextual information that is not imbedded in the language itself, such as inferences, spatial relationships, and so forth.

28. A: Canale and Swain. This theory determines that communicative competence consists of both organizational competence (competence with grammar and discourse) and pragmatic competence (sociolinguistic and speech acts) and is currently the objective of many language education programs.

29. C: Pre-production stage; early production stage; speech emergence stage; intermediate fluency stage. During the Pre-production stage, language is being absorbed and its meanings learned, but it is not being verbally produced. The early production stage features a willingness to initiate conversation with gesture or a single word and to answer questions with one or two words. Yes and no become commonly used. The speech emergence stage is characterized by developing comprehension and fewer errors in speech. By the intermediate fluency stage, a speaker exhibits greater comprehension, more complex sentence structures, a richer vocabulary, and more sophisticated errors.

30. B: Language acquisition develops unconsciously through use, while language learning requires instruction. Language acquisition is natural, subconscious, and concerned with message content. Language learning is formal, concerned with grammatical rules, and conscious.

31. C: Realia are concrete objects used in demonstrations, to develop vocabulary and encourage discourse. The use of realia during instruction offers students the chance to involve a range of senses. Objects that can be handled, carefully examined, smelled, tasted, or listened to offer a richer learning experience.

32. A: Increase comprehensibility. There is currently a great deal of research that supports the theory that the degree and types of language learning in L1 are a strong predictor of how well L2 will be absorbed and comprehended.

33. D: Competence in grammar, sociolinguistics, discourse, and communication strategies. Competence in grammar requires mastery of the rules of language; sociolinguistic competence requires an understanding of what is appropriate; competence in discourse requires the ability to organize messages into a coherent and cohesive whole; strategic competence refers to the use of communication strategies in ways that are appropriate.

34. D: Both my dog and my husband think I am a servant. My dogs thinks I am a servant, and my husband also thinks I am a servant. The third person singular form of to think, is "thinks." However, the use of the word "both" links the two singular subjects into a plural subject; hence, the verb form must change to "think" to be in agreement.

35. D: All of the above. "Thinking aloud" to demonstrate cognitive processes, differentiating instruction by teaching explicitly, asking "what if" questions to stimulate abstract thinking, challenging students by expecting maximum performance, and teaching test-taking and study skills are strategies that, taken together, will result in increased cognitive competency.

36. D: Understands and uses roughly 1,000 words. The early production stage lasts approximately six months beyond the pre-production stage and is characterized by an understanding and use of approximately 1,000 words in one-to-two-word phrases or by responding to questions with appropriate action.

37. A: No; parental permission is required. Under no circumstances can a student be placed in a special education classroom without the permission of a parent or a legal guardian.

38. B: Total Physical Response. TPR is an approach pioneered by James J. Asher in the late 1960s, which emphasizes physical activity as a means to increase language retention. It involves a set of detailed instructions or commands, which then require appropriate physical actions.

39. D: All of the above. Traditional methods of teaching English included immersion, also known as "sink or swim," which was used until the late 1960s and involved no instruction in a student's L1 and no instruction to teach L2; drills, in which students memorize and repeat sets of information; and teaching frequently used phrases, which has practical and immediate application, but does not teach a user to truly inhabit a language to the degree necessary to use it to express complex ideas.

40. C: "Dictated Stories" is another name for the Language Experience Approach. This strategy creates texts from students' own words, and uses it in reading lessons. A teacher or peer writes down the story verbatim, then reads the story back to the author. Next, the student reads the story himself, either aloud or silently. Students learn about encoding language by watching their own words being written, develop a bank of sight words, and develop fluency as they read their own words. Because this method permits students to record their own lives, it is particularly useful as a way to celebrate multicultural experiences.

41. D: Krashen. Acquisition-Learning, Monitor, Natural Order, Input, and Affective Filter hypotheses are central to Steven Krashen's highly respected theory of second language acquisition. Language Acquisition is subconscious and requires meaningful communication, while Language Learning is conscious and involves formal instruction; the Monitor is concerned with editing and correcting errors in speaking or writing; Natural Order finds there is a predictable natural order in which grammatical structures are absorbed; Input refers to the hypothesis that language is ultimately acquired and not learned, and the Affective Filter hypothesis explores ways in which positive and negative factors such as motivation, self-esteem, and anxiety help or hurt the acquisition of language.

42. B: Equal Educational Opportunities Act (1974) is a federal law banishing discrimination against all members of an educational community, including students, teachers, and staff. School districts are required to actively work to resolve situations in which students are denied equal participation. The EEOA, together with the Rehabilitation Act (1973), the Individuals with Disabilities Education Act (IDEA), and the Americans with Disabilities Act (ADA) regulate learning institutions.

43. C: The program must be based on sound educational theory; must be put into service with sufficient personnel, materials, and space; and must effectively overcome language barriers and handicaps. These are the three criteria that must be assessed as a result of Castaneda v. Pickard.

44. B: Because his first language is not developed, he will most likely obtain English vocabulary and skills much more slowly; the speed with which L2 learners develop proficiency can be anticipated by the degree of richness L1 exhibits. Research has demonstrated that the degree to which an L2 is obtained is related to the speaker's mastery of L1.

45. B: Content-based ESL models. The Cognitive Academic Language Learning Approach (CALLA) and Specially Designed Academic English (SDAE) and other sheltered-English approaches feature using content-area instruction as a vehicle for language instruction.

46. C: Inaccurate. A substantial number of research studies report that mastery of English (or any second language) should not be taken as an indication of the speaker's cognitive abilities. Learning a language is an ever-changing activity that is actualized at any given moment. Cognitive ability is the potential that is not yet actualized. To look at an ELL's control of English at any given moment of time and base assumptions about that individual's potential to think abstractly, organize knowledge into complex systems, and apply ideas across a wide spectrum would be a disservice.

47. D: Listening and speaking. At the intermediate level, listening and speaking practice enables learners to gain an enhanced comprehension of and insight into the complexity of thought and the means by which to express thoughts.

48. D: Privately meet with the bullies and explain that it's important to welcome Ricardo; ask for their help in doing so. Pair Ricardo with class members who have a gentle, accepting nature to do projects that do not need to be orally presented. Do not force Ricardo to speak publicly, but find opportunities for private, relaxed conversations about topics of interest to him. Do not correct errors; instead, model correct usage. It is important to lower his affective filter so that he will, with time, gain the confidence necessary to trust his ability to express himself using a second language.

49. B: The Bilingual Syntax Measure is a tool designed to assess bilingual students for both native and L2 (English) proficiency. As a result of Lau v. Nichols, schools have been issued a federal mandate to determine whether a child is an English Language Learner. Title III of the English Language Acquisition, Language Enhancement, and Academic Achievement Act additionally requires schools to assess bilingual students for both native language and English proficiency, and states must employ assessment measures that provide valid information gathered in a consistent and dependable manner. However, recent research indicates that a greater number of proficiency assessment tools fail to measure a student's true proficiency level, and that these tools generally do not give the same results.

50. D: Pull-out ESL classes. Of the program choices given, pull-out models consistently prove to be less effective.

51. A: Apply critical listening skills to deduce and evaluate ideas that may not be directly stated. The Texas Essential Knowledge and Skills for English as a Second Language requires K–3 ELL students "to listen attentively and engage actively in a variety of oral language experiences" and expects students to differentiate between listening for information, for understanding or for pleasure; to respond to questions and directions; to contribute to classroom discussions, songs, rhymes, and other language play; and to listen attentively.

52. B: Students' syntactic understanding. The teacher wants her students to understand the types of syntactical arrangements (grammatical structures) that are not allowed. For example, a sentence like "The quickly telephone and lonely" would not be possible because "quickly," an adverb, is modifying "telephone," a noun. In addition, "lonely" is an adjective, but has no noun to modify. Finally, the sentence has no verb. However, a silly sentence like "The quick telephone and forlorn toothbrush waltzed to the music of the moon" is grammatically possible, albeit absurd.

53. A: Development of CALP in L1. The Threshold Hypothesis (Cummins & Swain, 1986) finds that a higher proficiency threshold in the first language is a core contributor to the learner's acquisition of a second language. A speaker who did not achieve Cognitive Academic Language Proficiency in L1 will have more difficulty doing so in L2.

54. C: Always. Students with learning or communication challenges, emotional and/or behavioral disabilities, physical disabilities, and developmental disabilities are eligible for special services. LEP students experience challenges in communication.

55. B: Six months; 500. The Silent/Receptive (Pre-Production Stage) is a brief stage lasting only a few months, in which language learners develop a bank of approximately 500 words they understand but do not use verbally. Newly introduced words that are explained so that the student can understand them are readily added to this bank. It is important that teachers not force or push a student in this stage to speak. They may communicate by pointing or gesturing, can follow commands, and may answer questions with a nod or a single word.

56. C: Content-Based ESL Curriculum. The approach encourages ESL instruction to reach beyond a simply serviceable program of study in order to offer instruction that focuses on content rather than the rules of a language so that ELLs are becoming simultaneously more linguistically proficient and academically proficient.

57. A: Intermediate Fluency. This stage is marked by an increased level of complexity in speech, though some grammatical features and pronunciation aren't well set. Complex speech is starting to emerge, but errors do take place. Early production is a stage in which beginning language learners start to speak and have a relatively small vocabulary. Advanced fluency follows intermediate fluency and begins the process of naturalizing speech.

58. C: Teach a unit on prefixes and suffixes. Offer some examples of each. Next, group the students into teams and see which team comes up with the most words that use prefixes and suffixes. Challenge them by asking for a word with both a prefix and a suffix.

59. D: The learner's positive or negative level of emotional comfort in L2. According to Krashen, because learning a new language involves public practice, a language learner is more emotionally vulnerable. Negative emotions, such as shame, anxiety, or frustration, can obstruct the successful processing of unfamiliar words or grammatical constructions. Classrooms that foster positive feelings of self-esteem and success will encourage taking risks that are necessary to learning, thereby lowering a student's affective filter and encouraging a high degree of motivation.

60. B: Her ability to use the elements of language (syntax, phonology, morphology, semantics) together with an understanding of social expectations and to use spoken messages that are appropriate in terms of how they are manifested and when, in the course of conversation, they are used.

61. B: Incorporate extra-linguistic materials into instruction, such as realia, gestures, and enactments. Comprehensibility will be increased by direct, hands-on involvement and clues to meaning that exist in the physical context of the classroom.

62. A: Employ vocabulary the students understand and use it to teach new vocabulary; offer hands-on instruction; invite members of a mainstreamed class for peer tutoring. New vocabulary built on previous knowledge will be more readily understood and retained. Hands-on instruction allows non-linguistic experiences that can contribute to understanding. Peer tutoring challenges learners to reach for a higher level of communicative skills.

63. A: Neither Eric nor Tim admits he made a mistake. Eric and Tim are treated as a single subject in this sentence, so the verb must be in agreement. The pronoun "he" refers to either Eric or Tim, but not both. Hence, "he" is correct, and "they" is incorrect.

64. D: The teacher will write comments and questions in response, modeling correct English usage. Dialogue or Interactive Journals offer teachers the opportunity to engage students in the writing process. The teacher responds to a student's entry with questions or comments about the topic introduced by the students. The teacher doesn't correct errors, but instead models correct usage.

65. D: All the above. Some ESL students may not be able to interpret cursive handwriting. When asked a question directly, many students will agree, whether or not they understand what is being asked. Moreover, students may agree in order to avoid the embarrassment of admitting in public that they do not understand. The teacher's use of slang that has not been taught as idiom is more likely to confuse the students than clarify meaning for them.

66. C: Building literacy skills in all content areas will improve CALP and increase language and abstract thinking skills across the board. Cognitive Academic Language Proficiency requires specialized vocabularies for specific content areas and the ability to apply abstract concepts to areas that are not transparently related.

67. D: They do not accurately reflect native speakers' proficiency and therefore cannot accurately reflect non-native speakers' proficiency. A study examined the efficacy of the Language Assessment Scales-Oral, the Woodcock-Muñoz Language Survey, and the IDEA Proficiency Test by giving all three to both native English-speaking non-Hispanic Caucasian and Hispanic students from all socioeconomic levels. Interestingly, these L1 English speakers did not receive similar results from the three tests, which ostensibly assessed for the same information. In fact, none of the native English speakers who were given the Woodcock-Muñoz Language Survey were assigned fluent status. On the other hand, all students scored as fluent in the Language Assessment Scales-Oral, while 87% were described by IDEA Proficiency Test results as being fluent. L1 English speakers who do not uniformly score in the fluent range throw into doubt the assessment's ability to accurately reflect an L2's proficiency.

68. B: Degree of L1 development. The degree to which an L1 learner is successful in acquiring a second language is determined in part by the learner's motivation, age, previous instruction, opportunities to practice, willingness to practice, working and long-term memory, ability to process information, and the level of L1 proficiency.

69. B: LEP students: 3rd-12th use the RPTE.

70. C: A play in which a Korean student, a Hispanic student, and an American-born student perform a series of skits demonstrating how different cultures greet acquaintances and the confusion that can arise when people from two distinct cultures meet will best demonstrate the types of misinterpretation and confusion that can arise when two cultures bring different expectations to the same experience.

71. C: Scaffolding. Scaffolding provides a student with a combination of strategies to support independent learning, including hands-on activities; accessing prior knowledge; pre-teaching content-area vocabulary; and putting the lesson into context with visual aids and modeling.

72. C: Try to reestablish positive communication with his family, stressing the importance of the teacher and parents working as a team to find real-life solutions that can be consistently implemented at home and at school. The teacher in this example has violated nearly every principal of productive teacher-parent interaction. Rather than enlisting the mother's help in furthering her son's education, the teacher passes harsh judgment on the boy's behavior, implying fault is found at home. She neglects to realize that perhaps the mother isn't a Spanish speaker, but she is a Portuguese speaker. While his home environment might not be optimal, the teacher needs to do everything in her power to establish positive communication.

73. A: No. The students may believe that the character who dies was literally real rather than figuratively symbolic. Children from the countries the teacher has depicted as poor may feel shamed by their apparent poverty or frightened that they, too, might starve to death. Children from countries depicted as wealthy might either feel cheated, not being themselves wealthy, or entitled to the biggest and best of everything.

74. B: The Language Experience Approach, also called Dictated Stories, enlists the aid of volunteers who take down a story being dictated by a student verbatim. The stories are next read to the authors, and then each author reads her story silently or aloud. This approach utilizes several essential elements of literacy; encoding is modeled, sight word vocabulary developed, and the ownership a young author feels produces motivation.

75. C: An age equivalent score is used in a norm-referenced assessment to determine whether a student is working at, above, or below a level similar to her peers by studying the average age of others who got the same score as she did.

76. A: Develop tier 2 vocabulary; teach specialized vocabulary essential to a particular subject area; teach, offer ample practice opportunities, monitor, and re-teach more complex syntactical structures; offer instruction and practice in organizing ideas in terms of text. These are the necessary next steps once Basic Interpersonal Communication Skills have been gained.

77. A: Plyer v. Doe; 14th amendment. In 1975, Texas laws were revised, permitting districts to refuse to enroll illegal alien children. The Supreme Court used this case to strike down the Texas law, finding it in violation of the 14th Amendment, which gives equal rights to all people.

78. A: Introverts who lack confidence. Krashen's Monitor hypothesis places the role of editor in language learning, as opposed to language acquisition, which is intuitive and lacks the desire to revise and correct. The monitor plans, edits, and corrects language acts when the ELL is not rushed, is attending to the language's rules, and has fully integrated the rule under consideration. The monitor role should be a minor one since it is conscious of itself and therefore not intuitive.

79. A: Homophones. Homophones sound alike but are spelled differently and have different meanings. Synonyms share meaning, homographs share the same spelling, and homonyms are like homophones, that share the same sounds, but they also are spelled the same. An example of a homonym is "lie," which can refer to lying down or to untruth.

80. D: Incorporate gesture, pictures, manipulatives, and other extra-verbal tools into her teaching. The preproduction, or silent/receptive, stage of language acquisition is the first stage in which a learner must break into unfamiliar language that offers no easy entry. Visual images, coupled with the appropriate name, gestures indicating type or quality of movement, and other extra-verbal tools, will allow learners to begin to piece together the meanings that their first words carry.

81. C: It is a program that uses a student's culture of origin as a scaffold to teach her about her new culture. An Additive Educational Program is one that supports and celebrates bicultural identity and encourages acculturation, rather than assimilation.

82. D: All of the above. Hearing idiomatic expressions that have not been explained and aren't transparent will cause confusion in an L2 learner. English is particularly rich in words with multiple, frequently unrelated meanings; encountering a familiar word used in an unfamiliar way or having to decide in the course of a conversation which meaning out of several possibilities is the correct one can snarl understanding. Transporting syntax, vocabulary, and pronunciation from L1 and misapplying it in L2 (which is called negative transfer) will further render the language opaque.

83. B: The students will become bored. Students at Stage III: Speech Emergence are eager to practice their new skills and learn rapidly. The approaches the teacher is using are better suited to learners at Stage I (preproduction) or II (early production). Stage III learners will be challenged by entertaining and practical language practice, such as performing skits, participating in a mock trial, completing a job application form, writing alternate lyrics to a popular song, and so on.

84. B: He is experiencing a high affective filter due possibly to culture shock, which is heightened by being placed with younger students, as well as by his inability to freely communicate. He may feel shame, insecurity, embarrassment, frustration, or a combination of these, which he compensates for and covers up with anger.

85. C: Self-Contained Model. The One Teacher Approach is one in which a single teacher working in a self-contained classroom carries the responsibility for her students' linguistic and academic achievement. This allows for integration of language skills on a progressive scale while learning academic English.

86. C: Refer the student to the school counselor, who is trained to help in situations such as this. It is essential that the teacher not violate the child's trust by reading the journal or showing it to anyone else. Such a violation of trust at this time could be very damaging. While the teacher should certainly monitor the situation and give close attention to the student's moods and behavior, she should not delay bringing the situation to the attention of the counselor.

87. B: No. She is not a trained translator, and, for this reason alone, is not suitable for this task. The school is legally responsible for providing a trained translator or materials in Basque, if they are available. The teacher must advocate on behalf of the student and try to find a trained translator or the materials in Basque. The fact that the volunteer translator is both the boy's aunt and the teacher's friend compounds the problem, in that her objectivity could be affected by her feelings and desire to help.

88. D: Learning tasks are authentic, challenging, and meaningful. Shared learning activities give students the opportunity to absorb learning strategies employed by other students. Students involved in a shared learning activity will speak, discuss, argue, and consider quite naturally. The opportunity for authentic dialogue is especially useful for ELLs. The more meaningful the task, the more involved and motivated the students—and the more authentic their dialogue—will be.

89. A: Project-based learning. Swain's theory of comprehensible output has resulted in practitioners who have developed strategies that are designed to create opportunities for face-to-face communication that requires authentic negotiation to arrive at shared meanings. In addition to project-based learning, other suggested strategies include cooperative learning, student-teacher individualized communications, and working with a partner to study selected materials.

90. B: ESL models are English-only and employ a specific methodology to teach English and continue to develop L1. Bilingual models introduce instruction concepts first in L1 and over time transfer them into English.

91. D: CALP: academic language requires abstract thinking. Cognitive Academic Language Proficiency is necessary for academic communication, requires content-specific vocabularies and more sophisticated syntax, and does not rely upon external contextual information, thereby requiring users to be able to think abstractly.

92. B: A writing sample. The permanent record must contain parental approval; program entry dates, exit dates, and notifications; designation of language proficiency level; recommendation for placement; LEP identification; criterion-referenced test exemption dates, as well as all pertaining documents; and ongoing monitoring results.

93. B: Grade level content is essential. Simplifying language without simplifying content will help ESL students remain at grade level. Language is the vehicle for meaning. It matters less how a student arrives at a relatively full understanding of the intended meaning, as long as she arrives at it at roughly the same time as her peers.

94. C: Language acquisition is natural, subconscious, and concerned with message content. Language learning is formal, concerned with grammatical rules, and conscious. This describes the Acquisition/Learning hypothesis of Krashen's extremely influential theory of second language acquisition. Of the two, acquisition is the more important, as it imitates the subconscious absorption of language that mimics similar processes young children experience when learning a first language, and because it requires authentic use of the language. Learning is the result of formal instruction about a language and is useful in support of subconscious acquisition.

95. B: Differences in family or cultural values and school values are most likely at play in this scenario. Teachers should be aware of differences between a student's home culture and the dominant culture. American schools often value timeliness, efficient use of time, competition, order, and respect toward authority. This is not always the same in all cultures. Some schools in other countries may value humility, cooperation, and family.

96. C: Language registers are different tones, vocabulary, sentence structures, and even volume used in different situations. Consider how speaking during a presentation differs from working in small groups in a classroom. The classroom presentation register often includes things like eye contact, a strong voice that can be heard by the entire class, and a varied tone that keeps the audience's interest. Although being able to pronounce words is important, that has to do with phonology rather than discourse.

97. B: Considering the language level of learners is essential when considering learning activities that are appropriate. For beginning-level learners, fill-in-the-blank activities are appropriate. Although summarizing and paraphrasing may be an appropriate activity for intermediate or advanced-level learners, it would not be appropriate for beginning-level students. It is important to ensure that the activity also matches the purpose, which is to comprehend the text. Alternate activities should still achieve the same objective. Answers A and C do not fulfil the same objective of reading comprehension.

98. D: Early-advanced English learners can be challenged more than beginning-level students. Pre-reading activities should build interest and background knowledge rather than simply giving away the entire story before reading. Visuals can do that, but pre-reading activities should come before the reading, not during. Activating prior knowledge is key to pre-reading; however, a writing activity after reading does not constitute pre-reading.

99. B: Conducting home visits is the best way to understand the student's culture and build a relationship with the family. Teachers may attempt to learn the native language of the student;

however, because students may come from a variety of backgrounds, it is possible that teachers would only have the chance to learn basic greetings. Reading about the student's culture can be helpful as well, but it is important not to generalize findings. Newsletters should be written in both English and the student's home language to increase family involvement, especially if the language spoken at home is not English.

100. A: Additive multicultural curricula focus on adding to the curriculum what has previously been omitted. This might include a non-Eurocentric approach, such as perspectives from other cultures in social studies, including ways that other cultures solve math problems, and adding novels from diverse writers. More surface-level multicultural education approaches are known as contributions. These include one-off events such as celebrating Black History Month. Transformative multicultural education refers to expanding perspectives that were previously excluded, and social action includes having change projects.

MTTC Practice Test #2

1. A group of elementary intermediate-level English learners has difficulty identifying the differences between words like "there, they're, and their" as well as "eight and ate." Which of the following strategies is likely to be the most effective first step in addressing the students' difficulty?

a. Teaching minimal pair activities such as poems and songs to develop students' abilities to pronounce particular English phonemes
b. Repeating the words several times and asking students to review dictionary definitions of each of these words
c. Using sentence pairs with these words in context to teach homophones as well as explicitly teaching context clues
d. Reading aloud meaningful paragraphs with these words to expose students to different sentence types and language usage

2. Which activity is likely to be MOST effective in helping elementary school English learners develop familiarity with the concept of print?

a. Define the concept of print to students, and write the definition on the board.
b. Read aloud a book to learners while pointing at the words being read.
c. Encourage discussions in the students' first language, and translate into English.
d. Begin silent reading activities, so students develop a love for reading.

3. Read the sentence, and answer the question that follows:

They were playing soccer. Is finished the game?

Students in an intermediate English Language Development (ELD) class often make errors in their writing similar to the one underlined. The first step the teacher should take in addressing this problem is to help students learn how to do which of the following?

a. Teach pronouns and antecedents.
b. Distinguish between past participle and future indicative tenses.
c. Distinguish between gerunds and action verbs.
d. Teach subject and predicate order.

4. To develop pragmatic competence in oracy, a student must pay the most attention to which of the following?

a. Grammar and sentence formation
b. Register and body language
c. Literal and figurative language
d. Subject–verb agreement

5. Students in a second-grade beginning level English Language Development (ELD) class are practicing minimal pairs that differ by one phoneme such as "sap" and "tap." How does practicing in this way help promote English learners' phonemic awareness?

a. By enhancing their ability to distinguish different phonemes
b. By promoting their connected speech abilities
c. By supporting communicative competence
d. By differentiating rhymes that students need to learn

6. Which statement is a primary tenet of behavioral theories of language acquisition?

a. Classroom methodology should incorporate repetition and reward.
b. Cooperative grouping is essential to learning because humans are social creatures.
c. Language learners use interlanguage before they fully begin to use their second language.
d. Comprehensible input that is slightly higher than the student's level is key to learning.

7. A high school teacher notices that an English learner in his class is able to speak English with her peers during lunch and breaks; however, she has difficulty speaking English in his chemistry class. Which description offers the BEST explanation for this difference?

a. The student lacks syntactic knowledge used in chemistry.
b. The student is shy and doesn't like talking during class.
c. The student has acquired BICS but not CALP English language skills.
d. The student doesn't have a strong grasp of the pragmatic features of the English language.

8. A middle school English Language Development (ELD) teacher is teaching English learners Greek and Latin roots. What skill is this teacher developing?

a. Phonics
b. Syntax
c. Semantics
d. Morphemes

9. An elementary school English Language Development (ELD) teacher has several Spanish-speaking students in her class. She knows that Spanish and English share many cognates, but she is unsure of whether or not to explicitly teach them these words in case she confuses her students. What course of action should she take?

a. Teach Latin roots to support students' understanding of language instead of cognates.
b. Do not teach the cognates because there are many false cognates that will confuse the students. Instead, the teacher should focus on loan words.
c. Explicitly introduce cognates in Spanish and English while also including activities to show false cognates.
d. Read aloud a Spanish and English version of a story, and have students deduce the meaning of similar words.

10. An eighth-grade English language arts teacher is developing her students' persuasive academic writing skills. Which task would be MOST effective in supporting English learners' language development in this area?

a. Comparing and contrasting the vocabulary used in several different types of essays such as narrative, expository, and persuasive
b. Analyzing the purpose and structure of several persuasive essay examples provided by the teacher
c. Watching a video on academic writing for essays that describes sentence structure, organization, and language register
d. Discussing in small groups topics for essays and writing first drafts together

11. An intermediate-level English learner from Japan has difficulty with pronouncing words such as "this," "math," and "them." Which reason best explains why he has difficulties?

a. The Japanese language does not use phonemes with the /th/ sound.
b. He has a language learning disability that requires extra support as these are fairly common Tier 1 words.
c. New English learners have a silent period in which they do not produce any English words but are instead absorbing the language auditorily.
d. English learners from all backgrounds often have trouble with these words because they are abstract concepts.

12. An English teacher for early-intermediate-level English Learners from a variety of backgrounds wants his students to understand the subject–predicate pattern and agreement for sentences. Which activity best supports this goal?

a. Comparing and contrasting sentences in English and Spanish for the English learners who speak Spanish
b. Reading English passages aloud with students so they can infer the sentence pattern from the passages
c. Explicit teaching of subject–predicate syntax through pairing students who arrange index cards, each containing a word from a meaningful sentence
d. Developing worksheets to be filled out by students individually that require students to practice subject–verb agreement

13. Students in a second-grade beginning-level English Language Development (ELD) class are performing actions while the teacher gives oral commands that is being modeled by the teacher such as "stand" and "jump." This is known as what type of strategy?

a. Total physical response
b. Direct teaching and mastery learning
c. Common underlying proficiency
d. Call and response

14. A high school uses tracking to place students in classes of similar abilities. How might teachers at the school ensure a supportive school environment that offers equal opportunities despite this school practice?

a. Place English learners in low-track classes so that they are able to grasp the concepts that are presented at a more surface-level of depth.
b. Lower the affective filter of English learners by assigning them to nonacademic ESL classes that do not hold college credit, so they feel less academic stress.
c. Give intensive language support for English learner students who are in mid-level tracks, so they can be move to higher tracks.
d. Maintain high standards and consider academic knowledge of a subject beyond language limitations.

15. A veteran English Language Development (ELD) teacher notices that a new math teacher at the school has differentiated her homework for her English learners. English learners are asked to complete fewer math problems that still cover the same skills and concepts. What is an acceptable reason for the teacher to do this?

a. The math problems are difficult, so the teacher only assigns easy problems to the English language learners for them to be successful.
b. The math problems are language heavy, so English learners may take longer to complete the same number of problems.
c. The teacher knows that some of the English learners may not be able to complete the homework because a few of them have family obligations outside of school.
d. The teacher has fewer expectations of those students because of their language abilities.

16. A high school science teacher notices that her English learners use informal language such as "you know" and "gonna" in their writing. What area of language should she focus on to support her students in moving toward a formal register?

a. Pragmatic competence
b. Semantic shifts
c. Phonemic awareness
d. Syntactic competence

17. A middle school social studies teacher has several Spanish-speaking beginning- and advanced-level English learners in his class. He pairs each of the beginning-level students with an advanced-level student to allow them to use their primary language to understand an assignment on ancient Roman history. This pairing is most likely to achieve which outcome for English learners in his class?

a. It will decrease the self-esteem of the beginning-level English language learners because they are intimidated by the level of English proficiency of the other students.
b. It will increase the assimilation of the beginning-level English learners because they are exposed to more advanced-level English speakers.
c. It will expand learners' understanding of the content because students are able to move back and forth from their first and second languages.
d. It will decrease the motivation of students to learn English because they are able to speak in their primary language.

18. An elementary school class includes several intermediate-level English learners. Which activity is likely to be MOST effective in promoting their English-language development by encouraging communicative competence?

a. Students complete grammar drills that help them understand nouns, verbs, and adjectives.
b. Group students to practice role-playing a scenario in which students ask and give advice about school.
c. Students are asked to do a formal presentation to the class on heroes or heroines in their lives.
d. Assign an essay in which students must describe and explain a weather pattern such as rain or snow.

19. A middle school history teacher has assigned a presentation on Civil War heroes to his students, but he is worried that an English learner in his class is too anxious to present in front of the whole class. What factor affecting language development is he considering?

a. Background knowledge
b. Affective filter
c. First-language proficiency
d. Family acculturation

20. A teacher presents a lesson in which students in her English Language Development (ELD) class have paired up to come up with rhyming words such as "car," "bar," and "far." She focuses on phonemes from the English language that may not be common in other languages such as the /schwa/, /th/, and /r/. Each pair is given a word that they must find rhymes for and they present to the class. What domain of language is she developing in her students?

a. Phonology
b. Syntactics
c. Phonetics
d. Morphology

21. A high school English teacher wants to teach the importance of considering the audience in writing to her students. Which activity would promote this pragmatic feature?

a. Students watch their teacher model how to write a letter to her family, the principal, and to an author she admires, and then they compare these letters.
b. Students study different essays such as persuasive and expository and compare and contrast the different features of these texts.
c. Students discuss in cooperative groups topics that would interest them and write a joint poem to present to the class.
d. Students are asked to pretend to be news reporters for news organizations with different political stances and write articles showing that perspectives.

22. A fifth-grade social studies teacher notices that one of her beginning-advanced English learners is having trouble with a unit on the American Revolution. This student is unable to write on what she knows about George Washington. Which factor is the MOST likely to affect second-language development in this context?

a. Psychological factors such as low self-esteem around language competence
b. A lack of prior knowledge of American history
c. Cultural factors such as not showing off what one knows
d. An underlying learning disability in memory or cognition

23. A middle school science teacher has taught a lesson on the different planets. Which follow-up activity to the lesson would be the best activity to promote classroom discourse that improves English language development?

a. Using a worksheet matching activity in which students identify the different planets and their features
b. Asking questions to the class while calling on students to respond, following up with an evaluation of the answer given
c. Quizzing students on what they have retained from the lesson for the teacher to see what topics need to be retaught
d. Using instructional conversation in which the teacher acts as a facilitator to assist students' understanding of concepts

24. A new high school humanities teacher with diverse students including English learners in his class enforces spoken Standard American English during all conversation in class. What is the MOST likely effect this will have on his students?

a. Speakers of dialects and languages will feel subordinated because their language is not accepted in the classroom.
b. Students will greatly improve their English because only Standard American English is spoken in the class.
c. Students will feel their voices are heard and understood because everyone must communicate in the same way.
d. Students will experience cultural dissonance because some other students are not participating in the classroom.

25. Mr. Robinson notices that when he speaks individually with one of his English learners, the student often does not meet his eye contact. He wonders if this has to do with cultural differences. What feature of pragmatic language does this behavior relate to?

a. Nonverbal communication
b. Academic language structure
c. Leadership register
d. Family acculturation

26. A fourth-grade English learner has developed his basic interpersonal communication skills (BICS) fairly quickly since coming to the United States a year ago; however, his teacher has noticed that his cognitive academic language proficiency (CALP) is still behind other native English-speaking students. What advice would you give his teacher regarding his language development?

a. His teacher should be alarmed because CALP develops much more quickly than BICS.
b. His teacher should not be alarmed because it often takes 7 to 10 years for CALP to develop.
c. His teacher should refer him to get testing for special education services because his CALP is so far behind.
d. His teacher should expect his CALP to develop fairly soon as it takes only 2 to 3 years to develop.

27. A high school science teacher has a group of beginning-intermediate-level English learners in her class. She has students answer questions regarding the parts of a cell and share them with the class. Which is the best way of lowering students' affective filters in her class?

a. Collecting all written work and correcting every mistake that students make regarding grammar, spelling, and punctuation
b. Having students work together in small groups to share their answers
c. Calling students randomly to give answers so that she knows every student is engaged
d. Not choosing any of the English language learners to give answers, so they don't have to speak in front of the class

28. A third-grade English Language Development (ELD) teacher is hoping to learn more about her students' family acculturation patterns. Which strategy would help her MOST in developing an understanding of how her students' families have adapted to the new dominant American culture?

a. Have students fill out questionnaires about their lives
b. Visit the students' homes, and observe their media consumption
c. Present to parents on the differences between American culture and their home cultures
d. Have students take a language test that assesses their reading, writing, speaking, and listening skills

29. Read the sentence, and answer the question that follows:

This morning, I <u>eat</u> eggs for breakfast.

Students in a beginning-level English Language Development (ELD) class frequently make mistakes in their writing similar to the one underlined here. What is the first step that the teacher should take in addressing this problem to help students?

a. Teach verb tenses.
b. Distinguish between prepositions and appositives.
c. Developing use of phrasal verbs.
d. Understanding subject and predicate order.

30. Which of the following is NOT considered a dialectical difference?

a. Indi and Urdu
b. Beijing and Hong Kong Chinese
c. New York City and Los Angeles dialects
d. African American Vernacular English and Southern United States

31. Which of the following describes how positive language transfer can be used in the classroom to support second-language learning?

a. Allowing group work to enhance communicative competence
b. Monitoring errors in vocabulary and grammar in writing
c. Using dual-language examples in the classroom to teach sentence structures
d. Teaching common prefixes and suffixes

32. A first-grade English Language Development (ELD) teacher focuses on teaching grammatical features of English in a specific order. For example, he first teachers the use of the "–ing" verb form such as "walking." He then teaches adding "–s" to the end of regular third-person verb forms such as "She writes." What theory does this exemplify?

a. Interaction hypothesis
b. Affective filter hypothesis
c. Pivotal grammar
d. Natural order theory

33. For a classroom activity, students are asked to interview one another about their interests. The teacher provides students with a list of follow-up questions as well as coaches them on how to show they are listening by using eye contact and nodding.

In this scenario, which language feature is the teacher focused on?

a. Pragmatics
b. Syntax
c. Discourse
d. Morphology

34. Which is a primary tenet of the social constructionist view of language learning?

a. Language learning occurs within a cultural context that includes daily social interactions between children and adults.
b. Language learning is supported by the expectations placed on students by their families and teachers.
c. Language learners have an innate ability to learn language because all humans have internalized language rules from birth.
d. Language learners learn best when actively seeking meaning in a natural setting that applies to their lives.

35. What impact did the No Child Left Behind Act of 2001 have on school funding and English learners?

a. Schools must measure and share student results, including those of English learners, on state standardized tests to receive federal funds.
b. Schools should not include English learners in their school results for state standardized tests to receive funding.
c. All classes must have English language learners to receive federal funding so that they are integrated into mainstream classes.
d. Schools must offer all state standardized tests to English learners in the language of their choice and report that to the state.

36. What is the first step a school should take when an English language learner is enrolled in the school?

a. Administer a standardized test to identify his or her proficiency level.
b. Gather registration information like a home language survey.
c. Have the student take an English language assessment test to determine his or her English language proficiency level.
d. Place him or her in extra support classes to have him or her perform at grade level.

37. A ninth-grade English teacher is using "backwards" design to plan her unit on memoirs. She carefully chooses the English Language Development (ELD) Standards that she would like her students to achieve. What is the next step she should take to follow the method of "backwards" lesson planning?

a. Come up with activities that teach those particular standards.
b. Find texts that she could work with for the unit.
c. Develop a summative assessment that aligns with the standards she has chosen.
d. Consider how she will conduct formative assessments during the unit.

38. A middle school English teacher is planning a lesson incorporating Specifically Designed Academic Instruction in English (SDAIE) for a group of early-advanced English learners. Which of the following would be most appropriate and effective to use with students at this proficiency level to promote their English language development in reading?

a. Simplifying passages being used so that when students read, they are able to comprehend the text and answer questions
b. Choosing and displaying language development objectives for the reading lesson
c. Avoiding texts with figurative language and idioms to support student understanding
d. Giving students organizers with fill-in the blanks as they read to help them understand the passage

39. A 10th-grade math teacher has an early-intermediate English language learner in her class. She administers a math assessment on a unit on triangles that is predominantly comprised of word problems. What kind of test accommodations should she offer the student to address the English language learner's needs while still assessing her student's abilities?

a. Give the student an open book test, so he or she can look up formulas he or she doesn't know.
b. Allow the student to ask questions during the test.
c. Reduce the number of words in the word problem so the student only does the calculation portions.
d. Offer the student extended time to complete the exam.

40. Which of the following is not a component of using Specifically Designed Academic Instruction in English (SDAIE) to design a lesson for English learners?

a. Teacher attitude
b. Comprehensibility
c. Interaction
d. Structured English Immersion (SEI)

41. A sixth-grade science teacher is designing a lesson that clusters students into three groups based on their needs: an intensive group, a benchmark group, and a strategic group. She is teaching the three states of matter. Which is the MOST appropriate activity for the strategic group to complete?

a. Students write a detailed explanation of each of the three states of matter using their textbooks and additional texts that the teacher has selected.
b. Students collect different materials that show the three states of matter and organize data listing their characteristics using deduction.
c. Students discuss different states of matter in a class discussion after watching a quick video describing the three states of matter.
d. Students categorize different materials into the three states of matter in pairs using visuals and charts.

42. A 10th-grade British literature teacher has several intermediate-level English learners in his class. He has students give presentations on different British poets. Which approach aligns with Specifically Designed Academic Instruction in English (SDAIE) in supporting students' listening skills?

a. Encouraging students to ask questions to clarify any information they did not understand during the presentation
b. Asking students to compare and contrast two different poets that were presented in a short essay after watching the presentations
c. Giving students a list of the poets being presented before the class presentations so they can do research on one of the poets
d. Remind speakers to pace their speaking, speak clearly during the presentation, and use slides that highlights the key ideas

43. Which of the following is a primary tenet of a balanced reading program?

a. Combining a range of activities that address phonics, fluency, and comprehension
b. Using students' own stories to develop literacy
c. Focusing on vocabulary development to improve reading comprehension
d. Developing fluency as a means to build literacy

44. An English Language Development (ELD) teacher is looking at several different programs to implement in her school, including a front-loaded English program and a transitional bilingual program. What is one of the key differences between these two programs?

a. The goal of front-loaded English is to have students develop cognitive academic language proficiency (CALP), whereas the goal of transitional bilingual programs is to develop full biliteracy.
b. Front-loaded English programs use the home language throughout, whereas transitional bilingual programs only use it at the beginning of the program.
c. Front-loaded English programs use Specifically Designed Academic Instruction in English (SDAIE) content, whereas transitional bilingual programs deliver content in the primary language of the student.
d. Front-loaded English programs depend mostly on the skills of the SDAIE teachers, whereas transitional bilingual programs depend mostly on the content and curriculum being used.

45. An English Language Development (ELD) teacher noticed that when she had administered a listening test to her students twice, the scores were not reliable. What would indicate to her that the test is not reliable?

a. The scores were drastically different among all of the students.
b. The test took too long for students to complete the first and second time.
c. The test did not ask questions relevant to the topic that was being taught.
d. The scores were different the first and second time students took the test.

46. Which was NOT one of the impacts on English language learners of the *Lau v Nichols* U.S. Supreme Court Case in 1947?

a. Schools must communicate with parents in a language they can understand.
b. School are not allowed to assign English learners to vocational tracks instead of teaching them English.
c. Schools cannot deny children of illegal immigrants an education.
d. Schools cannot designate English learners into special education programs based on their English language skills.

47. An upper-level elementary school teacher is developing a unit on American history. How can he use formative assessments to support his students' English language and literacy development?

a. Create versions of the unit test to support learners with different linguistic needs.
b. Have English learners complete an alternative project that does not require essay writing such as a visual display of American history.
c. Use daily pop quizzes that relate to what the students have learned in the previous lesson to ensure they pay attention during class.
d. Conduct informal checks on the daily language objective of the lesson, so he can incorporate his observations into the next day's lesson.

48. A sixth-grade math teacher considers several tools and strategies to use with her beginning-level English learners that would support their vocabulary development in math. She is specifically teaching surface area. Which tool would best serve this purpose?

a. A calculator so they will not have to worry about making calculation errors
b. Worksheets with surface area practice problems
c. A page with pictures of three-dimensional objects and key terms that relate to these objects
d. A chart of essential formulas that they can use during tests and homework

49. Which example of a classroom display best describes a language-rich environment for English learners?

a. Posters of age-appropriate books that have a diversity of characters
b. Bulletin boards with exemplary student work to promote excellence
c. Labels of classroom items in both the primary language and English
d. Pictures of the many different cultures represented in the school

50. A second-grade teacher is planning a unit on measurements in his math unit. Which Specifically Designed Academic Instruction in English (SDAIE) strategy would best support his English language learners in their English language development?

a. Using rulers and scales to measure actual objects that the teacher collected
b. Shortening the language being used in word problems, so learners grasp the concepts faster
c. Activating prior knowledge by asking students about how their parents cook at home using measurements
d. Asking students to deduce how each unit of measurement is used based on their own research

51. An eleventh-grade anatomy teacher is administering a test for his unit on the bones in the body. Several of his essay questions require extensive writing to demonstrate knowledge of the skeletal system. What are ways he can ensure that for the English learners in his class, his assessment measures content knowledge rather than language skills?

a. Allow students to answer questions orally to the teacher.
b. Administer only half of the exam, so that they have time to write
c. Develop an alternative assessment that asks the student to draw pictures
d. Translate the test into the students' home language, and allow them to answer in that language

52. A high school history teacher plans to use authentic assessments for his unit on immigration during the 20th century in America. Which of the following would best serve this purpose?

a. Give students an Ellis Island computer simulation to complete and write a report on what happened.
b. Administer a pop quiz so he knows how much students truly know about the topic before he gives a final assessment.
c. Ask students to interview family and community members to learn about their immigration history.
d. Have students take the state standardized test for this unit, which is closely aligned with the state standards.

53. An upper-elementary school teacher is developing a rubric for a science project she will conduct with her fifth-grade students. Her class includes early-intermediate English learners. What is the first question she should ask herself when developing this rubric to ensure that it is fair and accessible for all of her students?

a. What type of task am I asking students to complete?
b. What is the level of language I should use when considering my English language learners?
c. How will I break up the rubric into categories such as hypothesis, observations, and results?
d. What should students be able to do and know at the end of the unit?

54. A middle school English Language Development (ELD) teacher notices that her students have difficulty reviewing for their social studies tests because their notes are incomplete. They explain that the teacher talks too quickly during class when they are writing notes, so they often miss some of the key words or ideas as they try to write everything down. Which strategy would best support these learners?

a. Give them all of the class notes so they don't need to worry about taking notes.
b. Teach them how to take better notes such as only writing key words, organizing based on topic, and underlining or highlighting main ideas.
c. Ask the teacher to record the lessons, so they can listen to the lessons again at home.
d. Tell the teacher that she must talk much more slowly.

55. A fourth-grade English Language Development (ELD) teacher is planning on conducting writing workshops with her students to develop narrative texts in which students write stories that incorporate their culture. What first step for students would best support the writing workshop approach?

a. Drafting topic sentences with the use of teacher-provided word walls and word banks
b. Sharing experiences with classmates in small groups to generate ideas
c. Using sentence stems provided by the teacher to begin writing
d. Learning grammatical structures that will be used in the narrative texts

56. A middle school drama teacher is focused on developing communicative competence with her English language learners. She has them role play scenarios that require that they ask each other clarifying questions and elaborate on their answers. What type of skill is she mainly fostering by encouraging questions?

a. Grammatical competence
b. Discourse competence
c. Strategic competence
d. Sociolinguistic competence

57. A fifth-grade elementary school English Language Development (ELD) teacher wants her students to be able to self-correct when pronouncing words during discussions. Which strategy would best support this goal?

a. Stopping the discussion any time a student mispronounces a word and having the entire class practice pronouncing the word several times
b. Creating a list of anticipated commonly mispronounced words for students to practice beforehand
c. Writing mispronounced words overheard during discussions without singling out students for students to refer to throughout discussions
d. Having students record themselves and the teacher listens to each recording to correct errors for the student

58. A third-grade science teacher is trying to teach the concept of cause and effect to his English language learners. Which activity would be LEAST beneficial in supporting his students' English language skills?

a. Providing a list of examples of cause and effect, such as when water is heated, it boils
b. Bringing in real examples of cause an effect, such as pushing a row of dominos
c. Writing on the board the definition of cause and effect for students to copy
d. Using sentence strips that students must match to show an appropriate cause and effect

59. A fourth-grade English Language Development (ELD) teacher notices that one of her early-advanced English learners often uses sentence structures similar to that in his primary language, Spanish. For example, he sometimes omits the subject in a sentence such as "buy apples" when he means "I buy apples." What is this phenomenon known as?

a. Communicative competence
b. Basic interpersonal language skills (BICS)
c. Interlanguage
d. False cognates

60. A ninth-grade world history teacher front-loads vocabulary from her unit on ancient Greece with a group of advanced-level English language learners. What effect will this have on her students?

a. Enable better comprehension of concepts that students may not know
b. Support diverse learning styles to increase language learning
c. Help build interpersonal language skills for when they will have group work
d. Reduce their schemata to help promote confidence and minimize anxiety

61. An eighth-grade English teacher models think-aloud reading to her class, which includes several intermediate-level English language learners. She reads aloud a section of *The Giver*, pauses, and says, "This reminds me of a time when I had never seen snow and was flabbergasted when I saw it in real life for the first time. I was astonished at how soft and cold it was as it fell from the sky." What is the MOST likely purpose that the teacher had in using the think-aloud?

a. The activity will expand students' vocabulary through the use of words like *astonished* and *flabbergasted.*
b. The activity will help them learn how to use complex sentences that use subordinating conjunctions such as *when* and *as.*
c. The activity will improve students' listening skills as they must pause in their reading to listen to something that is not written in the text.
d. The activity will model reading comprehension skills through the use of making connections to one's life.

62. According to Cummins's four quadrants theory, which of the following is NOT a task category that should be undertaken by students?

a. Tasks that are cognitively unchallenging but are also highly relatable
b. Tasks that are cognitively demanding but are abstract
c. Tasks that are cognitively undemanding and are unrelatable
d. Tasks that are cognitively challenging and are highly relatable

63. A 10th-grade chemistry teacher decides to use the Language Experience Approach (LEA) to develop English speaking and listening skills during a science experiment. In this experiment, different groups of students make observations of different unknown solutions as well as conduct tests such as a test identifying the pH levels of solutions. Which of the following would best utilize the LEA?

a. Students interview one another and write down a report of the results after the experiment.
b. Students compare their results with the teacher's results from her previous experiment with each of the solutions.
c. Students research about each of their own chemicals to try and identify what the solution must be.
d. Students complete a chart provided by the teacher with their results.

64. An 11th-grade English teacher has required texts he must teach in his classes. One play he must teach is *Hamlet.* What is the best way to incorporate effective resources to support his early-advanced English learners in his class?

a. Provide a summarized version for his English learners to read instead of the actual play.
b. Watch adaptations of *Hamlet* such as the animated film *The Lion King* to introduce the storyline to students.
c. Use technological resources such as websites that provide information on theme, symbolism, and character analyses.
d. Act out the play during class using props to make the play more comprehensible.

65. A 12th-grade English teacher has several Generation 1.5 English learners who have been part of the US education system since middle school and high school. He considers how he can best prepare them for higher education. Which statement demonstrates one of the Specifically Designed Academic Instruction English (SDAIE) strategies he can use to support their academic language skills?

a. Using a reading log to help students discuss their opinions on their reading
b. Focusing on basic interpersonal communication skills (BICS) language skills with daily discussions about common topics
c. Modeling effective use of context clues when coming across unknown vocabulary words in texts
d. Giving tips on how to memorize facts using mnemonics

66. A kindergarten teacher has several beginning-level English learners in his class. He reads aloud the story of "Goldilocks and the Three Bears" and assesses students' comprehension of the story. Which assessment would be the MOST appropriate for his English learners?

a. Rewriting the story in their own words
b. Creating their own stories based on what they heard
c. Placing pictures of events in the story in order
d. Drawing a picture of Goldilocks and the three bears

67. Which of the following describes a limitation of two-way immersion programs?

a. They depend primarily on the skills of the teachers involved and their ability to implement Specifically Designed Academic Instruction English (SDAIE) strategies.
b. English Language Development (ELD) and English language arts (ELA) are taught separately, or the language learning is slowed down for both groups.
c. They can often lead to subtractive bilingualism.
d. They can create segregation between groups because English learners are always separated from native English speakers in all classes.

68. A teacher notices that one of her English learners who was a top student in school in his home country often gets up in the middle of class to move around and will not stay in his seat. He does not seem to notice anything wrong with this behavior. What is the best explanation for why this student may behave this way?

a. The student is unengaged and wants to leave the class.
b. The student has an underlying attention deficit hyperactive disorder that needs to be further investigated.
c. The student comes from a different cultural school environment that allows for freedom of movement.
d. The student is unsure of what to do next and likes to see what others are doing.

69. A second-grade English Language Development (ELD) teacher invites parents to participate in an after-school event. She notices that communication with the family is only with the mother and never the father. She even called home, and when she spoke with the father, he said that she should speak with Amal's mother. Which of the following may be the best explanation for why this occurs?

a. In Amal's culture, the mother usually deals with children's education.
b. Amal's father does not care about his schooling.
c. Culturally, parents are uninvolved in school because they defer to the teacher.
d. Amal's father does not speak English well enough to talk about school.

70. Which of the following describes an internal cultural factor?

a. Clothing that is worn in the culture
b. Food that is common in the culture
c. Language spoken within that culture
d. Family structure typical of that culture

71. What is one of the main impacts of cultural assimilation?

a. Increased self-esteem and resilience
b. Loss of cultural identity
c. Rejection of the dominant culture leading to maladjustment
d. The ability to function in two cultures

72. A middle school has always had a no hat or headwear rule in its dress code policy. Recently, an immigrant from Iran who wears religious head garb enrolled in the school. The school allowed for her to wear something on her head as an exception to the policy but still maintained no headwear in other situations. What effect does this MOST likely have for the student?

a. The student will feel special and unique because she is allowed to wear religious head garb.
b. The student may feel different and singled out, creating an environment in the school that is not accepting of differences.
c. The student will be indifferent to this because at least she is able to wear her head garb.
d. The student may feel it is unfair toward other students that they also cannot wear anything on their heads and begin protesting.

73. An English Language Development (ELD) teacher notices that one of his 10th-grade English learners is refusing to use his home language in school. He has started to hang out with native English speakers and dressing similarly to them. What is this phenomenon known as?

a. Accommodation
b. Biculturalism
c. Culture shock
d. Assimilation

74. A teacher wants to encourage parents of English learners to be a part of the school governance, but many of them do not speak English fluently. What is a way that he can still help them get involved?

a. Asking the principal to create a representative parent–teacher groups for those parents
b. Sending minutes of meetings to parents in their home language
c. Giving parents an interpreter during those meetings
d. Thinking of an alternative way for involvement, such as class volunteer

75. An eighth-grade math teacher notices that his English learner is silent in class and often has a hard time answering when called upon. Aware that sometimes silence in his culture can mean respect rather than regret or embarrassment, he decides not to call on him in class. Before making this accommodation, what should the teacher do first?

a. Determine whether he feels that way about silence
b. Speaking to his counselor to determine his motivation
c. Consult with other teachers who have this student
d. Reading more about this student's culture

76. What was the result of cultural incompatibility theory being applied to schools?

a. Schools were more understanding of different cultures.
b. It perpetuated the status quo with the school, expecting home cultures to change.
c. Schools fostered multicultural perspectives through incorporating diverse curricula.
d. Schools demanded English-only programs.

77. The high school English Department is looking to reform its curriculum to become more multicultural. Which would be the best step to take to accomplish this?

a. Including books that feature diverse characters from around the world
b. Participating in professional development to incorporate technology in the curriculum
c. Brainstorming guest speakers who can come to talk about culture
d. Focusing on validating student's cultural identities through redesigning units

78. A fourth-grade teacher has a new English learner who has recently immigrated to the United States and enrolled in her class halfway through the school year. She notices that this student seems eager to participate and share about her culture. Which stage is this student experiencing in the acculturation process?

a. Euphoria
b. Cultural fatigue
c. Adjustment
d. Culture shock

79. In recent years, migrants from countries in Central America have arrived to the United States for various reasons. What is a pull factor that contributes to their decision?

a. Escaping from gang violence
b. Targeted persecution
c. Economic opportunities
d. High records of homicide rates

80. A third-grade teacher is seeking to foster a culturally supportive classroom. Which of the following best describes a strategy she can use to do this?

a. Fostering high standards by using Tier 3 academic language throughout her classes
b. Encouraging language development through English-only methods and practices
c. Providing simplified versions of activities for English learners to be successful
d. Maintaining high expectations by giving enough wait time for responses and smiling

81. Compared with immigrants in the late 19th century, immigrants after the 1960s were more likely to

a. be from Asian and Latin American countries.
b. immigrate due to religious persecution.
c. move to the East Coast of the United States.
d. come from Slavic-speaking countries.

82. A ninth-grade teacher has two students who do not get along with each other after having to work together in a group project. One learner is from Palestine, and the other is from Israel. In one instance, the students were calling each other names after school. Which of the following is the best approach the teacher should take in this situation?

a. Have students each explain what is upsetting them and try to understand the perspective of the other student.
b. Send them to the principal's office for possible suspension for their behavior.
c. Bring in each of the parents to defend their positions and have a chance to argue.
d. Leave it alone so that they can let it blow over because it did not occur during school.

83. Yin is an 11th-grade English learner from China. He has been taught at home to not speak to adults unless first spoken to. His science teacher believes that he is too passive in class because he does not volunteer to answer in class. What is this misunderstanding a result of?

a. The teacher holds incorrect stereotypes against Chinese students.
b. A cultural miscommunication is occurring due to a difference in cultures.
c. Yin has not yet assimilated to the minority culture.
d. Cultural pluralism is affecting the cultures that are a part of America.

84. A new teacher at a Navajo school notices that when he tries to play competitive games in the classroom, students are reluctant to participate. Which of the following offers a possible explanation for why this is the case?

a. Navajo culture does not foster a competition but instead cooperation.
b. The school does not allow for fun during school, so students are unused to the activities.
c. There are not many games in Navajo culture.
d. The teacher is new, so the students don't want to show off and give a bad impression.

85. A kindergarten teacher has suggested to parents that they read with their children at home to foster literacy. One parent of an English learner tells the teacher that this is not possible because she is unable to read English, only in Spanish. What suggestion should the teacher give the parent?

a. Do not read with the child but instead work on math.
b. Have the child read on his or her own.
c. Read books in a language the parent can understand.
d. Have the child stay after school with the teacher to read books.

86. A seventh-grade science teacher places diverse learners into groups that require cooperative lab work. She also praises times that students are able to work together despite their differences or when their differences bring multiple perspectives. What phenomenon is she seeking to reduce?

a. Social distance
b. Cultural relativism
c. Acculturation
d. Multicultural perspectives

87. An elementary school is preparing for parent–teacher conferences. Which of the following is NOT necessarily a consideration that the school and teachers should make with families of English learners?

a. Having appropriate interpretation services available
b. Being flexible for meeting times because some families work
c. Considering alternatives to in-person conferences
d. Providing refreshments for parents, so they feel welcome

88. From which country does the second-largest population of immigrants in the United States come?

a. China
b. Latin America
c. India
d. Mexico

89. A seventh-grade social studies teacher is aware of his cultural context and understands how he was raised affects his perspectives. He understands the values of different cultures but does not necessarily agree with all of them. What is this known as?

a. Ethnocentrism
b. Ethical relativism
c. Cultural pluralism
d. Cultural relativism

90. To foster good teacher–student relationships between the teacher and all students, which action should a teacher avoid?

a. Convey equality and commitment toward all students.
b. Change the level of physical contact based on the student's cultural norms.
c. Allow students to discuss their feelings and personal lives.
d. Communicate acceptance toward all students.

91. A 12th-grade math teacher has a new English learner in her class. Ever since he arrived, she noticed that he tends to take longer than other students on activities and does not always adhere to the bell schedule. She thinks this is due to different cultural values around time. What is a modification she can provide for the student?

a. Change his schedule, so he has flexible classes.
b. Talk to the principal about this issue, so they can come up with a solution.
c. Allow for flexible timing of activities within her class period.
d. Pair the student with another student who can help speed up the work.

92. An elementary school puts on a cultural day in which students share their food, folklore, traditional attire, and games. What level of multicultural education would this be considered?

a. Inclusive
b. Additive
c. Transformed
d. Exclusive

93. A teacher arranges diverse students to work together in cooperative learning groups. What is the likely impact of this action?

a. Students will have more conflicts because they may come from competitive cultures.
b. Students will develop semantic skills.
c. It fosters a culturally inclusive classroom.
d. It creates in- versus out-group dynamics that will divide the class.

94. Fahd is a 10th-grade student who shows signs of biculturalism. Which of the following would accurately describe how he behaves?

a. Fahd understands both Arabic and English but prefers to speak in Arabic in most cases.
b. Fahd feels ashamed of his home culture and only wants to speak English.
c. Fahd rejects American values and has strong ties to his home country and family.
d. Fahd easily switches back between English and Arabic depending on the situation.

95. A ninth-grade English teacher notices that one of her intermediate-level English learners tends to ramble in his written work. Before she writes down feedback regarding being concise and clear in his summaries, what should she keep in mind?

a. Because he is at the intermediate level, she shouldn't correct him so much.
b. His culture may use more storytelling in their discourse, which is reflected in his writing.
c. She should encourage his writing because at least he is trying hard.
d. She needs to try and give him feedback early on so that he is able to gain the skills he needs as soon as possible.

96. What is an important consideration when selecting diverse literature?

a. Is the author well-known to the students?
b. Does the book present stereotypical depictions of diverse characters?
c. Does the book include several different languages for students to read in?
d. Is the author still alive today and available for a talk at the school?

97. A second-grade English learner comes from a low socioeconomic background with parents who have not completed a middle school education. Her teacher notices that her parents are not involved in her schooling despite the class expectations that parents check over homework and read with the student. Which of the following explains why the parents do not get involved?

a. The family experiences cultural depravation due to poverty.
b. The family is not interested in education.
c. The family holds different values on family involvement in education.
d. The family is uneducated, so they cannot read.

98. A sixth-grade math teacher notices that one of her advanced-level English learners from China is not excelling in her class. She is worried that this student may have a learning disability. Which of the following offers the best alternative perspective to this explanation?

a. The teacher has ascribed to the model minority myth.
b. The student is experiencing culture shock.
c. The teacher has not adequately explained the assignments.
d. The student has a language barrier that interferes with her learning abilities.

99. Race tensions at a middle school have risen due to an increase of Latino immigrants in the area. What is the best way to resolve conflicts and support cultural understanding?

a. Dividing up classes, so each has a representative number of diverse students
b. Adding a mediation and conflict resolution elective course in the school
c. Increasing the disciplinary measures for racial intolerance at the school
d. Bringing in police surveillance to check for weapons

100. Which of the following best helps validate students' cultural identities?

a. Conducting naming interviews in which students learn about the origin of their classmates' names
b. Having a show-and-tell day in which students bring something that they are interested in to class
c. Focusing on author studies and the background of authors that students have read
d. Hosting a school field trip to a local museum with information on indigenous tribes from the area

Answer Key and Explanations

1. C: "There, they're, and their" and "eight and ate" are examples of homophones: words that sound the same but are spelled differently and have different meanings. Explicitly teaching homophones through the use of meaningful context gives students the chance to see the words used in different ways as well as identify the differences in meaning and spelling. This is more effective than reviewing dictionary definitions. Minimal pairs are words that change by one phoneme, helping students learn different phoneme sounds. In homophones, the phonemes are the same, so minimal pairs would not be a helpful activity.

2. B: Some students who do not have literacy skills in their first languages may not understand the concept of print. The concept of print includes that print has meaning, how to hold a book and turn pages, reading from left to right and top to bottom, understanding that there are letters and words with spaces that separate words, and so on. Reading aloud allows students to see this in action as modeled by the teacher.

3. D: The underlined phrase has the wrong word order with the predicate coming before the verb. Many languages such as Spanish often put the predicate before the verb, but English uses subject than predicate word order. Teachers may need to explicitly teach this if students have difficulty and put the verb before the subject. This sentence does not include pronouns or gerunds, which end in "–ing", nor does the error deal with tenses.

4. B: Pragmatic competence in oracy has to do with nonlinguistic factors such as body language, physical proximity, eye contact, and register. Register is how formally or informally the language is being used. In some situations, more formal language is required, whereas in other circumstances, more informal language or slang is appropriate.

5. A: Phonemes are the individual, smallest breakdown of sounds in a language. Not all languages have the same phonemes, and this can pose a challenge to English learners. Phonemic awareness is the skill acquired by speakers of a language connecting sounds to symbols or letters as well as identifying, hearing, and using individual phonemes. Rhymes are the vowel and consonants that follow the initial consonant sound in a word. The rhyme for both "sap" and "tap" is "–ap."

6. A: Behavioral theorists believe that the mind is a "blank slate," and students learn exactly what has been taught by the teacher. This method focuses on reinforcement through repetition and using rewards or punishments to support behavior. The main focus is on teacher output and a focus on student behaviors in response to the teacher.

7. C: BICS stands for basic interpersonal communication skills, which are language skills that focus on social situations. People generally learn BICS quickly in several months, even for a second language. On the other hand, cognitive academic language proficiency (CALP) often takes 7 to 10 years to develop. This language skill is used in academic settings such as the classroom, and it is highly formal, complex, and decontextualized. Syntactic knowledge refers to the patterns that govern sentence construction. For example, "A bird flies" follows the syntactic patterns of English, whereas "Flies a bird" does not. This is different from semantics, which is the study of the meaning of words and phrases.

8. D: Morphemes are the smallest units of language that have meaning. For example, "devalue" is made of the morphemes "de," which means opposite or not, and "value," which means something that is important or useful. These cannot be broken down further. Greek and Latin roots are morphemes that help all students understand the meaning of words as well as be able to infer the meanings of words they do not know.

9. C: Cognates are words that have similar meanings and spellings because they come from the same origin. Although false cognates do exist, students can benefit greatly from cognate awareness from as early as preschool. Teachers should teach cognates while also making students aware of false cognates.

10. B: Persuasive writing presents an argument supporting a point of view. Although comparing different types of essays may be helpful, to write a persuasive essay, students need to focus on purpose and structure rather than on vocabulary. Answer D, discussing and writing drafts, should come only after students have a firm understanding of key aspects of persuasive writing.

11. A: Several English phonemes are not found in other languages. The Japanese language does not contain phonemes such as /dg/, /th/, and the /schwa/. English learners who come from backgrounds that do not have certain English phonemes may have trouble with hearing and pronouncing these particular sounds. Although beginning-level learners do experience a silent period when learning a new language, intermediate-level language learners should be beyond this point.

12. C: Although students can acquire a language without explicit teaching of syntax, systematic and explicit teaching of syntax structures can expedite learning. Although comparing sentence structures from different languages is useful, it is important to consider the language background of learners. If all learners do not speak Spanish, it should not be the only method of teaching subject–predicate pattern and agreement. Worksheets can be helpful but should be used in moderation and come after explicit and direct teaching.

13. A: Total physical response (TPR) stems from a branch of behavioral theory that connects physical action to language. When teachers use TPR, they model an action while saying the word. Direct teaching and mastery learning also stem from behavioral theory; however, these strategies use rigid steps in which teachers follow a scripted lesson. Open Court is an example of direct teaching and mastery learning. Common Underlying Proficiency (CUP) refers to the idea that the primary language and the second language have shared underlying knowledge that allows competence in the second language. CUP is not a teaching methodology but relates to theories of second-language acquisition. Call and response is a strategy that uses choral replies between the teacher and the class, but it does not include physical actions.

14. D: Tracking can be a harmful school practice that precludes English learners along with many other students from accessing equal opportunities for education. Although teachers may not be able to immediately change this school-wide policy, teachers can continue to maintain high expectations, which are crucial to student success. In addition, it is essential that teachers consider academic ability beyond a student's language abilities. Ensuring appropriate grade-level academic content should be part of every English learner's education. Although affective filter is an important part of learning, students should not simply be placed in lower classes that can lead to disengagement and boredom. Intensive support is necessary, but all students should be supported, not just those who are tracked in mid-level classes.

15. B: Differentiation is an essential part of teaching; however, teachers should consider socio-cultural factors that influence instruction. If teachers believe that English learners are capable of less simply because of their language abilities, teachers set up students for failure. This can manifest in seemingly helpful ways by assigning only easy homework questions to English learners.

Instead, carefully constructing word problems, pre-teaching necessary vocabulary, and considering the cultural assumptions made in word problems would be a better approach. Cultural values such as family are an important factor to consider; nonetheless, making blanket assumptions about all English learners should be avoided. Students come from diverse backgrounds and may or may not all have the same values, even if they speak the same primary language.

16. B: Semantic shifts occur when writers move from different types of register such as informal and formal. Informal registers might use phrases like "you know" that are acceptable in spoken language but are not acceptable in academic writing. Pragmatic competence focuses on the context and how it shapes meaning, whereas phonemic awareness is the ability to distinguish and produce phonemes. Syntactic competence is understanding of sentence structures and word order. Although all of these are important to language, the errors that these students are producing relate to semantic shift.

17. C: Using the primary language to support learning has been shown to increase not only content learning but also learning of the English language. Advanced students can explain concepts in the primary language to beginning-level students, ensuring that they continue to grow in the content areas as they learn English. Assimilation is the erasure of a student's home culture, so allowing for home language in the classroom would not promote assimilation.

18. B: Communicative competence focuses on the importance of communication in interpersonal relationships to create understanding. This method allows students to produce and understand real language used outside of the classroom. This goes beyond grammar drills and focuses on how to use language appropriately in specific contexts. Activities that focus on communicative competence usually include interaction among students instead of having formal presentations or methods of communication.

19. B: Krashen developed the *affective filter hypothesis* in which he considers emotional factors in learning such as self-esteem, motivation, and anxiety. High levels of anxiety can block language learning, which is what the teacher is concerned about. Although background knowledge of the Civil War may also affect the learner's presentation, the question focuses on emotional availability of the student rather than knowledge.

20. A: Phonology is the study of sound patterns as it relates to language. This teacher's activity focuses on phonemes that are part of the English language but may not be present in other languages. This is often confused with phonetics, which is the study of specific speech sounds without context and does not require prior knowledge. Morphology is the study of the meaning of language units, whereas syntax is focused on sentence structure and formation.

21. A: Pragmatics deals with the impact of context on the meaning of language. Pragmatics is highly cultural as it requires a shared understanding among the people communicating. One aspect of pragmatics is considering the audience. A teacher can model this by showing how language changes depending on whomever is the recipient of the communication. This is best shown through comparing letters with different recipients.

22. B: Prior knowledge impacts students' English language development. Without the appropriate schema and background knowledge, students may have difficulty learning. Although psychological factors or learning disabilities may be at play, this particular learner is already at a beginning-advanced level, and a learning disability should not be the first conclusion a teacher jumps to when considering reasons for student difficulty. Cultural factors may also impact a student's performance at times; however, in this particular scenario, the student is not speaking in front of peers or showing off knowledge in a public way.

23. D: Instructional conversations are a discourse strategy that acts as an alternative to teacher-centered classrooms. Discourse is the study of language that considers language beyond grammar or vocabulary. It focuses on the communicative features of language in a particular context. Worksheets and quizzes would not promote discourse as discourse generally requires interaction whether orally or with a text. Although asking a question and seeking a student response is the typical discourse pattern in the classroom, it is teacher centered and promotes less student discourse.

24. A: By not accommodating and celebrating a variety of languages, student voices and the rich language diversity of English and other languages is lost in the classroom. Although this may in some ways improve academic English, forcing Standard Academic English across the board can lead to student disengagement, which will ultimately diminish language development. Students may experience cultural dissonance, but it would be due to a mismatch between the classroom culture and their own culture rather than because others are not participating.

25. A: Nonverbal communication includes how one holds oneself along with eye contact and gestures. Cultures have different body language and nonverbal skills that are normalized. In some cultures, eye contact can be seen as disrespectful. Academic language structure refers to the actual vocabulary, syntax, and structure of the language being used. Leadership register is a pragmatic feature that is associated with language used to denote leadership, which often includes commands. Family acculturation is a sociocultural factor that influences student behavior, but it relates to how a family adapts to a new culture and their attitudes toward the dominant culture.

26. B: Basic interpersonal communication skills (BICS) is the social language and register that is used in everyday life. Students can become proficient in BICS in 6 months or more. On the other hand, cognitive academic language proficiency (CALP), or formal academic language used in schools and workplaces, often takes much longer to develop. In fact, CALP often takes around 7 to 10 years to develop completely. For this student to be behind in CALP is normal because he has only been in the United States for a year.

27. B: Affective filter is activated when students are stressed, or their self-esteem is lowered. Teachers should create a supportive environment with constructive feedback to help students learn while lowering their affective filters. Correcting every mistake is often harmful for English learners at the beginning level as production is more important than precision at that stage. Cold-calling students can also heighten anxiety for students; however, ignoring students completely create an environment in which these learners are not included. Students may perceive this as English learners being less valued in the class.

28. B: To assess family acculturation, teachers should try as much as possible to learn about a student's family, ideally though home visits. Family acculturation refers to how they adapt to the new culture they enter. This facilitates language learning of the second language depending on the family's language engagement with the dominant language of the culture. If a family continues to read and watch news in the primary language, they may be less acculturated than families that read and watch TV in the dominant language. This is not to say that families should only consume media in the second language, but it can help teachers as they consider students' backgrounds.

29. A: The error in the sentence has to do with verb past and present tenses. The sentence should read "This morning, I ate eggs for breakfast." Some languages do not modify the verb to indicate past tense but instead use separate modifiers or context clues such as "this morning" to indicate tense. Appositives are clauses that are used to clarify the sentence. For example, "my fat cat" is an appositive in the sentence "My fat cat Marty was lounging on the couch." "Marty" is the noun associated with the appositive. Phrasal verbs are verbs in combination with another word, usually an adverb or a preposition, that are idiomatic expressions. For example, "bring up" and "cut off" are two examples of phrasal verbs.

30. A: Dialects refers to variations within a language that are understandable to the larger community as well. Indi and Urdu are treated as separate languages, although they are mutually intelligible. On the other hand, although written Chinese is the same, the dialects are so different that they are unintelligible for speakers from different regions. Common examples of dialects include differences in language due to region, such as New York City and Los Angeles.

31. C: Positive language transfer occurs when a student's first-language skills can be used to support learning the second language. This often occurs when languages are similar in structure and vocabulary. For example, an Italian speaker will have an easier time learning Spanish than Japanese due to positive language transfer. Teachers can use positive language transfer not only for language structure and vocabulary but also for skills such as phonemic awareness, knowledge of the reading process, and comprehension strategies.

32. D: Krashen's natural order theory posits that certain grammatical language structures are acquired in a specific order. The example here demonstrates this theory because research has demonstrated that "–ing" verbs are generally acquired before "–s" ending to verbs. Interaction hypothesis emphasizes comprehensible input and the importance of conversational interactions to develop language. Affective filter hypothesis focuses on how a student's level of stress affects learning a language. Pivotal grammar focuses on the transition children experience when moving from one- word to two-word utterances.

33. C: Discourse includes the way that people interact and use language. Whereas syntax and morphology look at the sentence and word level of language, discourse looks at language in a broader sense in texts as well as behaviors. In particular, discourse can focus on how speakers take turns or show behaviors around listening and using cues when interacting. Discourse is highly contextual and cultural. Language used in the classroom differs significantly from language used at a soccer game or on the playground.

34. A: Although Answer D seems like it could apply to social constructionist views, the key is that it focuses on meaning rather than the social context. This answer applies more to meaning-centered approaches rather than social constructionist views. Social constructionism focuses on the social interactions that children have with adults. Answer C is a tenet of transformational grammar, which views language as having structure that humans can naturally grasp.

35. A: The No Child Left Behind Act of 2001 required that for schools to receive federal funding, they must measure and report student achievement on standardized tests for all students, including English learners. This includes state assessments such as the California Standardized Testing and Reporting (STAR) Program. The Every Student Succeeds Act (ESSA), passed in 2015, gave states more power over choosing how to measure and report achievement rather than using a prescribed measure from the federal government. It also gave schools an exemption for reporting tests scores for English language students in their first two years of schooling.

36. B: The first step for any school when enrolling students is to determine which language is the child's first language and if it is a language other than English. This should be done before any assessments are given as sometimes assessments might include other languages such as Spanish. For example, the Brigance Diagnostic Assessment of Basic Skills (Brigance-D) is offered in Spanish. This allows schools to also measure the primary language proficiency and determine the student's needs. Students may or may not need extra support classes depending on the student's language proficiency level and past academic achievement.

37. C: According to "backwards" lesson planning, the next step after choosing the specific standards is to then develop a summative assessment that would reliably, validly, and practically measure how well students have achieved those standards. This should occur before activities are developed as the standards and assessments should tie closely together. Activities and formative assessments can be developed after the summative assessment is created. Remember, formative assessments occur during and throughout the unit, whereas summative assessments occur at the end of the unit.

38. B: Displaying objectives for language development is a key aspect to Specifically Designed Academic Instruction in English (SDAIE) in all subjects. Although modifying texts may be appropriate depending on the students' levels, it is important not to adapt the text in a way that does not simplify the content and still provides the same depth of understanding for the students. In addition, although figurative language and idioms can be difficult for English learners, it is essential, especially at the early-advanced level to expose students to these concepts and help build their knowledge of idioms. Organizers are often a great way to support students' reading comprehension; however, at the early-advanced level, fill in the blanks may be too easy. Instead, an organizer that provides headings and subheadings with spaces for students to write their own summaries and notes would be more appropriate for this level.

39. D: Extended time is most likely the best accommodation to offer the student. Extended time on assessments is often necessary for English language learners because of the additional time needed to process language. By reducing the word problems to mere calculations, the teacher is changing the nature of the examination and may not be assessing the same skills as in the original examination. In addition, if the student is able to use his or her notes, he or she may not show an understanding of formulas that the teacher is testing.

40. D: Structured English Immersion (SEI) is a separate program from Specifically Designed Academic Instruction in English (SDAIE). SEI focuses on teaching only in English along with strategies to increase comprehension. SDAIE, on the other hand, may include a student's primary language for support. There are several key components of SDAIE. Teacher attitude is one aspect of SDAIE. In particular, teachers should be open-minded and willing to reflect and learn. Comprehensibility and interaction are also both essential components of the SDAIE model. Comprehensibility means including strategies that enhance comprehension, and interaction means that students have opportunities to discuss the content and ask questions.

41. D: According to Kame'enui and Simmons (2000), the benchmark group may experience some small difficulties when learning concepts. The strategic group shows performance slightly below the benchmark group, whereas the intensive group often is frequently below performance on assessments. The intensive group may need special education support, whereas the strategic group may need additional support and modified curriculum. Students in the strategic group may need visuals and charts to support their learning. Using class discussion may exclude some students from the conversation. In addition, although videos can be helpful, speakers are often fast paced, making it difficult for English learners to pick up on all concepts being taught.

42. D: Asking presenters to speak clearly not only supports listening but also can enhance the speaker's speaking abilities. In addition, adding visual supports aids comprehension for English language learners as well as other classmates during a presentation. Although encouraging asking questions allows students to support their listening skills, teachers need to be mindful of students feeling self-conscious asking questions. Writing an essay may be an effective activity done after the presentations, but it assesses rather than supports listening skills. Research prior to the presentations may help build background knowledge, but if only done for one poet, students may still struggle with other presentations on others.

43. A: Balanced reading programs combine different aspects of reading that include phonics, fluency, and comprehension among other reading skills. Although vocabulary and fluency are both important, the balanced reading approach looks at all of these skills as important rather than building a single skill such as Answers C and D suggest. Using student stories for literacy can be a form of the Language Experience Approach.

44. C: Front-loaded English programs intensively teach English until it can be used for the language of instruction. Its goal is to develop cognitive academic language proficiency (CALP) through the use of English and uses Specifically Designed Academic Instruction in English (SDAIE) skills and content to support learning. On the other hand, transitional bilingual programs view bilingualism as a link to support English language development. It often lasts for around only three years until students can transition to fully English classes. Content instruction is given in the primary language and eventually is switched to English.

45. D: A test is reliable when it offers a relatively stable measure of the test taker's skills. This means that if the test is taken twice by the same person, the scores between the two should be similar. When an assessment is valid, this means that it measures what it should be measuring. For example, a test on reading comprehension should include questions regarding aspects of the passage rather than writing or speaking skills. An invalid test is demonstrated in Answer C. A practical assessment means that it does not take too much time or resources to administer. Answer B may be describing a test that is impractical.

46. C: *Lau v Nichols* was a landmark case for English language learners. It required that English learners have access to education that was adequate and accessible; however, it was not until *Plyer v Doe* in 1982 that the U.S. Supreme Court ruled that schools could not deny enrollment based on a child's immigration status. *Lau v Nichols* required that schools offer equal education to English language learners, meaning they should not be placed in vocational tracks as an alternative to learning English or placed in handicapped courses based on their language abilities. It also required that schools communicate with families in a language they understand.

47. D: Formative assessments are given throughout the unit for teachers to keep track of what concepts and ideas need to be retaught to students. Unit tests and projects are often thought of as summative rather than formative assessments. Although pop quizzes may help inform the teacher of his students' progress, the motivation for the pop quizzes is as a tool to garner attention rather than for aiding his teaching. Informing teaching with assessments is one of the most important components of formative assessments.

48. C: Although many of these tools may support students' learning, the tool that would best support vocabulary development is a page with key terms. Formulas are important, but in developing language, students should have a clear understanding of math terms related to this unit, such as surface area, sphere, and rectangular prism. Visuals aids can support students' vocabulary development.

49. C: A language-rich environment refers to classrooms that have a large amount of text and language present physically in the classroom. This includes posters, word walls, and student writing; however, the goal of a language-rich environment is to expose students to language rather than promote excellence as is stated in Answer B. Pictures of different cultures and books with diverse characters are not an example of language-rich environments, although they can support cultural inclusion.

50. A: Using real, physical materials is often a scaffolding strategy used for English learners to help support their learning and understanding. Shortening word problems can be helpful depending on how they are modified, but mere simplification is not a successful strategy because students will need to develop their language skills. Although activating prior knowledge is a key strategy, some families may cook with exact measurements, whereas others do not. Deduction is also a great learning tool with the appropriate supports, but individual research for English learners at this young age can be overwhelming without scaffolding.

51. A: Allowing students to give oral answers rather than written ones allows them to share their knowledge without having to write in English. Often, English learners' writing abilities develop slower than speaking skills, so it is easier to explain something orally than through writing. Although translating the test may assess the content knowledge of students, it would require the teacher to then be able to understand the primary language of the students. Furthermore, administering only half of the exam or offering an alternative exam may turn out to not assess the same skills as the original exam.

52. C: Authentic assessments are those that are similar to activities outside of the classroom. This includes experiments, interviews, and portfolios. Answer C is most authentic because students are asked to interview real people about their experiences and histories. Pop quizzes, standardized tests, and computer simulations are all valid assessment types but are not considered authentic assessments.

53. D: The first question a teacher should ask herself is what specific standards she would like students to demonstrate. This includes the knowledge as well as the skills. Remember, backwards planning starts with the objectives in mind rather than the task or activity. Although all of these questions are important to ask oneself as a teacher developing a rubric, the first should be an alignment of the rubric and the standards or objectives.

54. B: Although offering notes can support students in the immediate situation, the best long-term solution is to help students learn how to take notes. Research has shown that strong note-taking skills promote academic achievement. Asking the teacher to slow down is an important accommodation, but even if the teacher does slow down, English learners must still know how to identify key words and ideas being shared by any teacher. Recording the lesson may provide a short-term solution, but it will require an extensive amount of time for the learner, and it is possible that the students may not have access to technology that would allow them to listen to the recording.

55. B: The first step in writing workshops is prewriting. This includes activities such as brainstorming through the use of mind maps or graphic organizers. In addition, prewriting could include discussing ideas, reading texts, and creating role-playing activities. In prewriting, students are not yet crafting their texts, so sentence stems and word banks should come later in the writing workshop process. This means that Answers C and D are not the first step.

56. C: Within communicative competence, there are several different sub-competencies including grammatical, discourse, strategic, and sociolinguistic. Strategic competence is the ability to fix miscommunications or repair failures in understanding. By asking clarifying questions, students develop their strategic competence in this scenario. Grammatical competence requires individuals to use language accurately both orally and in written form. Discourse competence refers to the ability to combine language into meaningful paragraphs or statements, and sociolinguistic competence is the ability to consider the context in communication.

57. C: Self-correction is an important skill for students. When teaching students to self-correct, it is important to not single out students or stop the discussion to pinpoint errors. Instead, having students gain an awareness of mispronounced words during a discussion could include writing those words on the board. This ensures that one student is not embarrassed because conversation continues while students note words that they can refer to. Creating a list beforehand can be helpful but does not help students self-correct as the list is generated by the teacher.

58. C: Students benefit from a combination of both concrete and abstract representations of vocabulary concepts, especially ones like cause and effect. Teachers should consider if real objects or visual models can be used to demonstrate abstract concepts. This is represented in Answers A and B. Answer D is an application activity that helps strengthen understanding of cause and effect. Although it is helpful to define the concepts, student should discuss rather than merely copy the definition, meaning that Answer C is the correct answer because it is the least helpful compared to the other options.

59. C: Interlanguage is a transitional stage often seen when individuals learn a second language. Interlanguage occurs when the speaker applies rules from the primary language when producing utterances in the second language. They may overgeneralize grammar rules or even use vocabulary from the primary language when using the second language. Interlanguage is a normal part of language development and can be used to help support the learner's second language. Communicative competence refers to the theory that social interaction is key to learning a language. Basic interpersonal language skills (BICS) is language used in everyday interactions. Whereas "I buy apples" can be considered BICS, not using the subject in the sentence is not a form of BICS. False cognates are words that sound similar in the primary and second language but do not have the same meaning.

60. A: Front-loading vocabulary means that the teacher is pre-teaching key words that are part of a reading. This strategy helps improve comprehension because students have a better understanding of key concepts that are introduced in the passage. Front-loading builds rather than reduces schemata or background knowledge. It may improve communication skills but does not necessarily relate to interpersonal language skills. Front-loading vocabulary does not necessarily support diverse learning styles that require multiple modalities.

61. D: Although each of these answers can be correct, think-alouds are most often used to promote reading comprehension through modeling what a good reader does while reading. Many students benefit from being explicitly taught how readers engage with the text rather than absorb passively as is shown in Answer D. Students may learn vocabulary or sentence structures, which are represented in Answers A and B, but think-alouds are used as a metacognitive strategy. Using new vocabulary words can help build students' language knowledge but does not necessarily relate to think-alouds. Furthermore, although this strategy does work on listening comprehension, the main purpose is to develop strategies around reading comprehension. To further support students, the teacher can write down what he or she has said to aid with visual support.

62. C: According to Cummins's four quadrants model, teachers should strive to begin lessons with tasks that are relatively cognitively undemanding but are relatable. As time goes by, tasks should increase in cognitive demand but should remain highly contextualized so that students can relate to the material. Finally, students should move toward engaging in tasks that are both demanding and abstract. Tasks described in Answer C are often seen as busywork because they are undemanding but also unrelatable, which creates disengagement.

63. A: The Language Experience Approach (LEA) is a strategy that focuses on students sharing their experiences with one another to learn and support English language learning rather than learning through texts or outside sources. A key aspect of the LEA is the interaction shared among students. Comparing with the teacher's results or researching independently, although possibly effective, does not constitute the LEA. The LEA uses students' own words rather than language from outside texts or sources.

64. D: When choosing resources for English learners, it is important not to oversimplify the content, as is suggested in Answer A. It is also important to choose age-appropriate materials as well as ensure that students are still practicing the skills and content objectives, such as identifying theme and analyzing characters. This means choosing films and other outside sources that are age appropriate. In this case, *The Lion King* may not be the most age-appropriate film to show an 11th-grade class. Acting out the play is one way of supporting comprehension through adding visual and kinesthetic elements while maintaining rigor.

65. C: In higher education, students will need to be able to independently read and understand an incredible about of academic literature and texts. By modeling how to use context clues to understand academic vocabulary, the teacher can show students how to do that on their own when they read. BICS are basic interpersonal communication skills that are important but do not always play a large role in the higher education classroom. A reading log can support comprehension but would be less helpful than skills to tackle academic language. Memorization is an important skill for higher education but must be paired with comprehension for it to be useful for academic language.

66. C: In kindergarten, English learners may or may not have writing skills, so assessing them through rewriting the story would be inappropriate both for the grade level and the language level of students. Although drawing a picture of a character may seem appropriate, to assess their comprehension, students should be tasked with placing events in the story in order. This can be done through ordering pictures of events in the story or can be done by asking students to draw the main events in a story.

67. B: Two-way immersion programs provide content in both the primary language and in English. Classes are ideally split between students who have a home language of English and students with a home language other than English. Skills in both languages are developed, but this can also mean that English is taught separately for these two groups as a primary language versus a second language, or both groups will be slowed down to accommodate for the developing language skills of both groups. Because classes are taught together, there often is not segregation. Specifically Designed Academic Instruction English (SDAIE) strategies are not required in two-way immersion programs.

68. C: English learners from different countries may have different experiences and expectations of schooling. Some schools have rigid structures and value efficiency and timeliness, whereas others value a cooperative and flexible approach. It is important to examine the underlying values of the school as well as consider the values of the culture from which the student comes.

69. A: Lack of communication does not always mean disengagement or lack of caring. Different cultures may have different levels of parental involvement in schooling and may have gendered roles for who is responsible for a child's education. Answer C does not seem to be the answer because the scenario depicts Amal's mother being involved despite his father being uninvolved. Furthermore, although language barriers may be a factor that has to be considered, this deferral to the mother indicates possible gender roles within the culture.

70. D: Culture includes both concrete aspects and intangible aspects of a group of people. Internal cultural factors are those that are not visible, such as family structure. Other internal cultural factors include values, customs, perspectives, beliefs, nonverbal communication norms, roles for gender, and ideas around social status. Clothing, food, and language are all examples of external cultural factors. These are concrete and can usually be seen or observed. Other external cultural factors include things like the arts, entertainment, hobbies, sports, religious structures, technology, and language.

71. B: Assimilation is the process in which an individual rejects his or her home culture to adapt to the dominant culture. This includes language, beliefs, and views along with other observable aspects of culture such as dress and food. Although assimilation may lead to increased self-esteem, assimilation is often associated with negative psychological impacts such as anxiety and depression. Instead, individuals who assimilate often experience a loss of cultural identity or deculturation. Assimilation is the opposite of rejecting the dominant culture. Finally, the ability to function in two cultures is known as biculturalism, not cultural assimilation.

72. B: By singling out students who may dress differently due to cultural or religious differences, those students may feel ostracized or different from other students. It is important for schools to closely examine their dress code policies along with other school policies to determine if they are inclusive of all cultures and backgrounds. Although it is possible that the student may feel unique, it will most likely not make her feel special. Moreover, because she is the only student in the school who wears head garbs, she will most likely notice the differences. Especially in middle school, students are developmentally aware of their peers and may seek to fit in rather than stand out.

73. D: Assimilation is the process in which an individual tries to adopt the culture of the dominant culture and rejects his or her culture. Accommodation is a process in which members of the mainstream culture and the minority culture both learn to adapt to one another. Biculturalism is when an individual is able to function in two different cultures. Culture shock occurs once the initial excitement of being in a new culture wears off and the individual feels frustrated by the confusion and differences between the two cultures.

74. A: It is important to involve families not only in the classroom but also in school governance. Parents can form representative groups that report to the principal and other governance bodies to help voice the needs of their particular communities. Simply sending minutes is not an effective way to get parents involved as it reports what has happened but does not actively solicit their participation. Interpreters can also be effective; however, few schools have the resources to be able to have an interpreter for every language at every meeting. Answer D simply avoids school governance, which does not answer the question.

75. A: Silence can mean a number of things in different cultures. In the dominant American culture, silence often indicates embarrassment and regret, but in many other cultures it may symbolize power, respect, reference, and self-control. Before ascribing a particular value and reason behind the silence to a student, it is essential to determine if the student views silence in this manner. The student may actually not know the answer or be unsure of how to communicate. Being careful not to generalize is important to ensuring students are not stereotyped.

76. B: The cultural incompatibility theory is the belief that the difference between home and school culture leads to lower academic success in students. Neither culture is seen as right or wrong, but instead, the values are "mismatched." This has put the onus on teachers to change the conditions in the classroom to accommodate for all students' cultures; however, the result has been that schools continue the status quo with the expectation placed on the home culture adapting to the school culture. Although the goal was to foster multicultural perspective and an understanding of different cultures, ultimately the cultural incompatibility theory has not positively impacted schools' abilities to support English learners.

77. D: Validating cultural identities of the students is a great step toward creating a multicultural curriculum. It is important to distinguish between multiculturalism and globalism. Globalism refers to the cultures around the world, whereas multiculturalism focuses on different cultures within the United States. Although Answer A is an excellent strategy for schools to undertake, it promotes globalism rather than multiculturalism. Professional development is also another key aspect of changing a curriculum; however, Answer B focuses on technology rather than on teacher cultural self-reflection or understanding minority cultures in the United States. Guest speakers are also a great asset to building a multicultural curriculum, but these are often one-off events, which can be more surface level.

78. A: Euphoria is the initial stage that individuals generally experience due to the excitement of being a new culture. Cultural fatigue and culture shock are the same stage in which newcomers are disoriented and frustrated by the difference between cultures. The final stage is adjustment, which is sometimes known as adaptation. This is when the individual adjusts to the new culture and is able to successfully integrate into the dominant culture.

79. C: Pull factors are reasons that cause individuals to immigrate to another country. These factors are appealing opportunities that are part of the new country or area that one desires to go. Pull factors include job opportunities, political or religious freedom, and reunion with family members. On the other hand, push factors are unappealing factors that cause individuals to leave their home country or area. These include factors such as violence, persecution, war, and natural disasters. Answers A, B, and D all are push rather than pull factors that are part of the reasons why immigrants from Central America come to the United States.

80. D: Culturally supportive classes are those that are inclusive of all cultural backgrounds. Some key aspects of these kinds of classes include high expectations; however, it is important to balance high expectations with unrealistic ones. Using high-level academic vocabulary that is inaccessible for students can create frustration and confusion. Furthermore, culturally supportive classrooms allow for the use of the primary language to support learning. Finally, modifying and differentiating activities for learners is important, but it should not lead to oversimplifying all activities for English learners.

81. A: During the late 19th century, there was an influx of European immigrants. Due to the Chinese Exclusion Act of 1882 and other legislation that put quotas on how many immigrants could live in America from different countries, many individuals and families from Asian and Latin American countries were barred from entering the United States. Congress passed the Immigration and Nationality Act in 1965, which removed the quotas. This led to a change in the immigration pattern, with more immigrants coming from Latin America and Asia.

82. A: Conflicts between students can be difficult to resolve; however, teachers must be sensitive to cultural differences and take immediate steps to come to a resolution. Cultural conflicts can be proactively avoided through steps such as developing negotiation skills in students as well as being inclusive of a variety of cultures in the school. If conflict does occur, there are several strategies such as empathizing, building cooperation between parties, managing emotions, and offering creative solutions. Answer A is one method of building empathy between parties and developing an understanding of other perspectives. Although disciplinary action may need to occur as is suggested in Answer B, suspension should not be the first choice. Suspension can lead to reduced academic achievement. Teachers should not turn a blind eye toward conflicts, and when involving parents, it is important to approach parties with respect rather than defensively.

83. B: Cultures have differing forms of communicating both verbally and nonverbally. In some cultures, speaking loudly over one another is acceptable, whereas in others younger individuals do not speak unless spoken to. Stereotypes are preconceived beliefs about a particular group that overgeneralizes and is harmful. Although stereotypes do play a large role in the classroom and should be an area of reflection for teachers, it is not the cause of the misunderstanding. Assimilation is a rejection of one's home culture to accept the values and beliefs of the dominant culture, not the minority culture. Finally, cultural pluralism is the idea that many cultures exist within a society. This is not what is at play in this scenario.

84. A: Cultures differ in their level of cooperation and competitiveness. In particular, some indigenous cultures promote cooperation rather than competition. Although it is important not to generalize and instead gain a deeper understanding of the culture, this can offer the best explanation from the choices. Although the school may be strict, it does not mean that students will not embrace fun during school. Furthermore, most cultures have different games and aspects of play and entertainment.

85. C: Developing literacy skills in the primary language can help support second-language development. Although reading alone can also foster literacy, because this student is of a young age, it can be helpful for parents to be involved by reading in their native language with the child. Building a culture of reading at home, whether in English or the native language, provides great benefits for the student. Doing math instead of reading does not develop literacy, and although staying after school to read with the teacher can promote literacy, by reading at home, students associate reading with learning outside of school as well.

86. A: Social distance is the perceived separation between individuals based on social groups such as gender, ethnicity, and language. Social distance can create prejudice and bias in individuals. To reduce social distance, teachers can foster relationships among diverse students as well as highlight the value of multicultural education. What the teacher has done is actually support multicultural perspectives and cultural relativism. Cultural relativism is the idea that all thoughts, words, and actions exist in a cultural context. With more perspectives added, one's cultural relativism increases. Acculturation is the adaptation to another dominant culture. These activities could increase acculturation if individuals from the dominant culture are involved.

87. D: Although refreshments can be a nice touch, they are not an essential part of parent–teacher conferences. It is important for schools and teachers to consider having an interpreter if parents do not speak English. Moreover, there may be cultural differences in perceptions of time as well as of involvement in schools. It is important to communicate these expectations and create alternatives to allow for these cultural differences. Furthermore, some families may be working during the school day, making it difficult for parents to come to school during that time. This doesn't apply to only English learners but all learners.

88. A: According to Pew research conducted in 2017, the top second country with the largest number of immigrants coming to the United States is China. At the time of the poll, 2.9 million immigrants in the United States came from China. The top country is Mexico, with 11.2 million immigrants. Latin America is not a country. India has the third-largest group of immigrants at the time of the poll (source: https://www.pewresearch.org/fact-tank/2019/06/03/key-findings-about-u-s-immigrants/).

89. D: Cultural relativism is the idea that all thoughts, words, and actions exist in a cultural context. On the other hand, ethnocentrism is the idea that one's culture and cultural values is the norm. In this perspective, individuals are unable to understand other cultural values and beliefs. Cultural relativism, however, is not the acceptance of all values as is shown through ethical relativism. With cultural relativism, one does not have to agree with all behaviors and abandon one's own cultural values. Cultural pluralism is the idea that there are many different cultures within a society or country.

90. B: Although it may seem like changing the teacher's level of physical contact based on the student's perceived comfort levels and cultural norms, it would not be wise for the teacher to do so because it can be construed as favoring certain students over others. Furthermore, it can confuse students as to what the norm is around physical contact between a figure of authority such as the teacher and the student. Maintaining clear and consistent expectations and behaviors helps students learn what the norm is for the school's culture.

91. C: Cultural concepts about time differ across different countries and cultures. Some cultures such as the United States value strict organization around time as well as efficiency and speed. Intelligence is often associated with speed in the American context. Other cultures, however, may not value time in the same way. It is important for teachers to be aware of their own time values and work within the school structure to support the student. This means that they may not be able to completely change the schedule or force the student to speed up.

92. D: According to Morey and Kilano (1997), there are three levels of incorporating diversity. The first level is exclusive, which includes more surface-level and stereotypical depictions of culture. These are elements of cultures such as the food, the dress, and the games associated with a culture. Inclusive is the enhancement of the curriculum through adding diverse perspectives; however, it often holds the same central structure at the original curriculum. Transformed curriculum is built on completely new perspectives and is developed with a completely different structure. Additive refers to Bank's model on multicultural education, which is similar to the inclusive level.

93. C: Cooperative learning groups foster higher levels of interaction among students, which provides a classroom that supports diverse learning environments and is inclusive. Although conflicts may occur, with proper support, students will be able to overcome issues and work together. Semantic skills deal with understanding the meaning of language. Cooperative groups do not necessarily enhance semantic skills, although it might support better communication skills. Finally, it won't necessarily divide the class unless competition among groups is a prominent part of the class structure.

94. D: Biculturalism is a term used to describe individuals who are able to fully function within two different cultures without having to reject either culture. Individuals who are bicultural often are able to connect with their primary culture and that of the dominant culture. Answer A describes an individual who is perhaps acculturated but still is more comfortable in his primary culture and language. Answer B describes an individual experiencing assimilation, and Answer C is someone who has rejected the dominant culture.

95. B: Various cultures have differences in their written discourse. In America, features of written academic language tend to be distant, authoritative, concise, and clear. In other cultures, discourse may focus on storytelling and being less direct. Language is not only a reflection of knowledge but also culture, so it is important for teachers to take this into consideration as they teach and grade writing. Although it is important to explicitly teach the expectations of academic writing in the American setting, it is important to also allow flexibility and types of writing activities that build on students' cultures.

96. B: Simply including diverse literature in the curriculum is not enough to create an inclusive environment. Many "diverse" books can include stereotypical depictions of minority characters, including women. Although having multiple translations can be helpful, it is not essential when thinking about what texts to choose to teach. Well-known authors may be beneficial as it can draw the interest of students, but it is not required, and considering the author for a talk at the school depends on the funding available, which may not always be possible.

97. C: There are a multitude of reasons that may be an explanation for why the parents are not involved. These might include different values around family involvement in education. Some cultures do not have heavy family involvement in schooling due to a number of reasons such as respect toward the teacher. Lack of involvement, however, should not be confused with cultural depravation or disinterest in education. On the contrary, many families have reported that they are supportive of their children's education. Moreover, although parental education has an impact, it does not mean that they are illiterate, especially because the student is in second grade.

98. A: The model minority myth is the destructive belief that Asian Americans all excel in academic areas, especially math and science. This myth is dangerous in that it can lead the teacher to believe that the student does not have any problems. When self-reflecting, teachers should consider factors such as if other students are also struggling, which could indicate that they have not taught the content in a way that is accessible to all students. The teacher should also consider the language level of the student. In this case, the student is at the advanced level, so it is possible that the student is not experiencing culture shock nor has a language barrier that is causing these difficulties.

99. B: Several schools have added negotiation and mediation courses for students that have proven effective in reducing violence and vandalism as well as improving race relations. It is important that schools consider holistically a variety of strategies to implement rather than going with a single solution. Simply placing diverse students in the same classes alone does not improve cultural communication, and making disciplinary measures more stringent may actually have a negative effect.

100. A: Naming interviews are seen as an activity that helps affirm students' identities because names are often deeply rooted in culture. Names hold value within a culture and are associated with certain meanings. By allowing students to discuss this in the classroom, students are able to bring an important aspect of themselves—their names—in to light. Although show and tell can be culturally affirming, it doesn't necessarily have to do with a student's cultural identity. Activities that validate students' cultural identities should focus on the student.

How to Overcome Test Anxiety

Just the thought of taking a test is enough to make most people a little nervous. A test is an important event that can have a long-term impact on your future, so it's important to take it seriously and it's natural to feel anxious about performing well. But just because anxiety is normal, that doesn't mean that it's helpful in test taking, or that you should simply accept it as part of your life. Anxiety can have a variety of effects. These effects can be mild, like making you feel slightly nervous, or severe, like blocking your ability to focus or remember even a simple detail.

If you experience test anxiety—whether severe or mild—it's important to know how to beat it. To discover this, first you need to understand what causes test anxiety.

Causes of Test Anxiety

While we often think of anxiety as an uncontrollable emotional state, it can actually be caused by simple, practical things. One of the most common causes of test anxiety is that a person does not feel adequately prepared for their test. This feeling can be the result of many different issues such as poor study habits or lack of organization, but the most common culprit is time management. Starting to study too late, failing to organize your study time to cover all of the material, or being distracted while you study will mean that you're not well prepared for the test. This may lead to cramming the night before, which will cause you to be physically and mentally exhausted for the test. Poor time management also contributes to feelings of stress, fear, and hopelessness as you realize you are not well prepared but don't know what to do about it.

Other times, test anxiety is not related to your preparation for the test but comes from unresolved fear. This may be a past failure on a test, or poor performance on tests in general. It may come from comparing yourself to others who seem to be performing better or from the stress of living up to expectations. Anxiety may be driven by fears of the future—how failure on this test would affect your educational and career goals. These fears are often completely irrational, but they can still negatively impact your test performance.

Review Video: 3 Reasons You Have Test Anxiety
Visit mometrix.com/academy and enter code: 428468

Elements of Test Anxiety

As mentioned earlier, test anxiety is considered to be an emotional state, but it has physical and mental components as well. Sometimes you may not even realize that you are suffering from test anxiety until you notice the physical symptoms. These can include trembling hands, rapid heartbeat, sweating, nausea, and tense muscles. Extreme anxiety may lead to fainting or vomiting. Obviously, any of these symptoms can have a negative impact on testing. It is important to recognize them as soon as they begin to occur so that you can address the problem before it damages your performance.

Review Video: 3 Ways to Tell You Have Test Anxiety
Visit mometrix.com/academy and enter code: 927847

The mental components of test anxiety include trouble focusing and inability to remember learned information. During a test, your mind is on high alert, which can help you recall information and stay focused for an extended period of time. However, anxiety interferes with your mind's natural processes, causing you to blank out, even on the questions you know well. The strain of testing during anxiety makes it difficult to stay focused, especially on a test that may take several hours. Extreme anxiety can take a huge mental toll, making it difficult not only to recall test information but even to understand the test questions or pull your thoughts together.

Review Video: How Test Anxiety Affects Memory
Visit mometrix.com/academy and enter code: 609003

Effects of Test Anxiety

Test anxiety is like a disease—if left untreated, it will get progressively worse. Anxiety leads to poor performance, and this reinforces the feelings of fear and failure, which in turn lead to poor performances on subsequent tests. It can grow from a mild nervousness to a crippling condition. If allowed to progress, test anxiety can have a big impact on your schooling, and consequently on your future.

Test anxiety can spread to other parts of your life. Anxiety on tests can become anxiety in any stressful situation, and blanking on a test can turn into panicking in a job situation. But fortunately, you don't have to let anxiety rule your testing and determine your grades. There are a number of relatively simple steps you can take to move past anxiety and function normally on a test and in the rest of life.

Review Video: How Test Anxiety Impacts Your Grades
Visit mometrix.com/academy and enter code: 939819

Physical Steps for Beating Test Anxiety

While test anxiety is a serious problem, the good news is that it can be overcome. It doesn't have to control your ability to think and remember information. While it may take time, you can begin taking steps today to beat anxiety.

Just as your first hint that you may be struggling with anxiety comes from the physical symptoms, the first step to treating it is also physical. Rest is crucial for having a clear, strong mind. If you are tired, it is much easier to give in to anxiety. But if you establish good sleep habits, your body and mind will be ready to perform optimally, without the strain of exhaustion. Additionally, sleeping well helps you to retain information better, so you're more likely to recall the answers when you see the test questions.

Getting good sleep means more than going to bed on time. It's important to allow your brain time to relax. Take study breaks from time to time so it doesn't get overworked, and don't study right before bed. Take time to rest your mind before trying to rest your body, or you may find it difficult to fall asleep.

Review Video: The Importance of Sleep for Your Brain
Visit mometrix.com/academy and enter code: 319338

Along with sleep, other aspects of physical health are important in preparing for a test. Good nutrition is vital for good brain function. Sugary foods and drinks may give a burst of energy but this burst is followed by a crash, both physically and emotionally. Instead, fuel your body with protein and vitamin-rich foods.

Also, drink plenty of water. Dehydration can lead to headaches and exhaustion, especially if your brain is already under stress from the rigors of the test. Particularly if your test is a long one, drink water during the breaks. And if possible, take an energy-boosting snack to eat between sections.

Review Video: How Diet Can Affect your Mood
Visit mometrix.com/academy and enter code: 624317

Along with sleep and diet, a third important part of physical health is exercise. Maintaining a steady workout schedule is helpful, but even taking 5-minute study breaks to walk can help get your blood pumping faster and clear your head. Exercise also releases endorphins, which contribute to a positive feeling and can help combat test anxiety.

When you nurture your physical health, you are also contributing to your mental health. If your body is healthy, your mind is much more likely to be healthy as well. So take time to rest, nourish your body with healthy food and water, and get moving as much as possible. Taking these physical steps will make you stronger and more able to take the mental steps necessary to overcome test anxiety.

Mental Steps for Beating Test Anxiety

Working on the mental side of test anxiety can be more challenging, but as with the physical side, there are clear steps you can take to overcome it. As mentioned earlier, test anxiety often stems from lack of preparation, so the obvious solution is to prepare for the test. Effective studying may be the most important weapon you have for beating test anxiety, but you can and should employ several other mental tools to combat fear.

First, boost your confidence by reminding yourself of past success—tests or projects that you aced. If you're putting as much effort into preparing for this test as you did for those, there's no reason you should expect to fail here. Work hard to prepare; then trust your preparation.

Second, surround yourself with encouraging people. It can be helpful to find a study group, but be sure that the people you're around will encourage a positive attitude. If you spend time with others who are anxious or cynical, this will only contribute to your own anxiety. Look for others who are motivated to study hard from a desire to succeed, not from a fear of failure.

Third, reward yourself. A test is physically and mentally tiring, even without anxiety, and it can be helpful to have something to look forward to. Plan an activity following the test, regardless of the outcome, such as going to a movie or getting ice cream.

When you are taking the test, if you find yourself beginning to feel anxious, remind yourself that you know the material. Visualize successfully completing the test. Then take a few deep, relaxing breaths and return to it. Work through the questions carefully but with confidence, knowing that you are capable of succeeding.

Developing a healthy mental approach to test taking will also aid in other areas of life. Test anxiety affects more than just the actual test—it can be damaging to your mental health and even contribute to depression. It's important to beat test anxiety before it becomes a problem for more than testing.

Review Video: Test Anxiety and Depression
Visit mometrix.com/academy and enter code: 904704

Study Strategy

Being prepared for the test is necessary to combat anxiety, but what does being prepared look like? You may study for hours on end and still not feel prepared. What you need is a strategy for test prep. The next few pages outline our recommended steps to help you plan out and conquer the challenge of preparation.

STEP 1: SCOPE OUT THE TEST

Learn everything you can about the format (multiple choice, essay, etc.) and what will be on the test. Gather any study materials, course outlines, or sample exams that may be available. Not only will this help you to prepare, but knowing what to expect can help to alleviate test anxiety.

STEP 2: MAP OUT THE MATERIAL

Look through the textbook or study guide and make note of how many chapters or sections it has. Then divide these over the time you have. For example, if a book has 15 chapters and you have five days to study, you need to cover three chapters each day. Even better, if you have the time, leave an extra day at the end for overall review after you have gone through the material in depth.

If time is limited, you may need to prioritize the material. Look through it and make note of which sections you think you already have a good grasp on, and which need review. While you are studying, skim quickly through the familiar sections and take more time on the challenging parts. Write out your plan so you don't get lost as you go. Having a written plan also helps you feel more in control of the study, so anxiety is less likely to arise from feeling overwhelmed at the amount to cover.

STEP 3: GATHER YOUR TOOLS

Decide what study method works best for you. Do you prefer to highlight in the book as you study and then go back over the highlighted portions? Or do you type out notes of the important information? Or is it helpful to make flashcards that you can carry with you? Assemble the pens, index cards, highlighters, post-it notes, and any other materials you may need so you won't be distracted by getting up to find things while you study.

If you're having a hard time retaining the information or organizing your notes, experiment with different methods. For example, try color-coding by subject with colored pens, highlighters, or post-it notes. If you learn better by hearing, try recording yourself reading your notes so you can listen while in the car, working out, or simply sitting at your desk. Ask a friend to quiz you from your flashcards, or try teaching someone the material to solidify it in your mind.

STEP 4: CREATE YOUR ENVIRONMENT

It's important to avoid distractions while you study. This includes both the obvious distractions like visitors and the subtle distractions like an uncomfortable chair (or a too-comfortable couch that makes you want to fall asleep). Set up the best study environment possible: good lighting and a comfortable work area. If background music helps you focus, you may want to turn it on, but otherwise keep the room quiet. If you are using a computer to take notes, be sure you don't have any other windows open, especially applications like social media, games, or anything else that could distract you. Silence your phone and turn off notifications. Be sure to keep water close by so you stay hydrated while you study (but avoid unhealthy drinks and snacks).

Also, take into account the best time of day to study. Are you freshest first thing in the morning? Try to set aside some time then to work through the material. Is your mind clearer in the afternoon or evening? Schedule your study session then. Another method is to study at the same time of day that you will take the test, so that your brain gets used to working on the material at that time and will be ready to focus at test time.

Step 5: Study!

Once you have done all the study preparation, it's time to settle into the actual studying. Sit down, take a few moments to settle your mind so you can focus, and begin to follow your study plan. Don't give in to distractions or let yourself procrastinate. This is your time to prepare so you'll be ready to fearlessly approach the test. Make the most of the time and stay focused.

Of course, you don't want to burn out. If you study too long you may find that you're not retaining the information very well. Take regular study breaks. For example, taking five minutes out of every hour to walk briskly, breathing deeply and swinging your arms, can help your mind stay fresh.

As you get to the end of each chapter or section, it's a good idea to do a quick review. Remind yourself of what you learned and work on any difficult parts. When you feel that you've mastered the material, move on to the next part. At the end of your study session, briefly skim through your notes again.

But while review is helpful, cramming last minute is NOT. If at all possible, work ahead so that you won't need to fit all your study into the last day. Cramming overloads your brain with more information than it can process and retain, and your tired mind may struggle to recall even previously learned information when it is overwhelmed with last-minute study. Also, the urgent nature of cramming and the stress placed on your brain contribute to anxiety. You'll be more likely to go to the test feeling unprepared and having trouble thinking clearly.

So don't cram, and don't stay up late before the test, even just to review your notes at a leisurely pace. Your brain needs rest more than it needs to go over the information again. In fact, plan to finish your studies by noon or early afternoon the day before the test. Give your brain the rest of the day to relax or focus on other things, and get a good night's sleep. Then you will be fresh for the test and better able to recall what you've studied.

Step 6: Take a practice test

Many courses offer sample tests, either online or in the study materials. This is an excellent resource to check whether you have mastered the material, as well as to prepare for the test format and environment.

Check the test format ahead of time: the number of questions, the type (multiple choice, free response, etc.), and the time limit. Then create a plan for working through them. For example, if you have 30 minutes to take a 60-question test, your limit is 30 seconds per question. Spend less time on the questions you know well so that you can take more time on the difficult ones.

If you have time to take several practice tests, take the first one open book, with no time limit. Work through the questions at your own pace and make sure you fully understand them. Gradually work up to taking a test under test conditions: sit at a desk with all study materials put away and set a timer. Pace yourself to make sure you finish the test with time to spare and go back to check your answers if you have time.

After each test, check your answers. On the questions you missed, be sure you understand why you missed them. Did you misread the question (tests can use tricky wording)? Did you forget the information? Or was it something you hadn't learned? Go back and study any shaky areas that the practice tests reveal.

Taking these tests not only helps with your grade, but also aids in combating test anxiety. If you're already used to the test conditions, you're less likely to worry about it, and working through tests until you're scoring well gives you a confidence boost. Go through the practice tests until you feel comfortable, and then you can go into the test knowing that you're ready for it.

Test Tips

On test day, you should be confident, knowing that you've prepared well and are ready to answer the questions. But aside from preparation, there are several test day strategies you can employ to maximize your performance.

First, as stated before, get a good night's sleep the night before the test (and for several nights before that, if possible). Go into the test with a fresh, alert mind rather than staying up late to study.

Try not to change too much about your normal routine on the day of the test. It's important to eat a nutritious breakfast, but if you normally don't eat breakfast at all, consider eating just a protein bar. If you're a coffee drinker, go ahead and have your normal coffee. Just make sure you time it so that the caffeine doesn't wear off right in the middle of your test. Avoid sugary beverages, and drink enough water to stay hydrated but not so much that you need a restroom break 10 minutes into the test. If your test isn't first thing in the morning, consider going for a walk or doing a light workout before the test to get your blood flowing.

Allow yourself enough time to get ready, and leave for the test with plenty of time to spare so you won't have the anxiety of scrambling to arrive in time. Another reason to be early is to select a good seat. It's helpful to sit away from doors and windows, which can be distracting. Find a good seat, get out your supplies, and settle your mind before the test begins.

When the test begins, start by going over the instructions carefully, even if you already know what to expect. Make sure you avoid any careless mistakes by following the directions.

Then begin working through the questions, pacing yourself as you've practiced. If you're not sure on an answer, don't spend too much time on it, and don't let it shake your confidence. Either skip it and come back later, or eliminate as many wrong answers as possible and guess among the remaining ones. Don't dwell on these questions as you continue—put them out of your mind and focus on what lies ahead.

Be sure to read all of the answer choices, even if you're sure the first one is the right answer. Sometimes you'll find a better one if you keep reading. But don't second-guess yourself if you do immediately know the answer. Your gut instinct is usually right. Don't let test anxiety rob you of the information you know.

If you have time at the end of the test (and if the test format allows), go back and review your answers. Be cautious about changing any, since your first instinct tends to be correct, but make sure you didn't misread any of the questions or accidentally mark the wrong answer choice. Look over any you skipped and make an educated guess.

At the end, leave the test feeling confident. You've done your best, so don't waste time worrying about your performance or wishing you could change anything. Instead, celebrate the successful completion of this test. And finally, use this test to learn how to deal with anxiety even better next time.

Review Video: 5 Tips to Beat Test Anxiety
Visit mometrix.com/academy and enter code: 570656

Important Qualification

Not all anxiety is created equal. If your test anxiety is causing major issues in your life beyond the classroom or testing center, or if you are experiencing troubling physical symptoms related to your anxiety, it may be a sign of a serious physiological or psychological condition. If this sounds like your situation, we strongly encourage you to seek professional help.

Thank You

We at Mometrix would like to extend our heartfelt thanks to you, our friend and patron, for allowing us to play a part in your journey. It is a privilege to serve people from all walks of life who are unified in their commitment to building the best future they can for themselves.

The preparation you devote to these important testing milestones may be the most valuable educational opportunity you have for making a real difference in your life. We encourage you to put your heart into it—that feeling of succeeding, overcoming, and yes, conquering will be well worth the hours you've invested.

We want to hear your story, your struggles and your successes, and if you see any opportunities for us to improve our materials so we can help others even more effectively in the future, please share that with us as well. **The team at Mometrix would be absolutely thrilled to hear from you!** So please, send us an email (support@mometrix.com) and let's stay in touch.

If you'd like some additional help, check out these other resources we offer for your exam:
http://MometrixFlashcards.com/MTTC

Additional Bonus Material

Due to our efforts to try to keep this book to a manageable length, we've created a link that will give you access to all of your additional bonus material:

mometrix.com/bonus948/mttcesl126